How to Do
Everything™

Adobe® Acrobat® X

DISCARD

About the Author

Doug Sahlin is an author and Acrobat instructor living in Lakeland, Florida. He is the author of more than 25 books on computer applications, including the popular *How to Do Everything: Adobe Acrobat 9.0*. He is also a professional photographer and the author of *Digital Photography QuickSteps*. Sahlin has written and coauthored books on digital photography, image-editing applications, and video-editing applications. He uses Acrobat to create interactive electronic documents for his clients. He has taught local businesses and government organizations how to create paperless offices with Acrobat.

About the Technical Editor

Jennifer Ackerman Kettell has written and contributed to dozens of books about software applications, web design, and digital photography. She is a freelance web designer and has managed several online communities. Jenn has lived all over the United States but currently calls upstate New York home.

Adobe® Acrobat® X

Doug Sahlin

New York Chicago San Francisco Lisbon
London Madrid Mexico City Milan New Delhi
San Juan Seoul Singapore Sydney Toronto

The **McGraw·Hill** Companies

Cataloging-in-Publication Data is on file with the Library of Congress

McGraw-Hill books are available at special quantity discounts to use as premiums and sales promotions, or for use in corporate training programs. To contact a representative, please e-mail us at bulksales@mcgraw-hill.com.

How to Do Everything™: Adobe® Acrobat® X

1 2 3 4 5 6 7 8 9 0   QFR QFR   1 0 9 8 7 6 5 4 3 2 1

ISBN   978-0-07-175293-0
MHID   0-07-175293-5

Sponsoring Editor	**Copy Editor**	**Art Director, Cover**
Roger Stewart	Bart Reed	Jeff Weeks
Editorial Supervisor	**Proofreader**	**Cover Designer**
Patty Mon	Paul Tyler	Pattie Lee
Project Manager	**Indexer**	**Interior Designer**
Patricia Wallenburg	Karin Arrigoni	Jane Tenenbaum
Acquisitions Coordinator	**Production Supervisor**	
Joya Anthony	George Anderson	
Technical Editor	**Composition**	
Jennifer Ackerman Kettell	TypeWriting	

Dedicated to the memory of George Harrison,
the quiet Beatle who spoke volumes with his music.

Contents at a Glance

Contents

x Contents

Acknowledgments

Thanks to Roger Stewart for making this project possible. Many thanks to the talented folks at McGraw-Hill for taking my words and turning them into a finished product. Thanks to Patty Mon and Patty Wallenburg for overseeing the production of this book. Thanks to Jennifer Kettell for being an exemplary technical editor. Special thanks to the lovely and talented Margot Hutchison for being a stellar literary agent.

Special thanks to the love of my life, Roxanne, for being here and changing my life for the better. Special thanks to my fellow authors for their continued support and inspiration. Thanks to my friends, family, and mentors, especially you, Karen and Ted. Honorable mention to my social secretary, Niki the Cat, also known as the Queen of the Universe, and her younger brother Micah, who we believe is the reincarnation of Curly Howard.

Introduction

Acrobat X Pro is a full-featured application that enables the end user to convert documents into PDF (Portable Document Format) documents. PDF documents can be read by anybody who has the free Adobe Reader installed on his or her computer. Many people who own Acrobat don't utilize many of the incredible features the application has available. My goal for this book is to make Acrobat X Pro more accessible for everyone who uses the application and to explore the powerful features that enable the end user to convert vanilla PDFs into interactive forms, multimedia presentations, and much more.

This book covers features of Acrobat X Pro and is divided into three parts. Part I is an introduction to Acrobat that discusses the new features of Acrobat X Pro, explores the workspace, and shows you how to navigate a PDF document. Part II shows you how to convert Microsoft Office documents, paper documents, and web pages to PDF files. This part of the book also shows you how to add interactive elements to PDF documents and create navigation for PDF documents. Part III shows you how to edit PDF documents, review and mark up PDF documents, add security to PDF documents, create PDF forms, and add multimedia to PDF documents.

PART I

Welcome to Adobe Acrobat X

1

Get to Know Adobe Acrobat X

HOW TO...

- Utilize the power of Acrobat
- Create PDF documents
- Create PDF documents for the Web
- Capture websites as PDF documents
- Optimize PDF documents

Most computer users are familiar with Acrobat in some form or another. Many Windows computer users think Acrobat is the application that pops up when they double-click a file with the .pdf (Portable Document Format) extension. That application is known as the Adobe Reader. But there's much more to Acrobat than the Reader. Major corporations, software manufacturers, and businesses use the full version of Acrobat to create and publish documents for electronic distribution. Forms are another important feature of Acrobat. Interactive forms can be created in all versions of Acrobat or Adobe LiveCycle Designer and distributed online. Forms can be filled in with Acrobat Standard, Pro, and Adobe Reader 6.0 or newer. The fact that you're reading this book probably means you either own the full version of Acrobat X Pro or will soon purchase the application to create interactive PDF documents that retain the appearance of the original document.

If you've used Acrobat before, you know it's chock full of features—so many features that it takes a while to learn them all. If you're brand new to Acrobat, the prospect of publishing sophisticated electronic documents might seem a bit daunting. As you read this book, though, you learn to harness the power of Acrobat X Pro to create and publish electronic documents you never thought possible. Whether you need to create a simple electronic memo, an employee manual, an indexed electronic catalog, or a sophisticated form, Acrobat is the tool for you.

In this chapter, you also learn about the different components that come with Acrobat and the many uses for the software. If you just upgraded from Acrobat 9.0, you likely already noticed many changes to the software. If you're an experienced Acrobat user, you may be tempted to skip this chapter. However, even if you're an

Acrobat publishing veteran, I suggest you browse through this chapter, especially when you consider the numerous new features, enhanced PDF Portfolio creation, and the new interface. As you read this chapter, you may discover an application for the program that you never knew existed. As you learn about the new features and enhanced functionality of Acrobat X, you may develop ideas of how to best utilize the application for your publishing needs.

About Adobe Acrobat

Adobe Acrobat has been around for some time now. Adobe created the product for individuals and corporations who needed to publish documents for distribution in electronic format (which became known as e-paper after Acrobat had been out for a while). The original goal was to create a paperless office. Acrobat X well and truly makes that goal a reality.

The first versions of the application made it possible for authors to distribute electronic documents that had the look and feel of the original document. A PDF file can be viewed by anyone, on any computer, with the only required software being the free Adobe Reader. This saves time, money, and valuable resources.

Early versions of Acrobat found great favor with software manufacturers who used Acrobat to create electronic manuals for their products. The manuals could easily be bundled on program installation disks with a free copy of what is now known as Adobe Reader. Many software manufacturers opted to publish program manuals only in PDF format. Software companies selling applications with manuals published in this manner saved on packaging and shipping costs, enabling them to price their software more competitively. Help manuals published in PDF format are easy to navigate and read. The PDF format is also a favorite of authors who self-publish their work. PDFs can be read on all of the major e-book readers, including Kindle and iPad. Figure 1-1 shows an e-book that was created using Adobe InDesign and exported as a PDF file, as viewed in Acrobat Pro.

As Acrobat grew in popularity, Adobe added more features to the product. Newer versions of the software featured enhanced usability, the addition of document security, and the capability to create a searchable index of multiple PDF documents. Users of the software found new applications for PDF documents; the documents soon appeared as corporate memos, portable product catalogs, and multimedia presentations for salespeople. Most popular browsers support the Adobe Reader plug-in, so many companies post PDF documents on their websites. The PDF acronym aptly describes the published file, because it is truly a *portable* document, viewable by anybody with Adobe Reader 6.0 or later, and earlier versions of the Acrobat Reader installed on their computers. The Adobe Reader used to be called Acrobat. However, too many users confused the Acrobat utility used to read PDF documents with the full version of Acrobat that's used to author PDF documents. To end the confusion, Adobe changed the name to Adobe Reader.

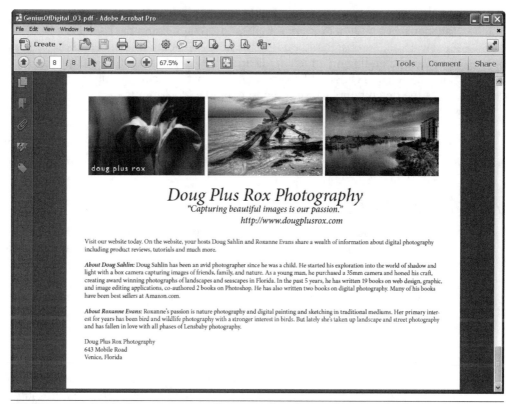

FIGURE 1-1   PDF documents can be viewed with Acrobat Standard, Acrobat Pro, or Adobe Reader.

About the PDF Format

If you've used computers for any length of time, you're probably familiar with the PDF format. As you may know, PDF is the acronym for Portable Document Format. PDF files are designated with the .pdf file extension and are, indeed, portable. You can view them on any computer with the free Adobe Reader X. For example, if someone sends you a PDF file of a document created on a Macintosh computer using Adobe InDesign, you can view it on a Windows PC that has Adobe Reader X. The file you view with Adobe Reader X on a PC looks identical to the PDF file published on the Macintosh computer. All the elements used to create the file on the Mac are saved when the author exports, prints, or saves (depending on the application) the file to PDF format, which is the reason it appears identical when viewed with Adobe Reader X on a PC.

Note   PDF files can also be viewed on the Apple iPad. However, as of this writing, Adobe does not have a version of the Acrobat Reader for the iPad. Owners of the iPad can add PDF documents to their iTunes library and view them using the free iBooks application after synching the iPad to their computer.

PDF files can also be viewed in supported web browsers, where Adobe Reader 9.0 functions as a plug-in or helper application. Whenever a user selects a PDF file posted on a website, Acrobat Standard, Pro, or Adobe Reader X launches in the user's web browser, depending on which application the user has on their computer. If a user has both the Adobe Reader and a version of Acrobat, whichever application was installed last is the default application used to read PDF documents.

Acrobat X Standard and Pro are full-fledged authoring applications used for publishing electronic documents in PDF format. If you've used previous versions of Acrobat, you're already familiar with the program's basic premise. In the sections to follow, you'll learn about the new features and uses for Acrobat X Pro.

Adobe Acrobat X

With the introduction of Acrobat 6.0, Adobe created two versions: Acrobat Standard, for the individual or small business needing to convert supported file formats to the PDF format, and Acrobat Pro, for task-oriented professionals needing to publish PDF files with objects such as form fields and multimedia elements. Acrobat X is distributed in Standard and Pro versions. Acrobat Pro has several features for the "power user." This book is for the Acrobat Pro user.

Acrobat Pro

Acrobat Pro has the same feature set as Acrobat Standard, but with some powerful additions. With Acrobat Pro, you can create PDF documents from within AutoCAD, Microsoft Project, and Microsoft Visio. Acrobat Pro also features additional commenting tools, enhanced multimedia support, and much more. Acrobat 7.0 for Windows featured the addition of the Adobe LiveCycle Designer, which enables you to create interactive PDF forms either by using preset templates or from scratch. Adobe LiveCycle Designer ES 2 (an enhanced version of the original Adobe LiveCycle Designer) is included with the Windows version of Acrobat X Pro.

Adobe Acrobat Pro Components

Adobe Acrobat Pro can be ordered as part of a suite, as a standalone application on DVD, or online as a downloadable application. Adobe Acrobat Pro X ships with the following components.

Adobe Acrobat X Pro

This is the core application. You use Acrobat to publish and edit PDF documents. In future chapters, you will learn how to use the program features to create and publish PDF files for a variety of destinations. You can also use Acrobat to capture web pages and save them as PDF files, as well as scan printed documents into Acrobat and save them as PDF files.

Adobe LiveCycle Designer ES 2

Adobe LiveCycle Designer ES 2 is installed with the Windows version of Acrobat Pro. This application, which can be launched from within Acrobat, gives you the power to create interactive PDF forms either from scratch or by using one of the many preset templates that ship with the application. In addition, you can edit existing PDF forms in Adobe LiveCycle Designer ES 2. Even though LiveCycle Designer ES is an integral part of Acrobat, it is a standalone application that is launched from the Windows Start menu. A LiveCycle Designer form can be filled in using Acrobat X Pro or Adobe Reader X.

Acrobat Distiller X

Acrobat Distiller X is used to create PDF documents from PostScript files in Encapsulated PostScript (EPS) or PostScript (PS) format. The Distiller Conversion Settings help you to optimize the document for its intended destination. Although Acrobat Distiller X is a separate application, you can launch it from within Acrobat.

What's New in Adobe Acrobat X

Acrobat X has many major enhancements. The program also has many new features. The major new features are listed here:

- **Improved scanning**   When you create a PDF document by scanning a document, Acrobat X Pro has better optical character recognition (OCR) than previous versions of Acrobat. The file sizes are also smaller with better image and color fidelity.
- **PDF Portfolios**   PDF Portfolios were introduced in Acrobat 9.0. Acrobat X gives you more options for customizing a PDF Portfolio with new layouts and themes. You can also customize PDF Portfolios by importing layouts created by third-party vendors.
- **Actions**   Use the new Actions Wizard to automate frequently performed tasks as a single action. You can use an action on a single PDF document or a batch of PDF documents in a folder.
- **Quick Tools**   You can add your most frequently used tools to the Quick Tools bar, which is below the menu bar. This option allows you to keep your favorite tools in one easy-to-access spot.
- **New interface**   All of the Acrobat tools are conveniently stored in the pane on the right side of the interface. The pane is divided into three sections: Tools, Comments, and Share.

Create a PDF Document

The flexible tools in Acrobat give you several options for creating and publishing documents for electronic distribution in PDF format. You create PDF files from within Acrobat by importing documents authored in other applications, by saving documents created in authoring applications such as Adobe Photoshop, or by using the Acrobat

PDFMaker to convert a Microsoft Office document. Several third-party plug-ins are available for working with PDF files in previous versions of Acrobat, a trend that is bound to continue with Acrobat X. Many scanning utilities, such as ScanSoft's OmniPage Pro 17, feature PDF output as an option. Third-party Acrobat plug-ins also have been tailor-made to suit specific industries.

After you convert a supported file type into a PDF document or open a PDF file created by another author, you can add interactive elements such as text hyperlinks, image hyperlinks, and multimedia elements, including QuickTime movies, Flash SWF movies, and sound files. You can append an existing PDF file by inserting other documents, deleting pages, inserting pages, or replacing pages. You can also do other housekeeping chores, such as cropping the physical size of a page, removing sensitive information from a document, or editing each page in the document to delete unwanted elements. You can also modify a PDF document by removing unnecessary pages, extracting pages to make a new PDF document, or adding pages to the document. Acrobat has a set of tools that let you make minor modifications to graphic and text elements in the document. A published PDF document retains the look and feel of the original. All the fonts and images you used in the original document are carried over to the PDF document. Figure 1-2 shows a document in Microsoft Word;

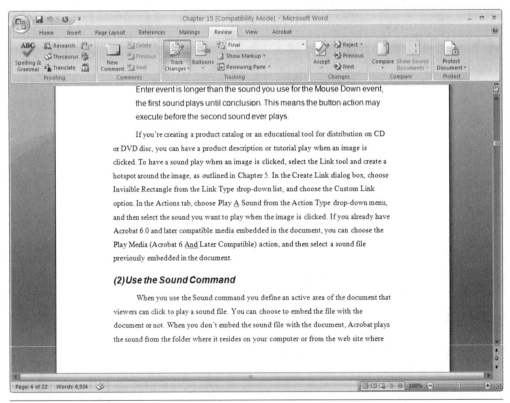

FIGURE 1-2   You can convert Microsoft Word files, such as this, into PDF documents.

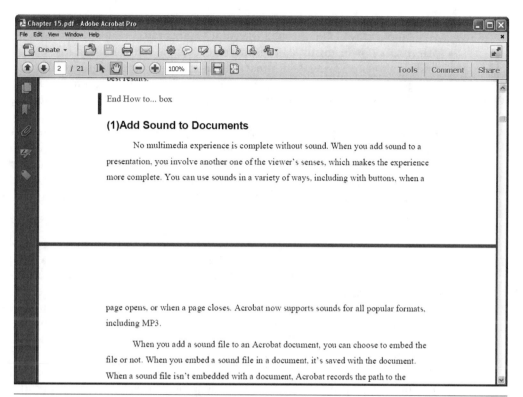

FIGURE 1-3   The PDF version of a converted Word document retains the look and feel of the original.

Figure 1-3 shows the same document after being converted to a PDF file. Other than the different interfaces, the documents look identical.

Create PDF Documents from Authoring Applications

The easiest way to create a PDF document is to create a file in an authoring application and then convert it to a PDF file. You can create PDF files from any of these popular Microsoft applications (Microsoft Office 2003 or newer):

- **Microsoft Word**   Microsoft Word is a word processing application. Within limits, you can add graphic elements to the content of a Word document.
- **Microsoft Excel**   Microsoft Excel is a spreadsheet program. Excel also has limited support for graphic elements.
- **Microsoft Outlook**   Microsoft Outlook is an application used to manage contacts, appointments, and e-mail. You can archive selected e-mail messages

or complete folders as PDF documents. All message attachments are archived as well, and are available through the Attachments tab.

- **Microsoft PowerPoint**   Microsoft PowerPoint is software used to create presentations. A PowerPoint presentation is similar to a slideshow. You can add graphic elements to your presentation and then convert it to a PDF file. Many slideshow transitions and other effects are preserved in the resulting PDF document.
- **Microsoft Project**   Microsoft Project is project management software. With this software, you can track schedules and project resources, as well as communicate and report the project status to others.
- **Microsoft Visio**   Microsoft Visio is used to create floor plans, flowcharts, software diagrams, and more. This software dovetails seamlessly with Microsoft Project to create project schedules.

When you install Acrobat X, the installer adds the Acrobat PDFMaker plug-in to any Microsoft Office application (with the exception of InfoPath, OneNote, and Groove, and any Microsoft application for Macintosh computers) and Internet Explorer. After installing Acrobat, you will see the Acrobat PDF shortcuts on your menu bar or in the Microsoft Office 2007 and 2010 Ribbon. You convert an Office document to PDF using the icons or menu commands in Office 2003, or by choosing options from the Ribbon in Office 2007 and Office 2010. You learn how to convert Microsoft Office documents to PDF documents in Chapter 4.

If you own certain Adobe products, such as InDesign, Illustrator, or Photoshop, you can use a menu command to export a document in PDF format. Other illustration programs, such as CorelDraw, also have the capability to export files in PDF format.

You can publish PDF files from any other application you use to generate images, illustrations, or text files. When you install Acrobat, Adobe PDF is added as a system printer. To publish a PDF file directly from an authoring application, choose the Print command and then choose Adobe PDF from the list of available printers. You can then open the resulting PDF file in Acrobat to add enhancements, such as links and form fields.

Create PDF Documents from PostScript Files

If you create illustrations and documents in illustration or page layout programs and publish the documents in EPS or PS format, you can convert these files to PDF format with Acrobat Distiller. After you launch Distiller and select an EPS or PS file, select one of the preset Distiller conversion settings or create your own conversion setting. You use conversion settings to optimize a PDF file for an intended destination, such as print, screen, or the Web. You can use Distiller to create a PDF proof of an illustration you're creating for a client. After you save the file in PDF format, you can then e-mail it to a client for approval.

You can quickly create a PDF document by dragging and dropping a supported file icon from your desktop onto the Acrobat shortcut icon. After you release the mouse button, the file opens in Acrobat. If the file isn't supported, Acrobat displays a dialog box noting that the file either is not a supported file type or may be corrupt. If you have the Distiller shortcut on your desktop, you can create a PDF document by dragging and dropping an EPS or PS file onto the Distiller icon.

Create PDF Documents for the Internet

If you design websites, you can use PDF documents in a variety of effective ways. For example, you can create a product catalog, create interactive PDF tutorials, create PDF forms, and publish a manual, all in PDF format. The website visitor can choose to view the document in the web browser or download the complete file for future viewing. Most popular web browsers support Adobe Acrobat and Adobe Reader X as plug-ins or helper applications. Figure 1-4 shows a published document as displayed in Internet Explorer. Note that the figure shows a document displayed in the plug-in version of Acrobat X Pro, not Adobe Reader X.

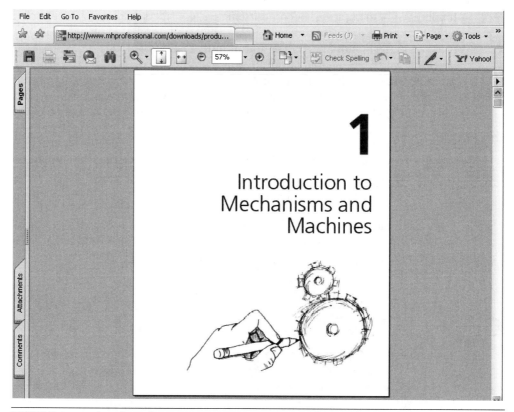

FIGURE 1-4   Acrobat also serves as an Internet Explorer plug-in that enables you to view PDFs from websites.

Capture Web Pages as PDF Documents

If you do a lot of research on the Internet, you can capture web pages for future reference. When you capture a web page, Acrobat downloads the text and graphic elements from the web page, complete with hyperlinks. If you want to add additional pages from the same site to the PDF file, simply click the desired hyperlink in the captured page and Acrobat will append the document by downloading the linked page. You can use the Acrobat File | Create | PDF From Web Page command (or choose the Create PDF From Web Page command from the Create Task button) to download complex tutorials from the Internet and save them as PDF files for easy reference. If you download numerous web pages for reference, you can create a searchable index of your reference files with the Full Text Index With Catalog command in the Document Processing section of the Tools pane. You will learn how to capture web pages in Chapter 5.

Convert Scanned Documents to PDF Format

If you have hard copies of documents such as contracts or product brochures that you need to share with coworkers or clients, you'll find Acrobat to be user friendly. You could send the documents by fax, but in most cases, what your recipient receives isn't anything near a reasonable facsimile of the original. To overcome the difference in resolution and quality of fax machines, create a PDF file for the document you want to share. If you have a scanner hooked up to your system, the Acrobat install utility adds the TWAIN information of the scanner as a scanner in the Create PDF From Scanner dialog box. Then, it's simply a matter of choosing Create PDF From Scanner from the Create Task button drop-down menu. After you scan the document into Acrobat, save it as a PDF file and then e-mail it. When your document is received and viewed in Adobe Reader X, it looks identical to what you scanned into Acrobat.

You can also use the File | Create | PDF From Scanner command to archive dog-eared magazine articles, for example, for future reference in PDF format. If you enable the Make Searchable (Run OCR) option, Acrobat converts the scanned document into searchable text—a powerful feature if you scan multipage magazine articles or documents for conversion to PDF files. You will learn how to convert scanned documents to PDF files in Chapter 5.

Create PDF Documents for Print

You also benefit from using Acrobat when you create PDF documents for print. Thanks to the available formatting and conversion setting options, all versions of Acrobat, as well as the Adobe Reader X software, make sure your published documents always print as you intended.

After you optimize a file for print, Acrobat X Pro gives you options for sending the file to the output device. The Print dialog box in Acrobat X Pro has an Advanced button. When you click the Advanced button, a separate dialog box opens that enables you to specify print resolution and output options. You can also specify options such as trim marks, transparency levels, and the capability of omitting images when printing a proof of the PDF file. Viewing and printing separations are only two of the many options available when creating a PDF to be used by a printing service. You can find more options for creating a PDF for a printing service under the Print Production section of the Tools Pane.

Create Interactive PDF Documents

When some Acrobat users create PDF documents for the first time, they tend to think the document will be read in linear fashion. However, you can use the Acrobat Link tool to create documents that can be navigated like web pages. You can use the Link tool to change static text or images into hyperlinks. When you create a link in a PDF document, it serves many purposes. You can use the link to open another PDF document, to navigate to a specific page in the current PDF document, to link to a URL on the Web, and much more. A link in a PDF document functions exactly as a link in an HTML page. When you position your mouse over the link, the cursor changes to a pointing hand. Interactive navigation for PDF documents is covered in Chapters 6 and 7.

Create PDF Documents for Multimedia Presentations

The age of electronic education is very much upon us. Fluctuating demands in the workplace make lifelong learning a necessity. People in all stages of life need to increase their knowledge base. Most lifelong learners don't have time for formal classroom education and, instead, use online education to learn at their own pace. Online learners can log on and take a lesson according to their schedule. Other lifelong learners purchase interactive CD-ROMs and play the discs in their spare time to educate themselves. PDF documents are an excellent way to educate online because they can contain multimedia content and are viewable in the student's web browser.

If, on the other hand, you're authoring a PDF document for an online or CD-ROM presentation, you can accomplish the task with Acrobat Pro. When you create a PDF document for an online or CD-ROM presentation, Acrobat X Pro provides you with the necessary tools to elevate your presentation to the next level. Multimedia is the current buzzword for online education, educational CD-ROMs, and business presentations. With Acrobat X Pro, you can create PDF documents with multimedia elements, such as movie clips, music, and the spoken word. You can use the Sound command in the Multimedia section of the Content section of the Tools pane, or the Record Audio command found in the Annotations section of the Comment pane, to record an audio clip or add a prerecorded sound clip to a document. After you add interaction, you can create links within the document to play multimedia clips or have them play when a document page is opened. In Chapter 15, you learn to create PDF files with multimedia elements.

Create PDF Documents for Internal Distribution

Many modern companies realize that using paper to distribute information is not efficient. Paper is bulky, it takes up room, and it's an expensive way to distribute written information with a short lifespan. If the company is a multilocation operation, there's also the cost of transporting published documents between locations. A PDF document is a much better solution for disseminating information efficiently over the corporate intranet, sent via e-mail, or distributed on disk. An employee manual in print form might take up hundreds of pages, plus a hefty portion of the employee's workspace. The same document can be created in PDF format and distributed to employees on a floppy disk or CD-ROM. A PDF employee manual uses fewer resources, is easier to distribute, and is easier to use. An employee looking for specific information can use the Advanced Search options, which are accessed from the Search dialog box (as shown in Figure 1-5) to find specific information in a PDF document.

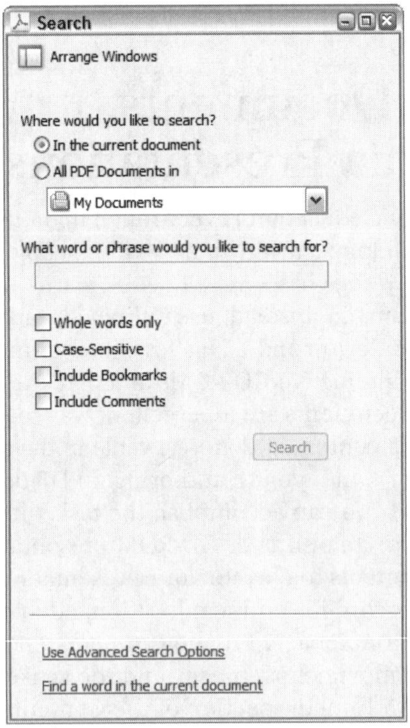

FIGURE 1-5 You can easily find relevant information using the powerful Search command.

You can also use PDF documents to distribute memos. If you author a confidential memo, you can password-protect the document and add other Acrobat security measures to prevent editing or viewing by unauthorized personnel. If you need to edit a confidential document, you can always change the security settings to allow editing and then disable editing after you make the changes.

When you create a document for internal distribution, recipients can sign off on the document using the Digital Signature feature. Digital signatures and document security are discussed in Chapter 10.

Optimize Documents for Distribution

Acrobat also enables you to optimize a PDF document for an intended destination, whether it be a CD-ROM presentation, a customer proof (a PDF document that serves as an example of a design in progress, such as a brochure or website), a document for a website, or a document that will be printed by a printing service. When you publish a PDF file optimized for a website and the website's hosting service supports byteserving (streaming a document into the viewers web browser), you can be assured the file will quickly download into the viewer's web browser.

Optimize Documents for Intended Destinations

If you've ever created images and documents for different destinations, you know a file needs to be formatted correctly for the intended destination. The file you create for print, the file you create for a website, and the file you create for a multimedia CD-ROM presentation all have different requirements. When you create files for print, you need to optimize them for the output device, matching the file as closely as possible to the printer resolution. If the file is destined for a commercial printing service, you use Acrobat X Pro's powerful Print Production options and save the document as a PDF/X or PDF/A file. On the other hand, when you create a PDF file for a multimedia CD-ROM application, you need to worry only about screen resolution. When you create a document for the Web, you need to achieve a happy medium between image quality and bandwidth. (*Bandwidth* is the amount of information that can be downloaded per second at a given connection speed—for example, 56 Kbps.)

Modify Conversion Settings

Acrobat Distiller comes with preset conversion settings to optimize a document for an intended destination. If you create a PDF file from a Microsoft Office application, the PDFMaker plug-in has several options available that can be changed using Preferences from the Acrobat menu, or if you own Office 2007 or Office 2010 by choosing Preferences from the Acrobat ribbon. If none of the presets suits the document you're publishing, you can modify a preset to create and save the parameters as a custom Adobe PDF Settings file with the .joboptions extension. Chapter 11 is devoted to optimizing PDF documents.

View PDF Documents

When you use different applications to publish documents for electronic distribution, the documents can be read only if the recipients have a copy of the authoring software installed on their computers. If you work for a large corporation and need to electronically distribute documents to a large number of coworkers, your employer ends up spending a fortune in software licensing fees. But if you publish the documents in PDF format, any coworker can read them as long as a copy of Adobe Reader X is installed on their computer. Adobe doesn't charge licensing fees when you distribute copies of Adobe Reader X. Therefore, sending documents in PDF format is a cost-effective way to distribute documents within large organizations. PDF documents created using Acrobat 10.0 format can only be read with the latest version of Acrobat or the Adobe Reader, and certain features may not be supported by earlier versions of Acrobat or the Adobe Reader. To make the document compatible with earlier versions of the software, you have to optimize the document for the version of the software or reader used by your intended audience.

If your published PDF documents are included on a website, most popular web browsers support Adobe Acrobat or the Adobe Reader, which enables viewers to display PDF files within their browsers. The plug-in used to view PDF documents in a web browser is installed when Adobe Acrobat or the Adobe Reader is installed on a user's computer. To accommodate any visitors to your website who don't have Adobe Reader 9.0 or an earlier version installed, you can add a direct link from your website to the Adobe website so these visitors can easily download the Reader for free.

Note Adobe Reader X is available for free at the following URL: http://get.adobe.com/reader/.

Another benefit you have as a PDF author is cross-platform compatibility. Any graphics you use are embedded in the published PDF document, and fonts can be embedded as well. When your published PDF documents are viewed with Adobe Reader X, they display as you created them, regardless of resources available on the viewer's operating system. If fonts aren't embedded in the document, and the viewer's machine doesn't have a font used in the PDF, Acrobat automatically uses a Multiple Master font to produce a reasonable facsimile of the font used in the original document. Embedding fonts is covered in Chapter 11.

Certain limitations are present. Generally speaking, sans serif and serif fonts are reproducible using the MM fonts. Fonts such as Wingdings and handwriting fonts, however, aren't reproducible.

Did You Know?

How Streaming Works

Many file formats viewed over the Internet are streamed into the user's browser. When a file is streamed into a browser, it doesnt have to download completely before the viewer can begin to see the file. The first part of the file (or *frame*, if the file is a Flash movie or a streaming movie) is displayed as soon as enough data has been downloaded. When a viewer opens a PDF document in a web browser, if the author has saved the document properly, the document downloads a page at a time, which is known as *byteserving* and is similar to streaming. As soon as enough data has downloaded, the first page of the document appears in the user's browser. After the first page has loaded, a user can elect to advance to a later page, which is then byteserved into the user's browser. While the user is viewing the desired page, the rest of the document is streamed in the background until it is loaded in the user's browser cache.

Use Acrobat as a Publishing Solution

If you read this chapter from the start, you're beginning to realize the power and diversity of Acrobat. You can use Acrobat X Pro as a publishing solution within a large corporation, to distribute documents over the Internet, to share documents with clients who don't own the software you used to create the original document, and to review documents. Acrobat can be used to create a simple electronic interoffice memo, a form for collecting data, or a complex presentation with interactive navigation and multimedia elements. Acrobat makes it possible for you to create a single document in an authoring program, such as Microsoft Excel, and publish the file as different PDF documents optimized for different destinations. With Acrobat X Pro, you can publish PDF documents with multimedia elements such as full-motion video and sound files.

Summary

In this chapter, you learned about the powerful new features in Acrobat X Pro and how you can utilize the software as a paperless publishing solution. In Chapter 2, you get a look at the nuts and bolts that make it possible for you to create a wide variety of PDF documents, and you learn how to navigate the Acrobat interface and use Quick Tools.

2

Navigate the Acrobat Workspace

HOW TO...

- Navigate the Acrobat workspace
- Utilize Quick Tools
- Select Acrobat tools
- Set Acrobat preferences

In this chapter, you will discover what you can accomplish with the wide variety of tools on the Acrobat X Pro toolbar and pane on the right side of the interface, which is divided into three sections: Tools, Comment, and Share. As an author of PDF documents, you spend a good deal of time working in Acrobat. In this regard, you'll find it useful to know the layout of the Acrobat workspace like the back of your hand. When you begin working with Acrobat, you'll see that the Navigation pane and Create task button are logically arranged for productive workflow. Knowing that no two people work alike, Adobe has designed Acrobat so you can easily add your favorite tools to the Quick Tools section of the toolbar. You can also change the settings in Acrobat's Preferences dialog box to suit your workflow.

But before we get started touring the Acrobat interface, here's something to keep in mind regarding the Adobe Reader. As an author of PDF documents, you may not feel learning how to use Adobe Reader X is imperative. After all, you'll do most of your work in Acrobat Pro X. The people who receive and view your PDF documents, however, may have only the Adobe Reader. Also, you will be sending PDF documents to people with varying levels of computer savvy. Occasionally, the recipients of your documents may require assistance with the Adobe Reader, so you should take some time to familiarize yourself with the application's menu commands and tool groups. This is especially important if you plan to include Adobe Reader X users in a document review cycle and enable them to fill in forms. Adobe Reader X has an interface similar to Acrobat X Pro, but without the robust toolset and menu commands used to author a PDF document, add security, and so on.

Navigate the Acrobat Interface

When you open a document in Acrobat X Pro, the workspace consists of the document pane, the Create task button, a toolbar, and a menu bar, as shown in Figure 2-1. The majority of the commands you use are accessed by clicking the Tools, Comment, or Share icon on the right side of the interface. The left side of the interface has icons you use to open the Page Thumbnails, Bookmarks, Attachments, and Signatures panes. In the following sections, you will find a brief overview of each tool group and the various menu commands for both versions of Acrobat. You can find concise information on how to use each tool in the subsequent chapters of this book.

Use the Navigation Pane

The Acrobat Navigation pane has four icons you can click to navigate to specific items in a document:

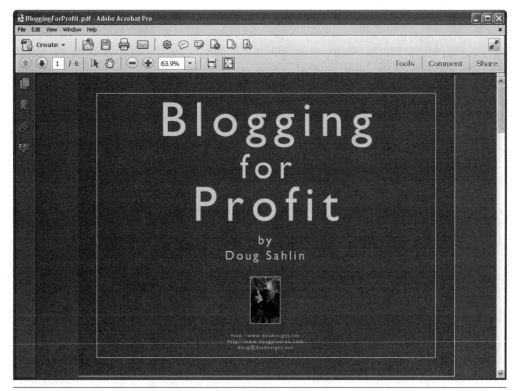

FIGURE 2-1 The Acrobat workspace consists of the Document pane, icons, a task button, a menu command bar, and a toolbar.

- **Page Thumbnails**   Provides thumbnail images of each page in the document
- **Bookmarks**   Displays a list of the bookmarks in the document
- **Attachments**   Enables you to manage any files attached to the PDF document
- **Signatures**   Lists the digital signatures applied to the document

These icons appear by default in the Navigation pane. You can open additional panels that you use frequently and dock them in the Navigation pane. Click an icon to open the Navigation pane to that particular panel and then click an icon or text area within the panel to navigate to a specific point in the document. Right-click a Navigation pane icon to add additional panels to the Navigation pane or to reset the pane to its default settings.

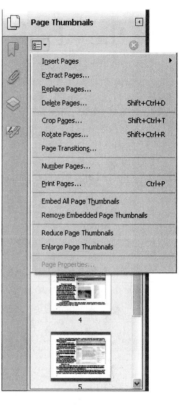

Tip   In addition to using these panels for document navigation, you also use them to perform specific functions, such as adding or deleting bookmarks; changing the size of thumbnails; extracting, inserting, replacing, or deleting pages; and so on. You click the Options icon, which is in the top-left corner of each panel, to open a menu with options that pertain to the panel, as shown next. The operations you can perform differ, depending on the selected panel. You will find many of the panel Options menu commands duplicated in menu command groups. You will learn the different ways you can achieve the same result when specific topics, such as bookmarks and digital signatures, are covered in upcoming chapters.

In addition to the Options menu, other icons vary in accordance with the tab you selected. A round red circle with a white X icon is used to delete selected items from the tab. In the upper-right corner of each panel's window, you'll find a left-pointing arrow, which you can click to close the Navigation pane.

About the Document Pane

You use the Document pane (the large window to the right of the Navigation pane, previously shown in Figure 2-1) to edit a PDF document, as well as to read it. At the top of the Document pane is a toolbar that contains tools you can use to navigate to a specific page or pan to a specific place in the document and the Create task button. You use the Read Mode command when you read a document, which hides all toolbars and the Navigation pane, to maximize your screen real estate. When you work in Read Mode, you can access a navigation menu by pausing your cursor over the bottom of the document you are reading. You can unhide the tools and panels with a keyboard shortcut or menu command. In Chapter 3, you will learn how to use this feature and all the other Acrobat tools.

Use the Acrobat Menu Commands

You find the Acrobat menu commands at the top of the interface, grouped by command type. Acrobat has five command groups, described in the following list in order from left to right on the menu bar. In upcoming chapters, you will learn to use the commands from these menus to unlock the powerful features of Acrobat, such as capturing web pages. Individual menu commands are presented in detail when they pertain to the topic of discussion.

- **File**   The commands in the File group are used to create PDF files; create PDF Portfolios; and to open, close, and save documents. Additional commands are used to attach the current PDF to an e-mail, share files online, view document information, and launch the new Action Wizard.
- **Edit**   As the name implies, the commands in the Edit group are used to edit the current PDF document. There are also commands to search for items in the current document, search for words or phrases in PDF documents stored in folders on your computer, find words or phrases in a document, check spelling in comments and editable text, and set Acrobat preferences (Windows). You will learn how to set Acrobat preferences in the later section "Set Preferences."
- **View**   The commands in the View group are used to change your view of the document. You use menu commands in this group to navigate to a specific page in the document, zoom in or out, change the manner in which the page is displayed, rotate the view, and so on. You will also find commands in this group to access Navigation panels and the toolbars.
- **Window**   The commands in the Window group are used to select documents you currently have open, split the view into two panes or spreadsheet view, as well as arrange the view of multiple documents. You can also view a document in full-screen mode by accessing a command from this menu. Another command enables you to open the active document in a new window.
- **Help**   In the Help command group, you can find access to complete program help, links to online help and program updates, as well as a feature you can use to repair the Acrobat installation if you feel something has gone awry. If you use Acrobat to read e-books, you can manage digital editions from the Help command group.

Use Acrobat Toolbars

Many of the tools you use in Acrobat are conveniently grouped and laid out as a task button and tool groups on a toolbar. You can access the rest of the Acrobat tools by choosing View | Show/Hide Toolbar Items and then selecting the desired tool from the submenu. In the default display of toolbars, you can find a Create task button that you use to create PDF documents. In the other toolbars, you find related tools to edit, view, and navigate documents, and to perform many other operations. In addition, the Quick Tools toolbar has what the Acrobat designers deem as tools that are frequently used by most Acrobat users. You can customize the Quick Tools toolbar to add your favorite tools, or remove tools you don't often use.

Many of the toolbars have drop-down menus containing other options. The page magnification options are a perfect example: The display and magnification options appear when the down-pointing arrow to the right of the current magnification option is clicked.

You can do much of your work in Acrobat using the toolbars, but many tools have equivalent menu commands. Most Acrobat users find it convenient to work with a combination of menu commands, tools, context menus, and shortcuts. Figure 2-2 shows the default display of Acrobat X Pro toolbars.

The following sections describe the default Acrobat display of task buttons and toolbars as they appear below the menu bar. In each toolbar section, individual tools are listed with a brief description of the task for which they are used. In future chapters, you find detailed information about using a specific tool in conjunction with a related task.

The Create Task Button

The Create task button, shown here, accesses commands used to create a PDF document. When you click this button, a drop-down menu appears with all the commands you need to create PDF documents from files stored on your computer, from web pages, from documents you scan into the Document pane, and from images you've copied to the system clipboard. These commands are as follows:

- **PDF From File**   Click the PDF From File button to navigate to a file on your computer and convert it to a PDF document. Creating PDF documents from supported files is covered in detail in Chapter 3.
- **PDF From Scanner**   Click the PDF From Scanner button to create a PDF document from a scanner or a digital camera attached to your computer. Capturing PDF documents from scanners is covered in detail in Chapter 5.
- **Create PDF From Web Page**   Click the PDF From Web Page button, and a dialog box appears in which you enter the URL of the web page you want to convert to

FIGURE 2-2   You use Acrobat task buttons and toolbars to create, edit, and navigate PDF documents.

a PDF document. After converting the web page, you can modify it by clicking Tools, clicking Document Processing, choosing Web Capture, and then choosing the desired command from the submenu. Capturing web pages is covered in Chapter 5.

- **PDF From Clipboard**   Click the PDF From Clipboard button to create a PDF document after using the Snapshot tool to select an area from an open PDF document and copy it as an image to the clipboard. You can also create a PDF after copying content to the clipboard from another application.
- **Combine Files Into A Single PDF**   Click this button to open the Combine Files dialog box, which enables you to create a PDF from supported files or existing PDF documents. The files can be mixed formats supported by Acrobat. In addition, you can specify which pages of each document are combined into the resulting PDF.
- **PDF Form**   Click this button to open the Create Or Edit Form dialog box. This enables you to use the current document as the basis for a PDF form, browse for a file that you make into a PDF form, or scan a paper form.
- **PDF Portfolio**   Click this button to open the Create PDF Portfolio dialog box, which enables you to create a sophisticated portfolio of documents in PDF format.

The File Toolbar

The File toolbar, shown here, consists of four tools you use to open, print, save, and e-mail PDF documents.

Here are the tools on the File toolbar:

- **Open**   Click this button to navigate to and open an existing PDF file stored on your computer or network.
- **Save**   This tool is used to save the current PDF document. This command is dimmed out (unavailable) if you open an existing PDF document. When you open an existing document and apply changes, the Save button becomes available.
- **Print**   This tool is used to print a document with a system printer.
- **Email**   Click this button to send a PDF document as an e-mail attachment using your default e-mail application. If you're logged onto the Internet, and your e-mail application supports automatic mailing, the message and attachment are sent. Otherwise, the message and attachment appear in the out basket of your e-mail application.

The Page Navigation Toolbar

The Page Navigation toolbar is composed of the tools you use to navigate from one page to the next. The toolbar has forward and back buttons, which you use to go to the next or previous page, respectively. You can also navigate to a page by entering its number in the text box.

The Select & Zoom Toolbar

The tools in this toolbar (shown here) are used to select objects, manually navigate to different parts of a document, and activate links in the document.

- **Select**   This tool enables you to select text, tables, or images in a PDF document. You can then copy selected objects to the clipboard for use in other applications.
- **Hand**   This aptly named tool is used to manually navigate through the pages of a PDF document. First, click the tool to select it; then, when you click inside the Document pane to navigate with this tool, your cursor becomes a closed fist. To navigate from the top to the bottom of a page, and vice versa, select the Hand tool, move the tool over the document, and then click and drag. Release the left mouse button to stop scrolling the page. The Hand tool is also used to find and activate links within the document. When you pass your cursor over a document link or a bookmark in the Bookmark tab, the cursor becomes a pointing finger. Click the link or bookmark to navigate to the specified destination within the document.
- **Zoom Out**   Click this tool to zoom out to the next lowest level of magnification.
- **Zoom In**   Click this tool to zoom in to the next highest level of magnification.
- **Magnification Window**   Acrobat displays the current percentage level of magnification in this window. You can click the triangle to the right of the window and select a magnification percentage from the drop-down menu, or you can enter the desired level of magnification directly into the window and then press ENTER or RETURN to apply. You can also specify a magnification level by choosing View | Zoom | Zoom To and then entering a value between 1 percent and 6400 percent in the Zoom To dialog box (the available range of magnification in Acrobat). Note that the lowest magnification level available from the Magnification drop-down list is 10 percent, but you can enter a value of 1 if desired.

The Page Display Toolbar

The Page Display toolbar, shown here, has two buttons by default. You use these buttons to control your view of the page.

Here are the buttons on the Page Display toolbar:

- **Continuous**   This page display option adjusts the width of the page to fit within the width of the Document pane. You can use the Hand tool to navigate within the page and scroll to different pages.
- **Single Page**   This option displays a single page. You can use the Hand tool to pan within the page and use the navigation tools to navigate to different pages.

Use the Panes

Acrobat has lots of tools and menu commands. Previous versions of Acrobat displayed most of the tools on the menu command bar. In Acrobat X Pro, you perform tasks by choosing menu commands that are conveniently located in panes on the right side of the interface. You have three panes with which to work: Tools, Comment, and Share.

Use the Tools Pane

In the Tools pane, you find commands to edit pages, edit content, create forms, use the Action Wizard, recognize text from scanned documents, and protect the document. To access the Tools pane, click the Tools icon. The illustration at left shows the default sections in the Tools pane. Click a section title to reveal a group of related commands. The commands in each section will be covered in future chapters of the book. The Tools pane is divided into the following sections.

Pages

The Pages section, shown left, has commands that enable you to edit pages, insert pages, and edit page design. You also find commands to rotate pages, delete pages, extract pages, replace pages, crop pages, insert a header or footer, insert a background, insert a watermark, and implement Bates Numbering.

Content

The Content section, shown right, has commands that enable you to add bookmarks, attach files, edit text and objects, add or edit interactive content, add links, add buttons, and select objects.

Forms

The Forms section, shown right, has commands that you use to create forms. After creating a form, you can add and edit form fields as well as distribute and track forms. Form creation will be covered in detail in Chapter 13.

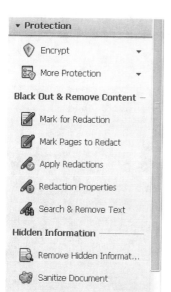

Action Wizard

The Action Wizard section, shown left, has commands to create and edit actions. You also find the default actions in this section of the Tools pane. Actions will be covered in detail in Chapter 14.

Recognize Text

The Recognize Text section, shown right, is used after you create a PDF by scanning a document. You can recognize text in a single document or multiple documents. You can also scan for suspects.

Protection

The Protection section contains commands that you use to protect documents. You can encrypt pages, remove sensitive information from documents, remove hidden information, and sanitize documents. Protecting documents will be covered in detail in Chapter 10.

Sign & Certify

In the Sign & Certify section, you can add digital signatures to a document and certify a document. These options will be covered in detail in Chapter 10.

Document Processing

In the Document Processing section, you find commands to optimize scanned PDFs, capture web pages as PDF documents, number pages, add page transitions, and much more.

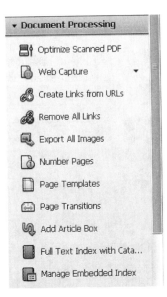

Print Production

In the Print Production section, you find commands to get documents ready for commercial printing services. You can add printer marks, convert colors, set the crop, art, and trim boxes, and much more. You can also access the Acrobat Distiller in this section. The Acrobat Distiller converts PostScript and Encapsulated PostScript files to PDF format.

Display Other Tools Sections

The tools sections previously discussed are shown by default in the Tools pane. You can access additional sections by clicking the Show/Hide Panels button in the upper-right corner of the Tools pane. The following sections describe the other sections in the Tools pane.

JavaScript

When you show the JavaScript section of the Tools pane, you find commands to debug JavaScript, edit JavaScript, edit document JavaScripts, and set document actions.

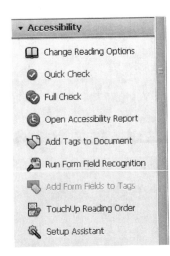

Accessibility

When you show the Accessibility section of the Tools pane, you find commands to add tags to a document, run checks to make sure the document is accessible to visually impaired people, run form field recognition, and much more.

Analyze

In this section, you find commands to analyze a document. You can check object data, measure distances, and check geospatial data.

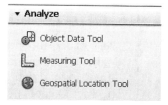

Use the Comments Pane

Acrobat has some powerful commands you use to review documents and collaborate with other members of your team. This pane has commands to add annotations to a document, mark up a document, and much more. The Comments pane contains the following sections.

Annotations

In the Annotations section, you can add sticky notes, add attachments, add sound annotations, add your stamp of approval to a document, highlight text, and much more.

Drawing Markups

In the Drawing Markups section, you can annotate a document with shapes, text, lines, pencil marks, and much more. There is also an eraser that you use to edit pencil marks.

Review

In the Review section, you can send a document for a shared review, send a document for e-mail review, collaborate live, and track reviews.

Comments List

In the Comments List section (not shown), you find a list of all comments in a document. You can also search comments.

Use the Share Pane

In the Share pane, shown here, there is only one section: Send Files. From within this pane, you can attach a file to an e-mail or share a file with Adobe SendNow.

Customize the Workspace

As you become more comfortable with Acrobat, you'll find you use certain tools more often than others. Adobe has engineered flexibility into the program, making it possible for you to customize the workspace to suit your working preference by floating toolbars and tabs as well as by adding more tools to the toolbars you frequently use.

Add Tools to the Quick Tools Toolbar

When you edit PDF documents and perform the same task numerous times, reaching up to select a tool from the menu bar or one of the panes can be distracting. To add a menu command to the Quick Tools toolbar, open the applicable pane, right-click the desired command, and choose Add To Quick Tools.

How to... Save Time with Context Menus

Acrobat Pro has context menus that can streamline your production and speed your workflow. Context menu options vary depending on the tool you use and the pane in which you work. For example, if you access a context menu in Acrobat after selecting a block of text with the Select tool, you have a list of several options or commands you can perform on the selected block of text. If you open the context menu in Acrobat while in the Signatures panel, you have a different set of options that pertain to digital signatures within the document and their properties. Individual panel context menu commands and options are discussed in detail in later chapters of this book. To open a context menu associated with a panel, position your cursor within the panel and then right-click. To open a context menu specific to an object, select the object and then right-click.

Tip

If you frequently use panels (such as the Destinations and Articles panels), you can dock them within the Navigation pane. To dock a panel to the Navigation pane, right-click inside the Navigation pane and then choose the desired pane. To restore the Navigation pane to its default, right-click inside the Navigation pane and choose Reset Panes.

Access More Tools

Acrobat has many features and many tools. Prior to Acrobat 8.0, the tools were all displayed on toolbars, which in some instances caused confusion because the tools had similar icons. In other instances, like tools were displayed on drop-down menus with the last-used tool being displayed on the toolbar. To alleviate interface clutter and possible confusion, with the release of Acrobat 8.0 the designers created toolbars with only the most popular tools displayed, a tradition that continued with Acrobat 9.0. The other tools can be accessed from menu commands. You can, however, modify the toolbars by displaying more or fewer tools by doing the following:

1. Right-click (Windows) or CTRL-click (Macintosh) the toolbar you want to modify to display a menu with all toolbars, as shown here.
2. Pause your cursor over the menu to which you want to add tools, and Acrobat displays all tools associated with that toolbar. A checkmark appears by all tools currently shown on the toolbar. The Page Navigation tools menu is shown next.
3. Click a tool to add it to the toolbar.

To reset a toolbar, right-click it, pause your cursor over the desired menu, and choose Reset Toolbar from the menu. To reset all toolbars to their default states, choose View | Show/Hide | Toolbars | Reset Toolbars. Alternatively, you can press F8 to reset toolbars.

Get Complete Acrobat X Help

This book covers every major aspect of Acrobat. However, if you need more information about a specific topic, you can search the Acrobat X Help document, which is online. If you're connected to the Internet, choose Help | Adobe Acrobat X Pro Help. After choosing this command, Acrobat Help appears in your default web browser.

Set Preferences

Many people find the Acrobat configuration easy to work with on installation. However, you can change many Acrobat defaults by selecting the appropriate title in the Preferences dialog box. A preference setting exists for virtually every Acrobat task you can perform. Unfortunately, the sheer volume of parameters you can change is beyond the scope of this book. When preference options are important to an individual task, the options are covered in that section of the book. Even casual computer users can easily understand many of the preference settings; therefore, they won't be covered. If you need more information on an individual setting, however, choose Help | Adobe Acrobat X Pro Help. After the Acrobat Help file opens, click the Search link and enter the keyword or phrase for the specific information you need. To open the Preferences dialog box, shown next, choose Edit | Preferences and then select the desired preference category from the left-hand column.

Summary

In this chapter, you learned to navigate the Acrobat workspace. You were also introduced to the toolbars and task buttons you'll use to edit and add interactivity to PDF documents. You were shown the differences between the Acrobat Standard, Acrobat Pro, and Acrobat Professional toolsets, and you learned how to customize the workspace to suit your working preferences. In the next chapter, you learn how to read PDF documents with Acrobat, as well as how to create PDF documents.

PART II

Create PDF Documents

3

Create a PDF Document

HOW TO...

- Create a PDF file
- Use Acrobat Distiller
- Set conversion settings
- Set document properties
- Save PDF files
- Save PDF files in other formats

Acrobat X Pro enables you to create PDF documents from many sources. You can create a PDF file from within many authoring applications, use an application's Print command and choose Adobe PDF as the printer, or create documents directly in Acrobat. When you create a document within Acrobat, you have many options available. You can save a document using Acrobat defaults, or you can modify the document properties and add security to confidential documents. You can even use Acrobat to save documents in other formats. In this chapter, you learn the nuts and bolts of creating a bare-bones PDF file.

Create a PDF File

You can use Acrobat to quickly create PDFs from existing files. You can choose between two methods: the PDF From File command and the drag-and-drop method. When you create a PDF file using one of these methods, Acrobat converts the original file into PDF format. After Acrobat converts the file, you can save it as a PDF file or export it using another supported format for use in another application. You can also create a PDF document from within an authoring application by exporting the file in PDF format (if supported) or by using the application's Print command and choosing Adobe PDF as the printing device. Creating a PDF file from within an authoring application is covered in Chapter 4.

Use the PDF From File Command

In Adobe Acrobat, you use the PDF From File command or task button to open supported file formats as PDF documents. When you choose this command and select one or more files to open, Acrobat converts each file from its current format into PDF format. You can open the following formats as PDF files:

- **3D File** You can create PDF documents from 3D files in the .U3D and .PRC formats.
- **Autodesk AutoCAD** You can create technical drawings using the popular Autodesk AutoCAD software. You can create PDF documents from AutoCAD documents with the DWG, DWF, or DST file extension.
- **BMP** You can export BMP files from the most popular photo-editing programs, such as Adobe Photoshop CS2, CorelDRAW Graphics Suite X, and Macromedia Fireworks 8. Image files saved in the BMP format can have color depth as high as 24-bit.
- **Compuserve GIF** Graphic Interchange Format (GIF) files have 8-bit color depth (that is, a maximum of 256 colors). You can open GIF files saved in the GIF 87 format or GIF 89a format as PDF files. You can also open an animated GIF, but only the first frame of the animation is converted to PDF format.
- **HTML** Hypertext Markup Language (HTML) files are created for use as web pages on the Internet. You can open HTML files as PDF documents. When you open an HTML file as a PDF file, Acrobat reads any image tags (< img src = "yourimage.jpg" >) and converts the associated files as images in the PDF document in the exact position they appear when the HTML document is opened in a web browser. If the image is not available, Acrobat creates a bounding box that is the size of the image and displays the Alt text. Converting a web page to PDF format is a great way to create a client proof of a website under construction. You can also use the Capture Web Page command to open a web page from your hard drive or download a web page from the Internet. Web capture is discussed in Chapter 5.
- **InDesign** Adobe InDesign is a popular page layout program. Adobe InDesign documents have the .indd extension.
- **JDF** Job Definition Format (JDF) files are created for PDF documents destined for output by a printing service. JDF files are instructions to the printing service center that contain information such as the client name, product name, number of copies to be printed, whether the job will have cover pages, the type of binding used, and so on. The command to create a PDF from JDF files doesn't create a PDF file, but instead opens the JDF file in the JDF Job Definitions dialog box.
- **JPEG** Joint Photographic Experts Group (JPEG) image files are used for web graphics and multimedia presentations. JPEG files are compressed for quick download from the Web or to save file space in a multimedia presentation.
- **JPEG 2000** JPEG 2000 can be thought of as JPEG's big brother. The file format features advanced image compression, which results in high-quality images with smaller file sizes. The format also features progressive download and will be used

by next-generation digital-imaging devices. JPEG 2000 files are designated with the .jpf, .jpx, .jp2, .j2k, .j2c, or .jpc file extension.

- **Microsoft Office Applications**   Microsoft Office is a suite of applications that enables you to create documents, spreadsheets, presentations, and much more. You can convert Microsoft Excel, Word, Publisher, and PowerPoint documents to PDF. You can also archive Microsoft Outlook messages as PDF documents.
- **Microsoft Project**   You use Microsoft Project to manage projects and communicate the status of a project, as well as manage project resources with colleagues in your organization.
- **Microsoft Visio**   You use Microsoft Visio to create diagrams and flowcharts that enable you to document and share information and ideas with colleagues.
- **Multimedia files**   Create PDF documents from Adobe Flash video files, Apple MOV files, and MPEG video files.
- **PCX**   Image files in the Windows-only Picture Exchange format can be exported from most popular image-editing programs. The .pcx format is native to the Windows Paintbrush program, but many applications, such as Photoshop CS2 and CorelDRAW Graphics Suite X3, offer full support of the .pcx format. The .pcx format supports 24-bit color depth and can be opened directly in Acrobat as PDF files.
- **PICT (Macintosh only)**   Image files saved in the Macintosh PICT (Picture) format support 32-bit color depth. Although PICT files can be created in Windows-based image-editing programs, only the Macintosh version of Acrobat can open PICT images as PDF files.
- **PNG**   Portable Network Graphics (PNG) files use lossless compression, which ensures better image quality than JPEG and GIF files. The file format supports 8-bit color, 24-bit color, or 48-bit color.
- **PostScript/EPS**   Encapsulated PostScript (EPS) files are used in illustration programs such as Adobe Illustrator, CorelDRAW, and Macromedia FreeHand MX. EPS files can be composed of vector and bitmap graphics.
- **Text**   You can open text documents saved in the TXT format as PDF documents. Text files can be created in programs as sophisticated as Microsoft Word or as humble as the Notepad utility, which is included with versions of the Microsoft Windows operating system (OS).
- **TIFF**   Tagged Image File Format (TIFF) files can be compressed or uncompressed and support 32-bit color. People who create images in both platforms for print favor this format because of the high image resolution and clarity.
- **XPS**   XPS (XML Paper Specification) is Microsoft's answer to the PDF. XPS is part of Windows Vista. XPS is in its infancy, so the impact on Adobe and the industry standard PDF will not be known for some time.

You have several options for creating PDF files. You can create a PDF from a single file or by combining multiple files. The upcoming sections cover both scenarios, and they show you how to choose compression and color management for images converted to PDF.

Use the Create | PDF From File Command

When you need to convert a single file into a PDF document, you use the Create | PDF From File command. To convert an existing file to a PDF document, do the following:

1. Choose File | Create | PDF From File to access the Open dialog box. Alternatively, click the Create task button and choose PDF From File.
2. Choose an option from the Files Of Type drop-down menu (Windows) or Show pop-up menu (Macintosh), or accept the default All Files option. If you select a specific file type, only files of that type are visible for selection.
3. Select the file you want to convert to PDF.
4. If you specify a file type, before you select a file, the Settings button may become available. The available settings options vary, depending on the selected file type. For example, if you select TIFF from the Files Of Type drop-down menu and then click the Settings button, you can specify compression and color management settings. These settings are covered in the next section.
5. Click Open. Acrobat converts the file to PDF format. Figure 3-1 shows a JPEG image converted to PDF format.

FIGURE 3-1   Use the Create | PDF From File command to convert supported files into PDF documents.

After you convert a file to PDF format, you can modify the document using the Acrobat commands and toolset. You can then save the file in PDF format or choose a supported file format. Saving files is covered in the section "Save PDF Files."

Choose Compression and Color Management Settings for Image Files

When you choose the Create | PDF From File command and choose an image format from the Files Of Type drop-down menu, the Settings button becomes available, which enables you to control how much compression is applied to the image and to specify color management options. The Settings option is not available when you convert Compuserve GIF or JPEG 2000 files to PDF documents, and the Compression settings are dimmed out when you choose JPEG from the Files Of Type drop-down menu. After choosing an image format that has editable compression settings, click the Settings button to display the Adobe PDF Settings dialog box, shown here.

With all image formats except Compuserve GIF and JPEG 2000, you can specify the following compression settings from the Adobe PDF Settings dialog box:

- **Monochrome**   For 1-bit monochrome images, choose CCITT G4 to achieve good image quality, JBIG2 (Lossy) for better image quality, and JBIG2 (Lossless) for the best image quality. When an image is compressed, data is lost—hence, the term "lossy."
- **Grayscale**   For 8-bit grayscale images, choose ZIP to convert images or documents with images that have large areas of similar color or repeating patterns, choose JPEG quality for photorealistic images, or choose JPEG 2000 to take advantage of the format's superior compression and progressive download. When you choose JPEG, you have five quality options, ranging from Minimum (high compression, small file size, and low image quality) to Maximum (minimal compression, largest file size, and best image quality). When you choose JPEG 2000, you have six options, ranging from Minimum (high compression, small file size, and low image quality) to Lossless (little or no compression, largest file size, and best image quality).
- **Color**   For images with thousands (16 bit) to millions (32 and 48 bit) of colors, you can specify ZIP, JPEG, or JPEG 2000 with the same compression settings as discussed in the previous bullet.

With all image formats except BMP, Compuserve GIF, JPEG 2000, and PCX, you can specify color management settings. From within the Color Management section of the Adobe PDF Settings dialog box just shown, you can specify color management for RGB (image colors composed of red, green, and blue hues), CMYK (image colors composed of cyan, magenta, yellow, and black hues), Grayscale, and Other by choosing one of the following options for each format:

- **Preserve Embedded Profiles**   Acrobat uses an ICC color profile that has been embedded with the image.
- **Off**   Acrobat color profiles will be used in lieu of color profiles embedded with the image.
- **Ask When Opening**   Acrobat displays color profiles embedded with the image, giving you the option of whether or not to use them.

Use the Create | Combine Files Into A Single PDF Command

You can use the Create | Combine Files Into A Single PDF command to create a PDF document from multiple files in formats supported by Acrobat. When you create a PDF document from multiple files, you can mix files of different formats and specify the order in which the files appear in the converted PDF document. You can also use this command to append all currently open PDF documents. Yet another option is to create a PDF Portfolio that creates a PDF that displays each file as an thumbnail that when clicked opens the file as a PDF. Click a bookmark to open the associated document.

To convert multiple files into a PDF document, follow these steps:

1. Choose File | Create | Combine Files Into A Single PDF to open the Combine Files dialog box, shown on the next page. (Alternatively, click the Create task button and choose Combine Files Into A Single PDF.)
2. Choose one of the following options:
   - **Add Files**   Click this button to open the Add Files dialog box. Navigate to and select the desired files and then click OK to exit the dialog box.
   - **Add Folders**   Click this button to open the Browse For Folder dialog box. Navigate to and select the desired files and then click Add Files to exit the dialog box. All supported files from the selected folder are added to the list.
   - **Add PDF From Scanner**   Click this button to scan a document from your scanner and add it to the list of files to combine.
   - **Add Webpage**   Click this button to open the Add Webpage dialog box. After you specify a URL, it gets added to the list of files to combine.
   - **Add From Clipboard**   Click this button to add the contents of the clipboard to the list of files to combine.
   - **Add Email**   This opens the Add Email dialog box, which instructs you to drag and drop e-mails from Microsoft Outlook or Lotus Notes into the dialog box to add them to the list. Note that this option is not available for the Macintosh version of Acrobat.

- **Reuse Files**   Click this button to open the Reuse Files dialog box. The left pane of the dialog box displays a list of PDF documents created with the Combine Files command, and the right pane displays a list of the files used to create each PDF document. Click a PDF document to display the files used to create the document. You can elect to add all files used to create a PDF by selecting a title from the right pane or by selecting individual files in the right pane of the dialog box. Click Add Files to add the selected files to the list of files to combine.
- **Add Open Files**   Click this button to open the Open PDF Files dialog box, which displays a list of all documents currently open in Acrobat. All files are selected by default. Click an individual file to select it, or CTRL-click (Windows) or CMD-click (Macintosh) to select multiple files. Click Add Files to add the selected files to the list of files to combine.
3. After adding files to the list, you have the following options:
   - **Move Up**   Moves the selected file to the next highest position in the list. The order in which the files appear in the list is the order in which they appear in the converted PDF document. You can click this button, as needed, to move the file further up the list. This button is dimmed out when you select the first file or reach the top of the list.
   - **Move Down**   Moves the file to the next lowest position in the list. You can click this button as needed to move the file further down the list. This button is dimmed out when you move a file to the bottom of the list or select the last file.

- **Choose Pages** This option becomes available when you select a PDF or Word document from the list. Click the button and then select the pages you want to appear in the resulting PDF.
- **Remove** Removes the selected file from the list.

4. Click an icon to determine the file size of the resulting document. Your choices are as follows (from left to right):
   - **Smaller File Size** Optimizes all files to achieve the smallest file size. This option produces a PDF suitable for monitor viewing and e-mail distribution.
   - **Default File Size** Uses the default PDF conversion method. All PDF files retain their original settings. This option creates a PDF suitable for high-quality viewing and printing of business documents.
   - **Larger File Size** Produces the highest quality PDF. If the original files are high quality, the resulting PDF is suitable for high-quality printing or printing on an inkjet printer.
   - **Options** Click this button to display the Options For Conversion Settings dialog box, which contains four options: Always Enable Accessibility And Reflow, which creates a document that is accessible for the impaired; Always Add Bookmarks To Adobe PDF, which creates bookmarks in the resulting PDF; Continue Combining If An Error Occurs; and Convert All Files To PDF When Creating A Portfolio.

Note When the Enable Accessibility option is selected, Acrobat adds PDF structure/tags to the PDF. This increases the size of the resultant PDFs, regardless of the size option selected.

5. Click a radio button to choose one of the following options:
   - **Single PDF** Combines the files into a single PDF. The resulting PDF has bookmarks for each file. If you choose this option, right-click a document from the list to display the context menu. The Edit Bookmark For File button is an option on the context menu, which, when clicked, opens the Edit Bookmark For File dialog box. Enter the desired bookmark name and then click OK. The new bookmark name is displayed. Choose Reset Bookmark from the context menu to revert to the original bookmark name.
   - **PDF Portfolio** The PDF Portfolio has many options that will be discussed in detail in the next section.
6. Click Combine Files to combine the files. At this stage of the process, the dialog box reconfigures and displays a progress bar for each file being converted.
7. Click Save to open the Save As dialog box. Navigate to the folder in which you want to save the combined file and then click Save.

Create a PDF Portfolio

The latest PDF Portfolio is a marked improvement to the PDF Portfolio introduced in Acrobat 9. The PDF Portfolio is fully customizable. You can specify the layout, import a custom layout, specify a color scheme, and specify the information displayed about each file. You can create a PDF Portfolio as outlined in the previous section, with the exception of choosing the PDF Portfolio option in step 5. The following steps show the process in detail:

1. Choose File | Create | PDF Portfolio. After you choose this command, the Create PDF Portfolio dialog box appears, as shown next.

2. Choose one of the following layout options shown here:
   - **Click-Through**   A thumbnail of each portfolio file is displayed at the bottom of the portfolio. The user clicks a thumbnail to see a larger version of the file. The larger thumbnail has navigation controls, or it can be clicked to display an even larger version of the document.
   - **Freeform**   The thumbnails for files in the portfolio are arranged in a freeform pattern. The thumbnails can be rearranged to suit your taste. Users click a thumbnail to view and navigate through the document.
   - **Grid**   The thumbnails for the files in the portfolio are arranged on a grid. Users click a thumbnail to see the associated PDF file.
   - **Linear**   The files are arranged in linear format. The currently selected file is displayed as a large thumbnail. Users can click a smaller thumbnail to view a larger version of the file. Double-click the larger version of the file to read and navigate through it.
   - **Wave**   The files are arranged in a spinning pattern that spirals off the screen. A slider is used to navigate from file to file. Users can also click a smaller thumbnail to make it the current document. Double-click the larger version of the file to read and navigate through it.
   - **Import Custom Layout**   Click this button to import a custom layout.

3. Click Add Files to open the Add Files dialog box. From this dialog box, you can select any file in a format supported by Acrobat.
4. After selecting the files, click Finish. The files are converted to PDF format, and Acrobat is reconfigured as shown next. Notice the icons on the right side of the interface. You can modify the layout, show details, or share the portfolio.

5. Choose File | Save Portfolio to save your portfolio, or modify the portfolio as outlined in the upcoming sections.

Change the Layout of a Portfolio

After you create a PDF Portfolio, you can modify it before you save it. When you create the Portfolio, Acrobat reconfigures with panes and commands you use to modify the Portfolio, as follows:

1. Choose one of the options in the Add Content section of the Layout pane. You can add files, add a folder of files, add content from the Web, or create a folder. The options are self-explanatory, except for the Create Folder option. When you choose this command, you can create a folder in the PDF Portfolio. Double-click the folder, and you can then add files to it. This is a handy way to manage files that have different content.

2. Change the portfolio layout by choosing a different layout in the Portfolio Layouts section.

3. Click Visual Themes. You can modify the Portfolio by choosing one of the following themes: Clean, Spring, Tech Office, Modern, or Translucent. The visual themes modify the background color and the frame around each thumbnail.

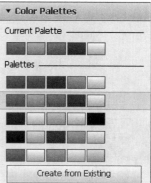

4. Click Color Palettes to change the color palette for your PDF Portfolio. When you open this section, the current palette is displayed, as shown here. Choose one of the available palettes, or click Create from Existing. When you choose the latter option, the hexadecimal value of each color is displayed. If you know how to specify a color using hexadecimal values, you can use this option to create a unique Portfolio.

5. Click Background to change the background color of your portfolio, as shown next. This option is useful if you choose None for the background image in the next step. You can make the following modifications:

   • Click the color swatch to choose a color from the Color Picker. This opens your computer OS color picker. You can click a swatch or enter the hexadecimal value for the desired color.

   • Choose an option from the Fill drop-down menu. You can choose a solid fill, which fills the background with the color you specified, a linear gradient, which creates a blend from white to the color you selected, or a radial gradient, which is a concentric fill from white to the color you selected.

   • Drag the Gradient Intensity slider to the left to display more of the lighter color or to the right to display more of the darker gradient color.

6. Choose an option from the Background Image drop-down menu. You can accept the theme default or choose None. When you choose the latter, you can create a custom background, as outlined in the previous step.

7. Choose a font face from the Font drop-down menu of the Portfolio Properties section. It's advisable that you stick with a standard font to avoid issues when the file is opened on other computers.

8. Click Embed Fonts if you choose a nonstandard font in step 7. Embedding fonts ensures that the Portfolio will look the same on any computer and any operating system.

9. In the Portfolio Properties section, choose an option from the Card Size drop-down menu. Note that this option is not available for the Click-Through, Linear, or Wave portfolio layouts.
10. Choose File | Save Portfolio or click Details to change the details of the files contained in the Portfolio.

After you save a Portfolio, it can be viewed with any version of Acrobat X or Adobe Reader X. Users can view the Portfolio in Layout version, which shows the template and all of the edits you've made, or the Portfolio can be viewed in Files view, which shows columns with information about each file you have in the Portfolio.

After you save the file, you can edit the layout by clicking Details and then clicking Edit. You then have access to the Layout and Details sections of the Portfolio.

Tip To add a header to your PDF Portfolio, click inside the blank area at the top of the Portfolio to open the Header Properties section. You can then add an image or text as the header. If you don't use an image, you can create a solid fill or gradient background.

Change Portfolio Details

After you modify the layout of a Portfolio, you can also modify details such as the name and the display name of the files that comprise the Portfolio. You can also add a description for each file in the Portfolio. Follow these steps to modify Portfolio details:

1. Click Details to display the details for each file in the Portfolio, as shown next.

2. Click inside the Name field to select and change the name of the file. Note that you must use the same file extension.
3. Click inside the Display Name field to select and change the display name of the file. The display name does not need a file extension.
4. Click inside the Description field and enter text that describes what the file is about.
5. In the Columns To Display section, click a column name with a checkmark to remove it from the display, or click a column name without a checkmark to add it to the display.
6. To change the order in which the columns appear, click a column name and then use the arrows to move the field to a different position in the hierarchy.
7. If desired, enter a name in the column field and then choose an option from the drop-down menu beneath the Add A Column text field. The type you choose from the drop-down menu determines how the field is formatted. For example, if you choose Date and then click inside the resulting field, a calendar icon appears that, when clicked, enables the user to enter a date and time from a pop-up calendar.
8. Click the Initial Sort drop-down arrow and choose a column name from the menu. This determines which column displays the sort arrow that, when clicked, will change the sort of the column from ascending to descending.
9. Choose File | Save Portfolio to save your changes.

Create a PDF File by Dragging and Dropping

You can quickly open one or more files as PDFs by dragging the file icon from your desktop or an open file folder and then dropping it on the Acrobat icon. You can also drag and drop a file from a file folder directly into the Acrobat application. If you select several files to open as PDF documents using the drag-and-drop method, Acrobat creates a separate PDF file for each file you select.

 If you have a project folder with several files you're converting to PDF documents, resize Acrobat and the open file folder so that both are visible on your desktop. Then it's a simple matter of dragging files from the folder and dropping them into Acrobat. If you select several files and drag them into Acrobat, a dialog box appears giving you the option of combining all files into a single document or creating a separate PDF document for each file.

 To launch Acrobat and create a new PDF, drop a supported file format on your Acrobat desktop shortcut.

Capture HTML Documents as PDF Documents

If you're a web site designer, you can use the Create | PDF From Web Page command to create a PDF proof for client approval. You can use this command to show your design to a customer before a web host is selected. Use this command to convert a single HTML document from your hard drive into a PDF document, or use it to convert the entire site into a PDF document, complete with links. To create a PDF document from HTML files, do the following:

1. Choose File | Create | PDF From Web Page to access the Create PDF From Web Page dialog box, shown next. If the command has been used before, the last site opened is listed in the URL field.

```
┌─────────────────────────────────────────────────────────────┐
│ Create PDF from Web Page                                  ⊠   │
│                                                               │
│  URL:  \\Das-003\d\Desktop\Phoenix\career.htm    ▼   [Browse] │
│                                                               │
│ ⦿ Capture Multiple Levels          [Create] [Cancel] [Settings...] │
└─────────────────────────────────────────────────────────────┘
```

2. If you want to open a single HTML page, accept the default Settings options. If you want to open the entire site in PDF format, click the Capture Multiple Levels button and choose the Get Entire Site option.
3. Click Browse. Acrobat opens the Select File To Open dialog box.
4. Navigate to the HTML file you want to convert to PDF format and then click Open. If you chose the Get Entire Site option, select the home page of the site.

Note The Get Only [ ] Level(s) option enables you to capture multiple levels of a website and is generally reserved for capturing websites from the Web, not creating client proofs, as discussed here.

5. Click Create. If you chose the Get Entire Site option, Acrobat displays a dialog box warning you of a potentially large download. Click Yes to begin the download; click No to abort. When you use this command to convert HTML documents stored in a folder on your hard drive, the conversion to PDF is relatively quick. However, when you download sites from the Web, the download time depends on the quality of your connection, your modem speed, your processor, and the size and complexity of the website. (Capturing web pages from the Web is covered in detail in Chapter 5.)

After you click Download, Acrobat begins converting the HTML pages into PDF format. Acrobat downloads the entire site, including images and accompanying files.

Save PDF Files

After you convert a file to PDF format, you can save it for future reference. When you save a PDF file, you can accept the Acrobat defaults, name the file, and save it. Alternatively, you can modify the document properties, name the file, and save it. The properties you modify determine how the document appears when opened and what information is available for the Search command (if the document is included as part of a PDF index). To save a PDF file using the Acrobat defaults, do the following:

1. Choose File | Save. Acrobat opens the Save As dialog box.
2. Navigate to the folder you want the file saved in and enter a name for the file. Accept the Save As Type default, which is Adobe PDF Files (*.pdf), and click Save.

After you click Save, Acrobat saves the file in PDF format using the default information, which appears in the Description section of the Document Properties dialog box. If you're using the document for your own reference, the Acrobat defaults may be acceptable. If you distribute the document to colleagues or customers, however, it's to your advantage to modify the information that appears in the Description section of the Properties dialog box, as discussed in the next section.

Set Document Properties

When you convert a file to PDF format or open a PDF document and modify it, you can change the document properties before saving the document, except if security has been applied to the document. You can edit the document properties to include information you deem pertinent to your viewing audience. For example, you can set the document's initial view to change or specify what the viewer sees when the document is opened, and you can set the document security to limit access to the document while adding custom information. To set document properties, choose File | Properties to open the Document Properties dialog box.

How to... **Add Headers and Footers to a PDF Document**

To add headers and footers to a document, click Tools, click Pages, and then choose Header & Footer to open the Add Header And Footer dialog box. The dialog box has two windows used to preview the header and footer. Above the header and footer windows are six windows to which you can add the date, page number, and custom text for the header and footer you're creating. You can also specify the range of pages on which the header or footer appears, and how the margins are configured. In addition, you can use spinner buttons to create headers and footers a page at a time.

Edit Document Properties

When you convert a file to PDF format, Acrobat records the document's properties. This information is gleaned from the original file and displayed in the Document Properties dialog box, which is divided into six tabs: Description, Security, Fonts, Initial View, Custom, and Advanced. You can modify a document's properties summary by following the steps described next.

1. Choose File | Properties to open the Document Properties dialog box.
2. Click the Description tab, shown next, and modify the information in any or all of the following text fields: Title, Author, Subject, and Keywords. Remember, this information is often the first information your viewers see concerning your document, especially if they use the Search command to locate the information. Keep this information as relevant as possible.

3. Click the Additional Metadata button to open a new window, which is designated by the filename of the document. In this window you can add additional metadata in several categories. You can add copyright information, IPTC (International Press Telecommunications Council) contact information, IPTC content information, and so on. This metadata can be used when searching a PDF index in which the document is included.
4. Click the Security tab to set document security options, as outlined in the upcoming section "Set Document Security."
5. Click the Fonts tab to display information about the fonts embedded and used in the document.
6. Click the Initial View tab to set viewing options when the document is opened, as discussed in the next section, "Set Document Initial View Options."

7. Click the Custom tab to define custom names and values for the document. Custom names and values can be specified as search options in PDF indexes.
8. Click the Advanced tab, shown next, to specify a base URL for the document, specify an index to be associated with the document, and set trapping options. When you specify an index and perform a search on the document, all documents in the index are searched as well.

9. In the Reading Options area of the Advanced tab, click the Binding drop-down arrow and choose Left Edge or Right Edge. Binding is used when thumbnails are displayed or when a multipage document is displayed using the Continuous Facing mode.
10. Click the Language drop-down arrow and choose a language. This information is used when the document is viewed with a screen reader.
11. Click OK to exit the Document Properties dialog box. When you save the document as a PDF file, Acrobat updates the information you entered along with other Description information, such as the date modified.

Saving a document with pertinent information in the Description section of the Document Properties dialog box makes it easier for other people who view the document to understand the information contained within. Time is valuable. In today's hustle-bustle world, people don't have the time to sift through a document to see if the information meets their needs. In addition to changing the Document Properties Description tab information, you can specify what your viewers see when they open a PDF document. The information you include in the Description tab of the Document Properties dialog box can also be used in a search if the document is included in a PDF index.

Set Document Initial View Options

If you save a PDF document with Acrobat defaults, when your viewers open the document, they see the first document page in the Document pane and all the Acrobat (or Adobe Reader) menus and tools. The Navigation pane is closed by default, but you can change a document's properties to have any of the tabs in the Navigation pane open when the document opens, which gives your viewers a way to navigate the document. The actual tabs available to viewers depend on the version of Acrobat or Adobe Reader they use to open the document. The default Initial View options work fine if you share the document with coworkers or work with a team of authors who will edit the document. When you create a document such as an e-book or multimedia presentation, however, you can change the default options by doing the following:

1. Choose File | Properties and click the Initial View tab, as shown next.

2. In the Layout and Magnification section, click the Navigation Tab drop-down arrow and choose from the following options:
   - **Page Only**   When the document opens, the viewer sees the full page with only the tab titles visible in the Navigation pane.
   - **Bookmarks Panel And Page**   When the document opens, the viewer sees the full page with only the Bookmarks panel of the Navigation pane visible.
   - **Pages Panel And Page**   When the document opens, the viewer sees the full page with only the Pages panel of the Navigation pane visible.
   - **Attachments Panel And Page**   When the document opens, the viewer sees the full page with only the Attachments panel of the Navigation pane visible.
   - **Layers Panel And Page**   When the document opens, the viewer sees the full page with only the Layers panel of the Navigation pane visible.
3. Click the Page Layout drop-down arrow and choose one of the following options:
   - **Default**   Acrobat configures the document according to the user's viewing preference.
   - **Single Page**   The document opens in single-page mode. Viewers will be able to use the Hand tool to navigate through a single page, but not to the next page.
   - **Single Page Continuous**   The document opens in continuous mode. Viewers will be able to use the Hand tool to scroll from page to page in the document.
   - **Two Up (Facing)**   The document opens with two pages arranged side by side in the Document pane.
   - **Two Up Continuous (Facing)**   The document opens with two pages facing side by side displayed in the Document pane. Viewers will be able to use the Hand tool to scroll to different spreads in the document.
   - **Two Up (Cover Page)**   The document opens with two pages arranged side by side in the Document pane, but the first page of the document is displayed as a single cover page.
   - **Two Up Continuous (Cover Page)**   The document opens with two pages facing side by side displayed in the Document pane, but the first page of the document is displayed as a single cover page. Viewers will be able to use the Hand tool to scroll to different spreads in the document.
4. Click the Magnification drop-down arrow and choose one of the following options:
   - **Default**   Acrobat sizes the document according to the general preferences of the user.
   - **Actual Size**   Acrobat sizes the document to its original dimensions.
   - **Fit Page**   Acrobat sizes the document to fill the entire Document pane when the file opens.
   - **Fit Width**   Acrobat sizes the document to fit the current width of the Document pane when the file opens.
   - **Fit Height**   Acrobat sizes the document to fit the current height of the Document pane when the file opens.
   - **Fit Visible**   Acrobat sizes the document so only visible elements fit the width of the Document pane. If you choose this option, no margins will be visible.

- **Magnification Levels**   Choose one of the preset magnification values (with the % symbol), and the document opens at that magnification. These values represent a percentage of the document size as it was originally published. You can also enter a value between 1 percent and 6400 percent in the Magnification field to have the document open at a level other than one of the defaults.
5. Enter the page number you want to be visible when the document opens.

To have PDF documents reopen to the last page you viewed, choose Edit | Preferences (Windows) or Acrobat | Preferences (Macintosh) and then click Documents. Enable the Restore Last View Settings When Reopening Documents option.

6. In the Window Options section, choose from the following options:
   - **Resize Window To Initial Page**   Acrobat resizes the Document pane to fit around the first page of the document.
   - **Center Window On Screen**   Acrobat opens the Document pane in the middle of the workspace.
   - **Open In Full Screen Mode**   Viewers see the initial page in Full Screen mode, without any toolbars, menu bars, or navigation tabs. Viewers are unable to scroll a multipage document viewed in Full Screen mode, but they can use the Page Down, Page Up, and arrow keys to navigate the document. Pressing the SPACEBAR will display the next page. If you choose Open In Full Screen Mode and your document will be distributed to parties with limited Acrobat knowledge, it is a good idea to create an index or buttons your viewers can use for navigation.
7. Click the Show drop-down arrow and choose one of the following options:
   - **File Name**   Acrobat displays the document filename in the application title bar.
   - **Document Title**   Acrobat displays the document title in the application title bar. If you didn't specify a document title in the Description tab of the Document Properties dialog box, the document filename and extension are displayed.

You can select every option in the Window Options section, but when options conflict, Acrobat applies the overriding option. For example, if you choose both Open In Full Screen Mode and Document Title, the document title isn't visible because the application title bar is hidden in Full Screen mode.

8. In the User Interface Options section, choose any or all of the following options:
   - **Hide Menu Bar**   Acrobat opens the document with the menu bar hidden. Press F9 to unhide the menu bar.
   - **Hide Tool Bars**   Acrobat hides the toolbar when the document opens. If you don't choose the Hide Menu Bar option in conjunction with this option, the user can press F8 or choose Window | Hide Tool Bars to unhide the toolbars.
   - **Hide Window Controls**   Acrobat opens the document with the Navigation pane hidden.

Note Even though it's possible for your viewers to reveal a hidden menu bar or toolbars using keyboard shortcuts, many of your viewers may not know this. Therefore, you may want to consider including some navigation aids for your viewers if you hide either the menu or toolbars. Alternatively, you can annotate the first page of the document with a note instructing viewers on how to reveal the menu and toolbars when they're hidden.

9. Click OK to apply the options and close the dialog box.
10. Choose File | Save.

When you save the document, the new Initial View options are saved with it and will be applied the next time the document opens. Of course, a viewer with the full version of Acrobat can modify any of the changes you make to the document. To prevent viewers from tampering with your handiwork, change the security level of the document, as described in the following section.

Set Document Security

You can add security to limit access to the document or prevent viewers from editing your document with the full version of Acrobat. You can use Acrobat Password Security to password-protect confidential documents. When you password-protect a document, you set document permissions; for example, you can prevent users from printing the document. Alternatively, you can choose to use Acrobat Certificate Security or Adobe Policy Server, both of which require a user to log in. When you use Acrobat Certificate Security, you specify which users can access the document. Acrobat security is covered in detail in Chapter 10.

Use the Save As Command

You use the Acrobat Save As command to save the same PDF document with different settings under another filename. Use this technique when you need to create different versions of the same document for different destinations—for example, to save a document optimized for print or to save a document optimized for a web page. To save the current PDF with a different filename, choose File | Save As to open the Save As Settings dialog box. Enter the new name for the document and click Save. When you use the Save As command, you also enable fast web viewing, which is discussed in Chapter 12.

You can also use the Save As command to save the document in another format. This is known as "repurposing content." After you save the file in another format, you can edit the resulting file in a program that supports that format.

Save PDF Files in Other Formats

When you open a document in Acrobat, you can save the file in PDF format or you can repurpose the document into another format. After you repurpose a document, you can edit the contents in another program. For example, if you repurpose all the text in a document by saving in Rich Text Format (RTF), you can edit the text in any word processing program that supports the RTF file format.

You can choose File | Save As and then choose one of the HTML or XML formats to save a PDF document as an HTML or XML file for use on your website. For additional information, refer to Chapter 12.

Save Text from a PDF File

Acrobat enables you to select text with the Select tool and copy it to the clipboard for editing in another application. However, you can repurpose a document by saving all the text in RTF format, as a text file, or as a Microsoft Word file and then edit it in your favorite word processing program. If you use Microsoft Word for your word processing tasks, you can export the edited text in PDF format. You can repurpose a PDF document as editable text by following these steps:

1. To save the text from a PDF file, choose File | Save As | Microsoft Word and then choose Word Document (DOCX format) or Word 97-2003 Document (DOC format). Acrobat opens the Save As dialog box.
2. Name the document, click the Save As Type drop-down arrow, and choose Microsoft Word Document (*.doc), Rich Text Format (*.rtf), Text (Accessible) (*.txt), or Text (Plain) (*.txt).
3. Click the Settings button to define parameters for the text option you chose. The settings vary depending on the file type you chose. The default options for each file type work well in most cases, but you can modify the settings to suit the application in which you'll be using the file. For example, you can choose whether to have Acrobat generate images when the PDF document is repurposed.
4. Click Save to save the document to a file.

Choose File | Save As | More Options. From this menu you can save a file as text, rich text, XML, PostScript, Encapsulated PostScript, HTML, PDF/X, PDF/X, or PDF/E.

Save PDF Files as Images

You can also repurpose PDF documents by saving them in image formats. You can save PDF documents in the following image formats: EPS (Encapsulated PostScript), JPEG, JPEG 2000, PNG, PS (PostScript), and TIFF. When you save a document in one of these image formats, you can modify the settings, which differ depending on the image format you use to save the file. The settings you choose determine parameters such as image compression, colorspace, and the resolution of the saved image. Most file formats have a Settings button that enables you to modify the default settings to suit the application in which you'll be using the file. The settings are self-explanatory for those who are familiar with the file format.

Create PDF Files with Acrobat Distiller

In previous sections of this chapter, you learned how to create PDF documents by converting supported file formats into PDF documents and then saving the files from within Acrobat. Acrobat Distiller is a separate program, but you can launch it from within Acrobat. When you install Acrobat, Acrobat Distiller is also added as a system printer under the moniker of Adobe PDF, which gives you the capability of printing a PDF file directly from within any application that supports printing. Printing from an authoring application is covered in Chapter 4.

Use Acrobat Distiller

Acrobat Distiller is a separate program that you use to convert EPS (Encapsulated PostScript) and PS (PostScript) files into PDF documents. With Acrobat Distiller, you have preset options available to optimize the file for an intended destination. Optimize a PDF document for a destination by choosing a specific setting. To create a PDF file using Acrobat Distiller, follow these steps:

1. Launch the program by choosing Acrobat Distiller X from your OS program menu. Alternatively, you can launch Acrobat Distiller from within Acrobat by clicking Tools, clicking Print Production, and then choosing Acrobat Distiller. If the Print Production section is not visible in the Tools pane, click the Show/Hide icon in the upper-right corner of the pane and choose Print Production from the drop-down menu. The Acrobat Distiller interface is shown here. As you can see, there isn't much of an interface at all—just a few menu options, an information section, and a progress section.

2. Click the Default Settings drop-down arrow and choose the option that best suits the intended destination of the document. Choose from the following:
   - **High Quality Print**   Choose this option when creating files that require higher image quality and will be printed.
   - **Oversized Pages**   Choose this option when creating files that will be used to view and print engineering drawings larger than 200 × 200 inches. The resulting file can be opened with Acrobat and Adobe Reader 7.0 and later.
   - **PDFA/1b 2005: (CMYK)**   Choose this option when creating documents using the CMYK color model that must be compliant with PDFA/1b and the ISO standard for long-term archiving of electronic documents. The resulting file can be opened and viewed with Acrobat and Adobe Reader 5.0 and later.
   - **PDFA/1b 2005: (RGB)**   Choose this option when creating documents using the RGB color model that must be compliant with PDFA/1b and the ISO standard for long-term archiving of electronic documents. The resulting file can be opened and viewed with Acrobat and Adobe Reader 5.0 and later.
   - **PDF/X-1a: 2001**   Choose this option when creating files that must conform to PDF/X-1a 2001 standards, which are compatible with Acrobat 4.0 (PDF 1.3).
   - **PDF/X-3: 2002**   Choose this option when creating files that must conform to PDF/X-3 2002 standards, which are compatible with Acrobat 4.0 (PDF 1.3).
   - **Press Quality**   Choose this option when you need the highest quality images in your files. This option is the way to go if you print your files on a high-end printer with PS capabilities. When you choose this format, minimum compression is applied to images.
   - **Smallest File Size**   Choose this option to create the smallest possible file size at the expense of image quality when the resultant PDF document will be distributed via e-mail or viewed on the Internet.
   - **Standard**   Choose this option when you create a PDF file for distribution across your corporate intranet or via CD-ROM for colleagues.

 You can modify a PDF setting to suit the intended destination for the document you distill. Modifying settings is discussed in detail in Chapter 11.

3. To apply security to the distilled PDF file, choose Settings | Security. For more information about Acrobat security settings, refer to the previous section, "Set Document Security," or Chapter 12.
4. Choose File | Open to access the Open PostScript File dialog box.
5. Navigate to the PS file you want to convert to PDF format, create a name for the file, and click Open.

After you click Open, Acrobat Distiller takes the reins and creates the PDF file. The Acrobat Distiller icon, which looks like a propeller, spins as the file is created. You can view information about the document in the PDF File window. If you distill a large multipage PS file, the distilling process may take some time. You can monitor the progress by viewing the Status bar in the Progress section. As the file is created, Acrobat Distiller shows you which page is being printed, the percentage of the job completed, and a visual reference in the form of a blue progress bar that moves across the window as the file is created.

By default, after completion of the distilling job, Acrobat Distiller creates a report that appears in the window at the bottom of the program interface. You can preview the PDF file in Acrobat by double-clicking its title in Acrobat Distiller.

Set Acrobat Distiller Preferences

Using Acrobat Distiller is a straightforward process: Choose a setting, load an EPS or PS file, and Distiller does the rest for you. The real power of Distiller is in the number of settings you can modify, which you learn how to do in Chapter 11. You can also modify Distiller to suit your working preference by doing the following:

1. Launch Acrobat Distiller.
2. Choose File | Preferences to open the Preferences dialog box. In the Startup Alerts section, you can modify the following options:
    - **Notify When Watched Folders Are Unavailable**   When you choose this option (the default), Acrobat Distiller has the capability of monitoring a folder or directory on your computer. Distiller automatically distills PS files placed in watched folders. You learn how to create watched folders in the following section, "Create Watched Folders."
    - **Notify When Windows TEMP Folder Is Nearly Full**   Distiller needs to write temporary files to disk when creating a PDF file. Choose this option, and Distiller warns you when the startup volume is less than 1 MB.
3. In the Output Options section, you can modify the following settings, all of which apply to Windows only:
    - **Ask For PDF File Destination**   When you enable this option, Distiller prompts you for a folder in which to save the converted PDF file. When this option is disabled (the default), the converted PDF file is stored in the same location as the PS file.
    - **Ask To Replace Existing PDF File**   This option is enabled by default and causes Distiller to prompt you when you try to overwrite an existing PDF file. If you enable the Ask For PDF File Destination check box, this option is unavailable.
    - **View PDF When Using Distiller**   When you enable this option, on completion of the distilling job, the default Acrobat viewer launches and the converted PDF file is displayed.
4. In the Log Files section, check Delete Log Files For Successful Jobs if you want Distiller to delete the log file of the job if the file is successfully distilled. A distiller log file is a text file, created during the distilling process, that records any distilling errors, even if a PDF file is not created.

 Macintosh Acrobat users have an option unavailable to Windows users: Restart Distiller After PostScript Fatal Error. When this option is enabled, Distiller automatically relaunches after encountering a fatal PostScript error.

Create Watched Folders

If you regularly create PostScript files and save them to certain folders, you can configure Acrobat Distiller to watch these folders and automatically convert PostScript files to PDF files. You can also choose to move the original PostScript files to the Out folder or delete them. Each watched folder can have unique Distiller settings. Here's how to create a watched folder:

Note   You cannot save PostScript files to watched folders on a network server. Set up a watched folder on your workstation for converting your files. Other authors who need to convert PostScript files to PDFs must set up a watched folder on their own workstations using a licensed version of Acrobat.

1. Launch Acrobat Distiller and choose Settings | Watched Folders to open the Watched Folders dialog box, shown next. (A folder to be watched has already been added.)

2. Click Add Folder to open the Browse For Folder dialog box.
3. Navigate to the folder you want Distiller to watch, select the folder, and click OK. The selected folder is added to the watched folders list. After you add the folder, Distiller automatically creates In and Out folders within the watched folder.
4. In the Check Watched Folders Every [ ] Seconds field, enter a value between 1 and 9999 seconds. This value specifies how often Distiller checks a watched folder.

5. Click the PostScript File Is drop-down arrow and choose an option to determine whether the converted PostScript file is moved to the Out folder or deleted.

6. Click the Delete Output Files Older Than [ ] Days check box and enter a value between 1 and 999 in the text field. Distiller uses this value to determine when to delete PostScript files in the Out folder.

7. After you add a folder to the watched folders list, you can click OK to close the dialog box or click Add Folder to add additional folders to the list.

Set Watched Folder Options

After you add one or several folders to the watched folders list, you can specify options for each folder, namely: Security Options, Job Options, Load Options, Add Additional Folders, or Remove Folders. To set options for a watched folder, do the following:

1. Launch Acrobat Distiller and choose Settings | Watched Folders.

2. Select the watched folder whose settings you want to modify. After you select a watched folder, additional buttons become available, as shown previously, for setting the following options:

   - **Remove Folder**   Removes the selected folder from the watched folders list.
   - **Edit Security**   After you click this button, the Security dialog box opens. You can apply Acrobat Standard Security to the PDF files that have been distilled. For information on individual security settings, refer to the previous section, "Set Document Security."
   - **Clear Security**   Removes security for files distilled from the selected folder.
   - **Edit Settings**   After you click this button, the Adobe PDF Settings dialog box opens. You can specify settings for all files distilled within the selected folder. You can find information for the options in this dialog box in Chapter 11.
   - **Load Settings**   Click this button to open the Select Adobe PDF Settings dialog box. Navigate to the folder that contains the settings file you want to load and click Load. Adobe PDF settings files have the .joboptions extension. For more information on creating custom settings, refer to Chapter 11.
   - **Clear Settings**   This button becomes available after you specify job options for files distilled from this folder. Click the button to clear Adobe PDF settings applied to the PostScript files being distilled from this folder.

3. Click OK to apply the new settings and close the Watched Folders dialog box.

Summary

In this chapter, you learned how to create PDF files from within Acrobat. You learned how to create PDF documents from single files and from multiple files. You also discovered how to save PDF documents in other file formats. In the latter part of the chapter, you saw how to use Acrobat Distiller to create PDF documents from PostScript files. In the next chapter, you will learn how to create PDF documents from within authoring applications such as Microsoft Word.

4

Create PDF Documents in Authoring Applications

HOW TO...

- Convert Microsoft Office documents to PDFs
- Set document conversion properties
- Convert documents to PDF files using the Print command
- Convert a document to PDF and then e-mail it

As discussed in Chapter 3, you can convert supported file types into PDF documents from within Acrobat. You can also create PDF files from within authoring applications. When you create a file in any application that supports printing devices, you can create a PDF file using the application's Print command. Other software, such as CorelDRAW, supports PDF exporting. You can also create PDF files from within Adobe graphics applications such as Photoshop CS5, InDesign, and Photoshop Elements. Adobe offers extensive PDF support with many of its image-editing, illustration, and page-layout applications. You can use the Acrobat PDFMaker to create PDF files from within Microsoft Office applications, except for Windows 2011 for the Mac. You can also create PDF documents from within Microsoft Outlook. This is a convenient way of archiving e-mail messages pertaining to a certain project. When you convert e-mail messages into PDF documents, the attached files are archived as well.

When you create a PDF file from within an authoring application, you gain many benefits. First, and primarily, you can save the original version of the file in its native format, which makes it available for future editing when needed. Second, you can export the file in PDF format without leaving the host application. If you have several documents to create and convert to PDF format, this is a tremendous timesaver. You can also export several PDF files from the original document, each optimized for a different destination.

Create PDF Files from Microsoft Office Software

When you install Acrobat, the install utility searches your machine for Microsoft Office applications. When a supported Microsoft Office application is found, Acrobat installs Acrobat PDFMaker as a helper utility. With Acrobat PDFMaker, you can create a PDF file that looks identical to the Microsoft Office file by clicking a Convert To Adobe PDF icon, which is added to your Microsoft Office 2003 application. If you own a Windows Microsoft Office 2007 or 2010 application, Acrobat creates an Acrobat ribbon with icons to convert files to PDF, attach files to e-mail messages, and so on. There are several default conversion settings for Acrobat PDFMaker. However, if you prefer more control over the conversion process, you can also modify the conversion settings to optimize a PDF file for its intended destination.

You can use Acrobat PDFMaker to create PDF files from within the following Microsoft Office applications:

- **Word 2003, 2007, and 2010**   Use Acrobat PDFMaker to convert documents you create with Word to PDF files. The resulting PDF file retains font information and embedded graphics, as well as header and footer attributes.
- **Excel 2003, 2007, and 2010**   Use Acrobat PDFMaker to convert an Excel spreadsheet to PDF format. The converted PDF file retains column formatting, as well as column and row headers and embedded graphics.
- **PowerPoint 2003, 2007, and 2010**   Convert PowerPoint presentations to PDF files and provide additional functionality to the presentation with many features of Acrobat PDFMaker.
- **Outlook**   Convert Microsoft Outlook e-mail messages to PDF files. This is a wonderful way of archiving selected e-mail messages or a folder of e-mail messages. File attachments are also archived with the PDF document.

The Acrobat PDFMaker plug-in is, for all intents and purposes, identical in all supported Microsoft Office applications, with the exception of the options available in each application when modifying conversion settings. The next section covers all the major features of the Acrobat PDFMaker plug-in and shows you how to use it to convert documents to PDF format (with examples from Microsoft Word 2010).

Create PDF Files from Microsoft Word Files

When Adobe Acrobat finds a supported application, as previously mentioned, three icons are added to the application toolbar, and a menu group is added to the application menu bar. Alternatively, if you use Microsoft Word 2007 or 2010, an Acrobat tab is added to the menu. When the Acrobat tab icon is clicked, a ribbon appears with the icons shown in Figure 4-1. These are used to convert a document to PDF format, to convert a document to PDF format and e-mail it, and to convert a

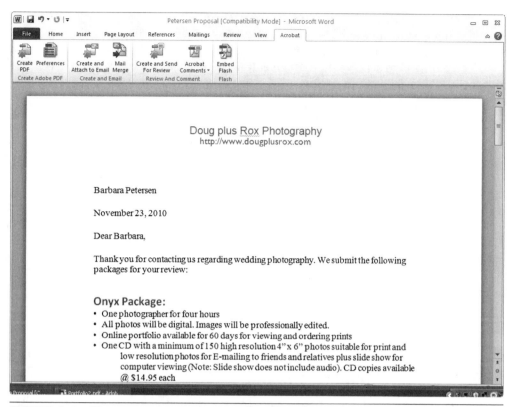

FIGURE 4-1   You can convert a Microsoft Office document into a PDF document by clicking an icon.

document to PDF format and initialize a review. In addition, there are icons to set preferences and to import comments from a PDF document into the current Word document. In Microsoft 2003 and earlier applications, the Adobe PDF menu group contains commands that duplicate the button tasks and allow you to change PDF conversion settings.

Convert Word Files to PDF Files

When you create a document in Word, you can apply styles to the document. When you convert the Word document to PDF format, Acrobat uses these Word styles to create corresponding bookmarks in the PDF document. The Acrobat PDFMaker default setting uses Heading styles to create bookmarks. If you want, though, you can change the conversion settings to include other styles that exist in the Word document, such as numbered or bulleted lists. When you convert the Word file to a PDF file, the resulting file retains the formatting and font information, as well as any graphics you may have embedded in the Word file.

The easiest way to convert a Word file to a PDF file is by using the Convert To Adobe PDF button in Microsoft Word 2003, or by accessing the ribbon in Word 2007 or Word 2010 and then clicking the Create PDF button. You can also use a menu command to achieve the same result in Microsoft Word 2003. To convert a Word file to a PDF file, do the following:

1. Click Acrobat to reveal the Acrobat ribbon and then click the Create PDF icon, previously shown in Figure 4-1. Alternatively, if you're working in Microsoft Word 2003, click the Convert To Adobe PDF icon or choose Adobe PDF | Convert To Adobe PDF.
2. Acrobat PDFMaker displays a dialog box stating the file must be saved. If you click Yes, the Save PDF File As dialog box opens. If you click No, Acrobat PDFMaker stops the conversion process.
3. In the Save PDF File As dialog box, accept the default name (the Word filename) and location (the directory the Word file is saved in) or specify a document name and directory.
4. Click Save to complete the conversion.

After you convert the document to PDF format, you can modify it in Acrobat by adding interactive elements, such as links to navigate the document, or by adding comments, annotations, or multimedia elements. Figure 4-2 shows a PDF file in Acrobat converted from a Word document. Word documents converted to the PDF format have bookmarks that Acrobat PDFMaker creates using Word's Heading styles. You can change the manner in which Acrobat PDFMaker creates bookmarks by changing conversion settings, which is covered in the upcoming section "Change Conversion Settings."

Tip A button can also convert a document to PDF format and send it for review. Chapter 9 covers reviewing PDF documents.

Convert a Word Document to PDF and Then E-Mail It

Thanks to the Internet and e-mail, it's now possible to efficiently conduct business with faraway clients. Whether you are a one-person entrepreneurship or work in a large organization, you can convert a Word document to a PDF file and then e-mail it to a client or coworker. To convert a Word document to a PDF file and e-mail it, follow these steps:

1. Choose Acrobat to reveal the Acrobat ribbon and then click the Create And Attach To Email icon. If you're using an earlier version of Microsoft Word, click the Create And Attach To Email icon. If you're using an earlier version of Microsoft Word, click the Create And Attach To Email icon.
2. Acrobat PDFMaker displays a dialog box prompting you to save the file. Click Yes to open the Save PDF File As dialog box.

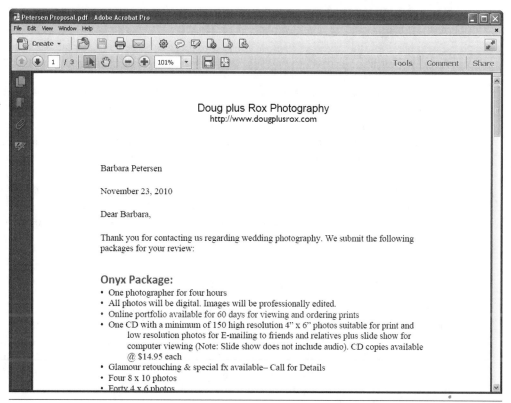

FIGURE 4-2   Use Acrobat PDFMaker to convert Microsoft Office files into PDF documents.

3. In the Save PDF File As dialog box, accept the default filename and location to save the file in or specify your own parameters.
4. Click Save. Acrobat PDFMaker converts the file to PDF format and launches your default e-mail application.
5. Enter the recipients' e-mail addresses and subject information, and add any message for your intended recipients.

The action that happens next depends on your e-mail application. If Outlook is your default e-mail application, the message is sent to the Outbox. Follow the e-mail application prompts to send the message. When you send the message, the PDF file is sent as an attachment.

Additional Acrobat Commands from Microsoft Office Applications

You have other options in addition to converting Microsoft Office files into PDF format, converting them to PDF documents, and then e-mailing them. Some options are available for Acrobat Pro or Acrobat Pro Extended only. The additional commands are:

- **Mail Merge**   Converts a mail merge document to PDF format and then sends it as a PDF file to mail merge recipients.
- **Create And Send For Review**   Converts the Office document to PDF format and then opens the Send For Shared Review dialog box in Acrobat. Follow the prompts to initiate the shared review and select the participants.
- **Acrobat Comments**   Enables you to integrate comments from a PDF file into a Microsoft Office document. This option is handy when you want to integrate comments from reviewers into the original Office document and then act on the comments. You also have options to accept changes in the document based on the comments or to delete all comments in the document.
- **Embed Flash**   Enables you to embed a supported video file in the document and then convert it to PDF.

Change Conversion Settings

When you convert a Word document to a PDF file, Acrobat PDFMaker uses the currently selected conversion settings. You can modify these conversion settings, as well as modify document security, specify how Microsoft Office features are converted to PDF, specify how Acrobat PDFMaker creates bookmarks, and specify display options. You change conversion settings by clicking the appropriate tab in the Conversion Settings dialog box. To open the Acrobat PDFMaker dialog box, choose Acrobat to display the Acrobat ribbon, shown next, and then click the Preferences icon.

When you first open the Acrobat PDFMaker dialog box that modifies conversion settings, the Settings tab is active, as shown next. Here you choose the setting that is the closest match for the intended destination of the PDF file, which you can then modify by following these steps:

1. Click the Conversion Settings drop-down arrow and choose one of the preset options: High Quality Print, Oversized Pages, PDF/A-1b 2005 (CMYK), PDF/A-1b 2005 (RGB), PDF/X-1a 2001, PDF/X-3-2002, Press Quality, Smallest File Size, Standard, or any custom conversion setting you have created. These options are the same as the Distiller Job Options discussed in Chapter 3. To apply the new settings, click OK. To modify additional conversion settings, click the appropriate tab and modify the parameters to suit the intended destination of your document, as outlined in Chapter 11.

2. In the PDFMaker Settings area, you can choose the following options, the first three of which are selected by default:
   - **View Adobe PDF Result**   Opens the document in Acrobat after the conversion process is completed.
   - **Prompt For Adobe PDF File Name**   Prompts you for a filename before the document is converted to a PDF file. If you deselect this option, the resulting PDF file adopts the filename of the Microsoft Office document you're converting.
   - **Convert Document Information**   Converts certain information (document title, author, keywords, and subject) from the Microsoft Office Properties dialog box into the PDF file's Document Properties, which can be displayed by opening the file's Document Properties dialog box.
   - **Create PDF/A-1a: 2005 Compliant File**   Creates a document that is compliant with PDF/A-1a: 2005 standards.
3. In the Application Settings area, you can choose the following options, the last three of which are selected by default:
   - **Attach Source File**   Attaches the source file to the converted PDF document. Viewers can open the source file by opening the Attachments panel and double-clicking the file title.
   - **Create Bookmarks**   Uses headings or styles from the Microsoft Office document to create bookmarks in the PDF document. You can specify which styles are converted to bookmarks on the Bookmarks tab of the Acrobat PDFMaker dialog box.

- **Add Links** Preserves any links present in the Microsoft Office file. The links in the converted PDF file maintain a similar appearance to those found in the original file.
- **Enable Accessibility And Reflow With Tagged Adobe PDF** Creates tags (objects that reference document structure objects, such as images and text objects) in the PDF document based on the structure of the source Microsoft Office file. This structure can be used to reflow a document when viewed on different devices.

4. Click OK to apply the settings. Alternatively, you can click a different tab to modify additional settings.

 You can create custom conversion settings by clicking Advanced Settings. After you click this button, the Acrobat PDFMaker dialog box opens the Adobe PDF Settings dialog box for the currently selected job option. For more information on creating a custom conversion settings file, refer to Chapter 11.

Change Document Security Settings

When you convert a Word file to PDF format, you can specify document security from within Microsoft Word. You can assign a password to the converted file and limit permissions. The default encryption level is 128-bit RC4, which is compatible with Acrobat 6 and later. Do the following to implement document security:

1. Open the Acrobat PDFMaker dialog box, as outlined previously.
2. Click the Security tab to reveal the security settings options. The encryption level is designated at the top of the dialog box.

3. To assign a password to the PDF file, check the Require A Password To Open The Document check box. When you choose this option, the Document Open Password field becomes active. Enter the password in this field.

4. To assign a master password to the PDF file, which enables you to require entry of a password to change permissions, click the Restrict Editing And Printing Of The Document check box. When you choose this option, the Change Permissions Password field (and the two fields below it) becomes available. Enter the password in this field.

5. Click the Printing Allowed drop-down arrow and choose one of the following options:
   - **Not Allowed**   Disables printing the document.
   - **Low Resolution (150 DPI)**   Enables users to print only a low-resolution copy of the PDF document.
   - **High Resolution**   Enables users to print the document at high resolution.

6. Click the Changes Allowed drop-down arrow and choose one of the following options:
   - **None**   Disallows users with Acrobat X to edit the document.
   - **Inserting, Deleting, And Rotating Of Pages**   Enables viewers with Acrobat X Pro to insert, delete, and rotate pages.
   - **Filling In Of Form Fields And Signing**   Enables viewers with Acrobat Standard, Pro, or Pro Extended to fill in form fields and digitally sign the document. Adobe Reader 8.0 and later users will only be able to fill in the form fields.
   - **Commenting, Filling In Of Form Fields, And Signing**   Enables viewers with Acrobat Pro X to add comments to the document, as well as fill in form fields and digitally sign the document.
   - **Any Except Extracting Of Pages**   Enables viewers with Acrobat X Pro to perform any editing with the exception of extracting pages from the PDF document.

7. When you require a permissions password to edit the document, the Enable Copying Of Text, Images, And Other Contents check box is deselected by default. This option is initially selected and grayed out until you choose the Use A Password To Restrict Printing And Editing Of The Document option. Check this box to enable document viewers to copy text, images, or other contents of the document.

8. The Enable Text Access For Screen Reader Devices For The Visually Impaired check box is selected by default. If you deselect this option, visually impaired readers will be unable to access text with their screen readers.

9. If you select the Enable Plaintext Metadata check box, any metadata is converted to plaintext and can be accessed even though the rest of the document is encrypted.

The default 128-bit RC4 encryption means the document can only be viewed with Acrobat 6.0 and later. For earlier versions of Acrobat (Versions 3, 4, and 5), you have to choose a conversion setting that supports 40-bit security. For more information on modifying document security settings, refer to Chapter 10.

10. To apply the security settings, click OK. To modify additional settings, click the appropriate tab and modify the parameters as desired.

Note When you assign a document password, a permissions password, or both, you will be prompted to verify the password(s) before the new settings are accepted.

Change Word Settings

The settings you modify on the Word tab of the Acrobat PDFMaker dialog box determine how Acrobat PDFMaker converts Word features. The actual wording of this tab varies, depending on the Microsoft Office program for which you're modifying conversion settings. For example, these settings have no tab in Microsoft Excel, Microsoft Outlook, or Microsoft PowerPoint. To change Microsoft Word settings, do the following:

1. Open the Acrobat PDFMaker dialog box, as outlined previously.
2. Click the Word tab to reveal the settings illustrated next:

3. In the Word Features area, you can modify the following settings:
   - **Convert Displayed Comments To Notes In Adobe PDF**   Converts Word document comments to notes in the resulting PDF document. If you choose this option, any comments in the document appear in the Comments window.

Comments are segregated by reviewer, and the number of comments entered by the reviewer is noted in the # Of Comments column.

- **Convert Footnote And Endnote Links (default option)**   Preserves endnote and footnote links in the converted PDF document.
- **Enable Advanced Tagging**   Enables you to integrate advanced tagging in the PDF.

4. If you choose Convert Displayed Comments To Notes In Adobe PDF in the Comments window, you can perform the following tasks:
   - Click the check box in a reviewer's Include column to include his comments in the PDF file.
   - Click the check box in a reviewer's Notes Open column to have a note created with this reviewer's name as the author open when the page on which the note appears opens.
   - Click the icon in a reviewer's Color column to select a color for the note. Each time you click the icon, it changes to a different color. You can choose different colors for other reviewers' comments in the document.

5. To apply the Word settings, click OK. To modify additional settings, click the appropriate tab and modify the parameters as desired.

Change Bookmark Settings

The settings you modify on the Bookmarks tab determine which Word text styles Acrobat PDFMaker converts to bookmarks. To change bookmark settings for the document conversion, do the following:

1. Open the Acrobat PDFMaker dialog box, as outlined in previous sections.
2. Click the Bookmarks tab and modify the settings, as shown here and as described in the following list:
   - **Convert Word Headings To Bookmarks (default option)**   Acrobat PDFMaker converts all Word headings in the document to PDF bookmarks. By default, Heading 1 through Heading 9 styles are converted to bookmarks. To modify which headings are converted to bookmarks, click a heading name in the Bookmark column to select or deselect it.
   - **Convert Word Styles To Bookmarks**   By default, no

Word styles are converted to bookmarks. When you choose this option, all Word styles used in the document are converted to bookmarks when Acrobat PDFMaker converts the document. You can deselect any style you don't want converted to a bookmark by clicking its check box. Remember, if you decide to have bookmarks created for styles, the conversion process *may take a long time*, especially if you have a large number of styles in the document.

- **Convert Word Bookmarks** Converts any user-created Word bookmarks to PDF bookmarks.

3. Click OK to apply the new settings, or click another tab to make additional modifications to the document conversion settings.

 After you modify conversion settings, they remain active until you modify them again. To restore the default settings, open the Acrobat PDFMaker dialog box, click the Restore Defaults button, and then click OK to complete the restoration. The next document you convert to PDF is converted with the default Adobe PDF conversion settings.

Create PDF Files from Microsoft Excel Files

You can also use Acrobat PDFMaker from within Excel 2003, Excel 2007, or Excel 2010 to convert spreadsheets to PDF documents. The only difference between Acrobat PDFMaker in Excel and Word is the available conversion settings. The Excel Acrobat PDFMaker dialog box has only two tabs: Settings and Security. You also have a menu command to convert the entire workbook to a PDF. With these exceptions, the process for converting an Excel spreadsheet to a PDF is identical to that outlined in the "Convert Word Files to PDF Files" section earlier in this chapter.

Create PDF Files from Microsoft PowerPoint Files

If you use PowerPoint, you know it's a powerful program for creating presentations. It seems PowerPoint presentations are everywhere these days, even on the Web. You can convert a PowerPoint presentation to PDF and enhance it with Acrobat features. For example, you can use the File Attachment tool to open another file during your presentation. From within Acrobat X Pro, you can embed 3D or Flash video in the converted document.

The PowerPoint Acrobat PDFMaker dialog box has two tabs: Settings and Security. The process to convert a PowerPoint file to PDF is identical to that outlined in the "Convert Word Files to PDF Files" section earlier in this chapter.

Create PDF Files from Microsoft Outlook

You can use Acrobat X to convert an e-mail message, a selection of e-mail messages, or a folder of e-mail messages in Microsoft Outlook into a PDF document. If you segregate e-mail messages in folders when you work on a project, or keep folders for important e-mail messages, you can archive the entire folder as a PDF document. When you archive e-mail messages, file attachments are saved as well. In addition, you can migrate previous PDF Outlook archives to PDF Portfolios.

When you create a PDF document from e-mail messages, you use the Filter settings to search for messages by date, sender, subject, personal folders, and so on. After sorting through archived messages, you can click Open to view a selected message in a new window.

Convert Selected E-Mail Messages to a PDF Portfolio

When you need to consolidate several e-mail messages pertaining to a certain subject, you can easily do so by converting them into a PDF Portfolio. You can select messages from within any folder or from your Inbox. Follow these steps to convert Microsoft Outlook e-mail messages into a PDF Portfolio:

1. Navigate to the folder in which the messages you want to convert to a PDF document are located.
2. Select the desired messages.
3. Click the Create Adobe PDF from Selected Messages button. Alternatively, choose Adobe PDF | Convert Selected Messages | Create New PDF.
4. In the Save Adobe PDF File As dialog box, enter a name for the PDF document and navigate to the folder in which you want to save the document.
5. Click Save.

Convert a Selected Folder of E-Mail Messages to a PDF Portfolio

When you work on a project or receive a lot of e-mail from a particular individual or client, it makes good sense to store the messages in a folder. This is a task you can easily accomplish within Microsoft Outlook. You can consolidate a Microsoft Outlook folder into a PDF Portfolio by following these steps:

1. Click the Create Adobe PDF From Folders button, shown previously, to display the Convert Folder(s) To PDF dialog box, shown on the next page.
2. Select the folder(s) you want to covert to PDF.

Convert folder(s) to PDF

Please select one or more folders to create PDF from.

- ☐ Archive Folders
- ☐ Personal Folders
  - ▪ Calendar
  - ▪ Contacts
  - ☐ Deleted Items
  - ☐ Drafts
  - ☑ Inbox
    - ☑ Superb Images
  - ▪ Journal
  - ☐ Junk E-mail
  - ▪ Notes
  - ☐ Outbox
  - ☐ RSS Feeds
  - ☐ Sent Items
  - ☐ Spam Mail
  - ▪ Tasks

☑ Convert this folder and all sub folders

[OK] [Cancel]

3. Click OK. A dialog box appears showing you the progress of the conversion to PDF. Acrobat also creates an index that is embedded with the PDF for faster searching.

How to... **Attach Files to E-Mail Messages as PDF Documents**

Acrobat's strong point has always been the capability to share a file with anybody who has the full version of Acrobat or the Adobe Reader installed on their system. In the past, you'd convert a file into PDF format and then attach it to an e-mail. With Acrobat X, Microsoft Outlook users can accomplish both tasks in one fell swoop. Supported file formats can be converted to PDF and attached to an e-mail message with the click of a button. Here are the steps to follow:

1. In Microsoft Outlook, click the New Mail Message button to open a blank e-mail message.
2. Click the Attach As Adobe PDF button to open the Choose File To Attach As Adobe PDF dialog box. If you're using Microsoft Outlook 2007 or 2010, choose Attach As Adobe PDF from the ribbon.
3. Select the desired file and click Open to display the Save PDF File As dialog box.
4. Enter a name for the PDF document and then navigate to the folder in which you want to save the document.
5. Click Save. The file is converted to PDF and attached to the e-mail message.
6. Enter the desired title in the Subject field, type your message, and send the e-mail.

Depending on the number of e-mails in the folder, this process can take a considerable amount of time.

Append Selected Messages to an Existing PDF

You can easily add selected e-mail messages to an existing PDF document. This feature is useful when you've received e-mail messages pertaining to a PDF document you're currently reviewing. You can also use this feature when you need to add new e-mail messages to those you've previously converted to a PDF Portfolio. Here are the steps:

1. Select the desired e-mail messages in Microsoft Outlook.
2. Choose Adobe PDF | Convert Selected Messages | Append To Existing Adobe PDF to display the Select PDF File To Append dialog box. Alternatively, you can choose a PDF you recently created from Outlook messages. The path to and the filename of the PDFs you recently created from Outlook appear beneath the Append To Existing PDF command.
3. Select the desired PDF file.
4. Click Open to convert the selected messages to PDF and append them to the selected PDF document.

To convert a folder to PDF and append the resulting file to an existing PDF, follow these steps:

1. Choose Adobe PDF | Convert Selected Folders | Append To Existing Adobe PDF to open the Convert Folder(s) To PDF dialog box, shown previously.
2. Select the folder(s) you want to append to an existing PDF.
3. Click OK to open the Select PDF File To Append dialog box.
4. Select the file and then click Open.

Create PDF Files Using an Application's Print Command

When you install Acrobat software, Adobe PDF is automatically added as a system printer. You can use Adobe PDF to print from the authoring application file to disk in PDF format in the same manner as you use a printer to print a hard copy of a file. You can create a PDF file from any authoring application that supports printing, by following these steps:

1. Choose the application's Print command.
2. Choose Adobe PDF from the application's Printer menu. The actual Print dialog box varies, depending on your operating system (OS) and the software from which you are printing the file.

3. Click Properties to reveal the Adobe PDF Document Properties dialog box, which has three sections, separated by tabs. Click the Layout tab, as shown next.

4. In the Orientation area, choose Portrait, Landscape, or Rotated Landscape.
5. Click the Pages Per Sheet drop-down arrow and choose an option from the drop-down menu. The default option of 1 displays one document page on one PDF page. If you choose one of the other options, multiple pages of the original document are displayed on a single PDF page. After you select the number of pages per sheet, the Preview window updates to give you an idea of how the finished document will look.
6. Click the Paper/Quality tab, shown on the top of the next page, and then click the Paper Source drop-down arrow and choose an option from the drop-down menu.
7. Click the corresponding icon to print the document in color or black and white.
8. Click Advanced to open the Adobe PDF Converter Advanced Options dialog box, shown on the bottom of the next page. All options have been expanded here, because they are discussed in the following steps.
   In the Paper/Output section, choose the following options:
   - **Paper Size** Click the drop-down arrow and choose one of the presets from the drop-down menu.
   - **Copy Count** Click Copy Count and enter a value for the number of copies to print. When you choose this option, the Collate option is available. This option is enabled by default and causes Acrobat to collate the pages for each copy printed.

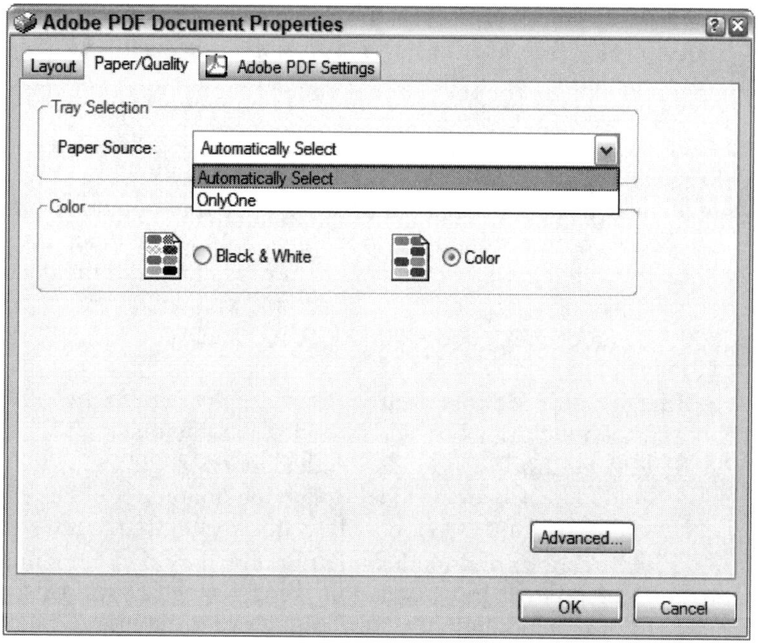
Adobe PDF Document Properties
Layout
Paper/Quality
Adobe PDF Settings
Tray Selection
Paper Source:
Automatically Select
Automatically Select
OnlyOne
Color
Black & White
Color
Advanced...
OK
Cancel

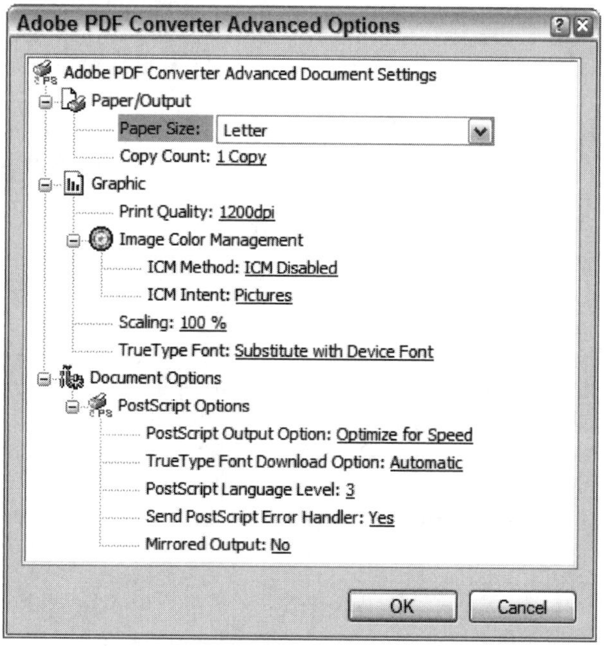
Adobe PDF Converter Advanced Options
Adobe PDF Converter Advanced Document Settings
Paper/Output
Paper Size: Letter
Copy Count: 1 Copy
Graphic
Print Quality: 1200dpi
Image Color Management
ICM Method: ICM Disabled
ICM Intent: Pictures
Scaling: 100 %
TrueType Font: Substitute with Device Font
Document Options
PostScript Options
PostScript Output Option: Optimize for Speed
TrueType Font Download Option: Automatic
PostScript Language Level: 3
Send PostScript Error Handler: Yes
Mirrored Output: No
OK
Cancel

You can match the paper size to the file you're printing by choosing PostScript Custom Page Size from the Paper Size drop-down menu and then entering the desired dimensions in the PostScript Custom Page Size Definition dialog box.

9. Click the plus sign (+) to the left of the Graphic title to set the following parameters:
   - **Print Quality**   Click Print Quality, click the drop-down arrow, and then choose an option from the drop-down menu. The default resolution, 1200 dpi (dots per inch), works well in most instances. If the document you're converting to PDF contains images and you will eventually print the file on a high-end printer, choose a resolution that closely matches the intended output device.
   - **Image Color Management**   Click the plus sign to the left of the Image Color Management title to set the following parameters:
     - **ICM Method**   Click ICM Method, click the drop-down arrow that appears, and then choose one of the following options: ICM Disabled, to disable color management; ICM Handled By Host System, to handle color management through the color management profile used by your computer; ICM Handled By Printer, to handle color management through the output device; or ICM Handled By Printer Using Printer Calibration. Refer to your printer operation manual to choose the right setting, or contact your service center if you are having the file printed professionally.
     - **ICM Intent**   Click ICM Intent, click the drop-down arrow that appears, and then choose one of the following options: Graphics, if the document predominantly contains images with large areas of solid color; Pictures, if the document is largely made up of full-color photographs; Proof, to create a black-and-white proof for a customer; or Match, to match the document colors.
   - **Scaling**   Click Scaling and then enter a value to which you want the document scaled when distilled to PDF format. This value is a percentage of the document size as created in the authoring application. Alternatively, you can click the spinner buttons to increase or decrease the scaling value.
   - **TrueType Font**   Click Substitute With Device Font (the default), or click the drop-down arrow that appears, and choose Download As Softfont. This determines how Acrobat Distiller handles TrueType fonts used in the original document. In most cases, the default option works well.
10. Click the plus sign to the left of Document Options and then click the plus sign to the left of PostScript Options to set the following parameters:
   - **PostScript Output Option**   Click the PostScript Output Option, click the drop-down arrow that appears, and then choose one of the following options:
     - **Optimize For Speed**   Choose this option to speed the distilling process. If you choose this option, though, you may be unable to take advantage of print spooling if you work on a network.
     - **Optimize For Portability**   Choose this option to have the distilled file conform to Adobe Document Structuring Conventions (ADSC). When

you choose this option, each PostScript page is independent of the other pages in the document. Choose this option if you're printing the file on a network spooler. When you use a network spooler, printing happens in the background, which frees up your workstation for other tasks. When you choose this option, the network spooler prints the PDF document one page at a time.

- **Encapsulated PostScript (EPS)**   Choose this option to create EPS files composed of single pages in the authoring application you intend to use in documents of other applications. Use this option if you want to create a high-quality image and use it in a document that will be printed from another application.
- **Archive Format**   Choose this option to improve file portability. When you choose this option, printer settings that may prevent the distilled PDF file from printing on other output devices are suppressed.
- **TrueType Font Download Option**   Click TrueType Font Download Option, click the drop-down arrow that appears, and then choose one of the following options:
  - **Automatic**   Choose this option to automatically embed any TrueType fonts from the source document to the resulting PDF file.
  - **Outline**   Choose this option to embed any TrueType font in the source file as outlines in the resulting PDF file.
  - **Bitmap**   Choose this option to convert TrueType fonts in the source file to bitmap images in the resulting PDF document. The resulting PDF document cannot be searched.
  - **Native TrueType**   Choose this option, and TrueType fonts will not be embedded with the document. The resulting PDF file will download font information from the source computer from which the document is viewed.
- **PostScript Language Level**   Click this option and then use the spinner buttons to select 1, 2, or 3. Alternatively, you can enter the desired value.
- **Send PostScript Error Handler**   Click this option and then choose Yes or No from the drop-down menu.
- **Mirrored Output**   Click this option and then, from the drop-down menu, choose No to print the PDF document the same as the source file, or click Yes to print the PDF document as a mirror image of the source document.
11. Click OK to close the Adobe PDF Converter Advanced Options dialog box.
12. Click the Adobe PDF Settings tab to set the parameters shown on the top of the next page.
13. Click the Default Settings drop-down arrow and then choose one of the presets from the drop-down menu. These are identical to the settings previously discussed in Chapter 3.
14. Click the Adobe PDF Security drop-down arrow and choose one of the following options:
  - **None**   No security is applied to distilled documents.
  - **Reconfirm Security For Each Job**   You will be prompted for security settings each time you use the Adobe PDF printer.

- **Use Last Known Security Settings**   On future printing jobs, Acrobat will use the last security settings you specified.

15. After you choose one of the preceding options, the Edit button to the right of the field becomes available. Click the Edit button to edit security settings. Acrobat security is discussed in detail in Chapter 10.

16. Leave the Adobe PDF Output Folder field at its default setting, Prompt For Adobe PDF Filename, which prompts you for a document name and a folder in which to save the document, or choose My Documents*PDF to save the file in your My Documents folder. Alternatively, you can click the Browse button and navigate to the folder in which you want to save the document.

17. Click the Adobe PDF Page Size drop-down arrow and choose the desired size for the resulting PDF document.

18. At the bottom of the Adobe PDF Settings tab, check one or more of the following options, as appropriate to your needs:

    - **View Adobe PDF Results**   This default option opens the resulting PDF document in Acrobat. Deselect this option to print the document without previewing the end result.

    - **Add Document Information**   This default option adds information from the source document to the PDF file as Document Information.

    - **Rely On System Fonts Only; Do Not Use Document Fonts**   No fonts will be embedded in the PDF; if the document contains an embedded font, it will be unavailable in the PDF. Instead, the MM (Multiple Master) fonts will be used to reproduce the font if it is not available on the user's system; otherwise, the font will be missing from the PDF.

    - **Delete Log Files For Successful Jobs**   Acrobat Distiller creates a log file whenever you use Adobe PDF to create a PDF file. By default, the file is deleted when the distilling job is successful. If you deselect this option, Acrobat creates a log file that can be viewed with a text editor.

- **Ask To Replace Existing PDF File**   Select this option if you want Acrobat to prompt you before overwriting a PDF file with the same filename as the one selected for the current printing job.

19. Click OK to apply the settings and then close the Adobe PDF Document Properties dialog box.
20. Click OK in the Application Print dialog box to print the document in PDF format.

If you are printing a multipage document with lots of embedded graphics, the printing process may take a while.

To print a document from a Macintosh computer, choose File | Save As | Adobe PDF Files. Alternatively, you can choose File | Save As | Adobe PDF Files Optimized. When you choose to save a document as an optimized PDF, the Settings button becomes active. Click the button to reveal the PDF Optimizer dialog box, which gives you options for image compression and embedded fonts.

Create PDF Files in Adobe Programs

Adobe has gone to great lengths to enhance interactivity between Acrobat and its graphics software. You can create a PDF file using the following Adobe software:

- **FrameMaker**   A page-layout program suitable for publishing long documents for viewing across multiple media. You can use the program to create content for the Web, CD-ROM, and print. FrameMaker offers extensive support for creating PDF documents. To create a PDF file in FrameMaker, you can use the application's Print command or the Save As PDF command.
- **Illustrator**   A vector-based illustration program. Programs like Illustrator use mathematics to define a shape, which means the shape can be greatly enlarged without loss of fidelity. You can convert Illustrator documents to PDF format using the Save command. Illustrator 9.0 and newer versions support transparency, which is preserved when you save an Illustrator document as a PDF file with Acrobat 7.0 (PDF 1.6) compatibility.
- **InDesign**   The latest page-layout software from Adobe, featuring extensive PDF support. Use the Export command to convert documents you create in InDesign to PDF format. You can export a PDF for a commercial printer using one of the PDF/X settings. Check with your printer for this preferred setting.
- **Photoshop CS5**   In the latest version of the award-winning image-editing application from Adobe, you use the Save As command and then choose the PDF format to save a Photoshop file in PDF format. When you use the Save As command to convert a Photoshop file to PDF, you can specify image compression and the color model. When you save a file from Photoshop in PDF format, layers are flattened. But if you open the resulting PDF file in Photoshop, any layers and objects from the original file are preserved and available for editing. You can choose File | Automate | PDF Presentation to save several images as a PDF

presentation or slideshow, complete with transitions. The option to create a PDF presentation is also available from within the Adobe Bridge.

- **Photoshop Elements** This image-editing application has almost as much power as its big brother, Photoshop CS5. Photoshop Elements also enables you to save a single image file as a PDF.
- **Photoshop Lightroom 3** This Adobe application is used by professional photographers to process and catalog images. From within the application, you can create a PDF slideshow.

Although the methods used to create PDF files among between Adobe programs, many of the options are similar. Consult your software application manual for specific instructions on exporting the file as a PDF document. After you export the file, you can modify it in Acrobat X Pro.

Create PDF Files from Vector-Drawing Software

If you create vector-based illustrations, you can convert them to PDF files by using one of the following methods:

- Save the file in either EPS or PS format and then use Acrobat Distiller to print the file.
- Use the vector-drawing program's Print command and choose Adobe PDF for the printer.
- Export the file in PDF format, if supported by the software.

Create Files from Adobe Illustrator

If you create illustrations with Adobe Illustrator, you can save documents in the PDF format. When you save an Illustrator document in PDF format, the Adobe PDF Format Options dialog box, which has seven sections, appears: General, Compression, Marks And Bleeds, Outputs, Advanced, Security, and Summary.

The settings you specify in each section determine the version of Acrobat with which the file is compatible, the amount of compression applied to images, which printer's marks are included with the document, whether the file is output with color conversion, whether to embed fonts, and whether to secure the document. Everything is neatly summed up in the Summary section.

Create PDF Files from CorelDRAW Documents

If you use CorelDRAW 10 or newer to create illustrations, you may be unaware that PDF documents you create in CorelDRAW or Corel PhotoPaint are produced with the Corel PDF engine. When you want to publish a CorelDRAW file as a PDF document, use the Publish To PDF command on the File menu. For more information on exporting a CorelDRAW illustration as a PDF document, consult your software user's manual.

Summary

In this chapter, you learned to create PDF documents from within Microsoft Office applications that support Adobe PDF. You also saw how to create PDF files from within applications that support printing, and learned to configure Adobe PDF as a PostScript printing device. In the next chapter, you will learn how to create PDF documents by capturing them from your scanner or from web pages.

5

Capture PDF Documents

HOW TO...

- Capture searchable PDF documents with your scanner
- Capture web pages
- Append web pages

You create most of your PDF documents in authoring applications and then convert them to PDF files from within the authoring application (if supported) or by using Adobe PDF to print the documents in PDF format. You can also create PDF files by using Acrobat Distiller to convert a PostScript file (*EPS or *PS) to PDF format. Both of these techniques are covered in Chapters 3 and 4. However, you can use other methods to create PDF documents.

PDF documents can also be created with your scanner or by capturing pages from websites. Either method is an excellent way to build an information library. You can scan magazine articles of interest, convert them to PDF format, and discard the original to avoid paper clutter. You can also capture single web pages or an entire website. With the wealth of information available on the Internet, capturing web pages is a wonderful way to build a PDF library on your hard drive. With any version of Acrobat, you can use the Full Text Index With Catalog command to create a searchable index of PDF documents captured from the Web.

Capture PDF Documents from a Scanner

If you have a scanner attached to your computer, you can capture PDF documents directly from your scanner by using the Acrobat Scan plug-in. With the Acrobat Scan plug-in, it's possible to scan a document into Acrobat without leaving the program. After you scan the document, you can use Acrobat tools or menu commands to modify the document before saving it as a PDF file.

Your scanner probably has an interface or other software that makes the scanning process a relatively simple task. Most scanner applications let you crop the scanned image, select a color model, and adjust the image resolution before capturing the image into an application. If your scanner is equipped with similar software, you can adjust the image to suit its intended destination before returning the scanned image to Acrobat.

Capture Images and Text

After you have a scanner up and running on your system that is a TWAIN device that Acrobat recognizes, you can scan any document into Acrobat and save it as a PDF file with searchable text. To capture a document into Acrobat with your scanner, follow these steps:

1. Insert the document you want to capture in your scanner.

To create a better-looking PDF document, make sure the document is square with the edge of your scanner. If the page is clipped from a magazine, trim and square the edges for better results.

2. Choose Create | PDF From Scanner and then choose one of the following options:
   - **Autodetect Color Mode**   Choose this option and Acrobat will automatically detect which color mode is used to convert the document to PDF.
   - **Black And White Document**   Choose this option if you're scanning a fax document.
   - **Grayscale Document**   Choose this option if you're scanning a black-and-white photograph.
   - **Color Document**   Choose this option if you're scanning a page from a magazine that contains primarily solid colors.
   - **Color Image**   Choose this option if you're scanning a color photograph or a magazine page with a detailed color photograph.
   - **Custom Settings**   Choose this option to create a custom setting to suit the documents you scan and your scanner. When you choose this mode, you can change the color mode, resolution, and paper size.

   After you choose an option, the scanning process begins, unless you choose Custom Scan. Here is the Custom Scan version of the dialog box.

3. Click the Scanner drop-down arrow and choose the appropriate TWAIN device for your scanner.

Tip The menu for TWAIN devices may show two or more listings for each item. For best results, choose the manufacturer's software for your scanner if it's listed. With some scanners, you may have to install special TWAIN drivers to make your scanner available as a TWAIN device in Acrobat.

4. Click the Scanner Options button to set options applicable to your scanner.
5. Click the Sides drop-down arrow and choose one of the following options: Front Sides (the default) or Both Sides. If your scanner supports double-sided scanning, and you're scanning a document with content on both sides, choose Both Sides; otherwise, accept Front Sides.
6. Choose the desired options from the Color Mode and Resolution drop-down menus. These options are only available if you use the Acrobat scanning interface instead of the native scanner interface and if you're using the Windows version of Acrobat.
7. In the Output section, accept the New PDF Document option (the default if you don't currently have a PDF document open) or click the Append radio button. If you select this option, you can choose a currently open document from the drop-down list. Alternatively, you can click the Browse button to navigate to the document you want to append and then open it.
8. Click the Make PDF/A-1b Compliant check box. The option creates a document compliant with PDF/A-1b standards, an ISO standard for the long-term archiving of electronic documents.
9. In the Document Settings section, drag the Quality slider to determine the quality of the resulting PDF document. Drag the slider to the left to create a PDF document smaller in file size with a lower quality or drag the slider to the right to create a PDF document larger in file size, but of higher quality.
10. Click the Options button to reveal the Optimize Scanned PDF dialog box shown here.
11. Accept the default option to apply adaptive compression. This results in a smaller file size. If you deselect this option, the document will not be compressed.
12. Click the Color/Grayscale drop-down arrow and then choose one of the following options:
    - **JPEG 2000** Optimizes the document for the JPEG 2000 format. The default option is recommended for most documents.

- **JPEG**   Applies JPEG compression to grayscale or RGB input. Choose this option when you're scanning a document that contains predominantly RGB and/or grayscale images.
- **ZIP**   Optimizes the document using the ZIP compression format. Choose this option for documents that contain objects such as logos or vector graphics.

13. Click the Monochrome drop-down arrow and then choose one of the following options:
    - **JBIG2 (Lossy)**   Applies the JBIG2 compression method to black-and-white input. This option is only compatible with Acrobat 5.0 (PDF 1.4) or later.
    - **JBIG2 (Lossless)**   Optimizes the document using the JPBIG2 (Lossless) method. This optimization does not compress the graphics and may result in a larger file size.
    - **CCIT Group 4**   Applies CCIT Group 4 compression to black-and-white input. This compression method is lossless, compresses the page quickly, and is compatible with Acrobat 3.0 (PDF 1.2) and later.

14. Drag the quality slider to determine the quality and file size of the resulting PDF. Drag to the left for lower quality and smaller file size, or to the right for higher quality at the expense of a larger file size.

15. In the Filters section, choose the following options:
    - **Deskew**   Rotates a page that isn't square with the scanner bed. Click the drop-down arrow and choose either On or Off.
    - **Background Removal**   This option works with color and grayscale portions of a scanned document, but has little or no effect on a document that is predominantly black and white. This option converts a background that is almost white to pure white. You have four options: Off, Low, Medium, or High. In most instances, the default setting of Low does a good job of cleaning up the background. If something printed on the other side of the page is visible, however, Medium or High may remove the objectionable bleed-through.
    - **Descreen**   Removes the halftone dots that appear when certain images, such as newsprint or magazine pages, are scanned. Your options are On and Off. In most instances, the default option of Automatic creates the best-looking PDF.
    - **Text Sharpening**   Choose an option from the drop-down menu to determine how crisply text is rendered when the document is scanned. Your options are Low, Medium, and High. The default option (On) removes halos that appear at high-contrast edges or images that have been oversharpened.

16. Click OK to exit the Optimize Scanned PDF dialog box.

17. Deselect the Make Searchable (Run OCR [optical character recognition]) option to create a PDF document without searchable text. If you accept the default option, click Options to reveal the Recognize Text – Settings dialog box, shown here.

18. Accept the default Primary OCR Language option (the language specified when you installed Acrobat) or choose a different language from the drop-down menu.

19. Click the PDF Output Style drop-down arrow and choose one of the following options:
    - **Searchable Image**   Captures the scanned document as an image, but also recognizes the text in the document. The PDF document can be searched, and text can be selected with the Select tool. Use this option when you need maximum image quality.
    - **ClearScan**   This option was introduced in Acrobat 9. It creates a Type 3 font that approximates the original font.

Note   If you deselect the Make Searchable (Run OCR) option in the Create PDF From Scanner dialog box, the PDF file created will be an image only and you cannot search the text from within Acrobat, nor can you index the document using the Full Text Index With Catalog command. The only real value in deselecting this option is the resulting unsearchable PDF has a smaller file size.

20. Click OK to exit the Recognize Text – Settings dialog box and return to the Create PDF From Scanner dialog box.
21. Click the Add Metadata check box to add information to the document, such as keywords. If you choose the option, the Document Properties dialog box appears after all pages of the document are scanned into Acrobat.
22. Click Scan. After you click the Scan button, the interface for the TWAIN device you selected opens. Follow the prompts to preview the scan and return it to Acrobat. Refer to your scanner user guide for specific instructions.
23. After the image is scanned into Acrobat, modify the document as needed and save the file.

Did You Know?   **How TWAIN Got Its Name**

When you install Acrobat, the install utility detects any TWAIN devices you have attached to your computer. As a note of interest, the name "TWAIN" was adopted from the phrase "and never the twain shall meet" in Rudyard Kipling's *The Ballad of East and West,* to reflect the fact that, when the technology was in its infancy, connecting a scanner to a personal computer was difficult. However, many people think TWAIN is an acronym for Technology Without An Interesting Name. A *TWAIN* device contains drivers that convert the optical input from a scanner or digital camera into a digital format that can be recognized by computer software. The TWAIN devices you have attached to your computer are listed on a drop-down menu in the Create PDF From Scanner dialog box.

Capture PDF Documents from Websites

The Web is a treasure trove of information. You can find out almost anything about any subject by typing relevant keywords into one of the many online search engines.

After you submit the search, the search engine usually returns several pages of links to websites containing information that pertains to your search. The first three or four pages contain links to the sites with information that closely matches your query, but searching through 10 or 15 websites can be time-consuming. If you have a slow Internet connection and the returned pages are filled with graphics, this exacerbates the problem. The solution is to use the Create | PDF From Web Page command to download the page into Acrobat. You can download a single page or the entire site. After the download is complete, you can save the page(s) in PDF format to review at your leisure. Figure 5-1 shows a web page that has been downloaded into Acrobat.

Download Web Pages

Whether you're surfing the Web for pleasure or browsing for product information or tutorials, you can quickly download a web page or an entire website using the Create | PDF From Web Page command. When you capture a web page in Acrobat, the entire page is downloaded, complete with images. When Acrobat encounters an unsupported object, a rectangular shape the color of the web page background is displayed in lieu of the unsupported object. If an animated GIF is part of the page being captured, only

FIGURE 5-1 You can download web pages for future reference.

the first frame of the animated GIF appears after Acrobat downloads the page. When you're on the Internet and find a web page you want to download, do the following in Acrobat:

1. Choose File | Create | PDF From Web Page to access the Create PDF From Web Page dialog box. Alternatively, you can choose the PDF From Web Page command from the Create task button.
2. In the URL field, enter the URL for the page you want to capture.

Tip   Some URLs are long. Instead of manually entering the entire web address, you can select the web address in your web browser and then press CTRL-C (Windows) or CMD-C (Macintosh) to copy the web address to your operating system (OS) clipboard. Switch to Acrobat, click inside the URL field, and then press CTRL-V (Windows) or CMD-V (Macintosh) to paste the URL into the field.

3. Click Capture Multiple Levels to expand the dialog box to include settings for capturing multiple levels, as shown next, from the current web page.

4. In the Get Only [ ] Level(s) field, enter the number of levels to download, or use the spinner buttons to increase or decrease this value. Alternatively, you can choose the Get Entire Site radio button to download every level (and subsequently every page) in the site.
5. If you specify the number of levels to download, you can specify the following options:
   - **Stay On Same Path**   Acrobat downloads all pages along the path of the specified URL.
   - **Stay On Same Server**   Acrobat downloads pages from the server of the specified URL only, disregarding links to URLs on other servers.
6. Click the Settings button to modify Acrobat web capture conversion settings. This feature is explained fully in the later section "Specify Web Page Conversion Settings."
7. Click the Create button to begin capturing the page(s). As the site is downloading, Acrobat keeps you informed of the download progress by opening the Download Status dialog box.

8. To save the captured page in PDF format for future reference, choose File | Save to open the Save As dialog box. Enter a name for the file, specify the folder to save the file in, and then click Save.

When the download is complete, Acrobat displays the captured page in the Document pane according to the specified web capture preferences. At the top of the document you'll find the title of the captured page. This same title is displayed in your web browser when you view the page on the Web. You can change the name of the document by choosing File | Properties and then entering another name in the Title field of the Description tab of the Document Properties dialog box. This changes the title as it pertains to a PDF index, to which the file is added. When you reopen the document after assigning the new title, the filename you saved the PDF document with appears in the Document pane, not the title you specified in the Description section of the Document Properties dialog box. You can, however, change whether the filename or title is displayed by changing the Show option in the Initial View tab of the Document Properties dialog box.

Certain web page features won't download, such as pop-up menus, multistate JavaScript buttons, and JavaScript image swaps. Pop-up menus and similar web page features are created using JavaScript. You should also be aware that Acrobat won't convert certain CGI files, Java applets, or RealMedia to PDF. Although JavaScript is supported in bookmarks, links, and form fields that you create in Acrobat, JavaScript features aren't downloaded with a web page.

Append Web Pages

After you successfully capture a web page, you may decide to add additional pages from the same site to the document, download the rest of the site, or append web pages from another site to the document. You can append the currently open PDF document that was captured from a website by clicking document links or using menu commands.

Use Web Links

As you view a captured page in Acrobat, you may decide that another page from the same site, or a page from another site that is linked to the captured page, contains information you would like to archive in PDF format. To append a page to your current document by using a web link, follow these steps:

1. From within a PDF created from a web capture, move your cursor over the link to the page you want to capture. Your cursor becomes a pointing finger with a *W* in it. This signifies that the linked page will be viewed in your default web browser.

2. Right-click the link and then choose one of the following from the context menu:
   - **Open Weblink In Browser**   Opens the linked web page in your default web browser.
   - **Append To Document**   Appends the linked web page to the PDF document.
   - **Open Weblink As New Document**   Creates a new PDF document of the linked page.
   - **Copy Link Location**   Copies the URL of the linked page to the clipboard. You can paste the link—CTRL-V (Windows) or CMD-V (Macintosh)—into the address bar of a web browser or into the URL field of the Create PDF From Web Page dialog box.
3. Continue right-clicking links to add additional pages to the document, or you can choose one of the other options.
4. When you finish adding pages to the document, choose File | Save.

Use the View Web Links Command

To view all the web links within a captured page, you use the View Web Links command. You can use this command to add additional web pages to the document, as the following steps explain:

1. Choose View | Tools | Document Processing, and Acrobat displays the Document Processing tab in the Tools pane. From the Document Processing tab, choose Web Capture | View Web Links, and Acrobat opens the Select Page Links To Download dialog box, shown here.

   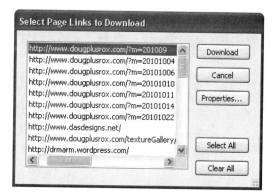

2. To create a selection of URLs to web pages you want to append to the current document, do one of the following:
   - To add contiguous links to the selection, click the first and last link you want to download while holding down SHIFT. To add noncontiguous links to the selection, click each link while holding down CTRL (Windows) or CMD (Macintosh).
   - To select all links, click Select All.
   - To clear the selection, click Clear All.
3. Click the Download button to begin the download. After you do so, Acrobat opens the Download Status dialog box and displays the progress of the operation. When the download is complete, Acrobat appends the downloaded pages to the document and adds additional bookmarks and thumbnails for the new pages.

If you download a web page with form fields, such as text boxes, check boxes, and submit buttons, these form fields are preserved in the PDF document. You can modify the properties of the fields, as outlined in Chapter 13.

Use the Append Web Page Command

You can use the Append Web Page command to add additional pages to the current document. If you're appending links from within the same site to the current document, either click a link within the document or use the View Web Links command to view the links within the document, and then select the links of the pages you want to add to the document. If, however, the page you want to add to the captured web page doesn't have a link on the page, do the following:

1. Choose View | Tools | Document Processing to open the Document Processing tab in the Tools pane. Choose Web Capture | Add to PDF From Web Page to open the Add To PDF From Web Page dialog box.
2. In the URL field, enter the address for the web page you want to add to the document.
3. Click Capture Multiple Levels to expand the dialog box, as shown here.

Add to PDF from Web Page   ☒

URL: http://www.dougplusrox.com   ▼   Browse

┌─ Settings ──────────────────────────────┐
◉ Get only   1   ⇕   level(s)   ○ Get entire site

☐ Stay on same path

☐ Stay on same server
└──┘

🔲 Capture Multiple Levels   Create   Cancel   Settings...

4. In the Get Only [ ] Level(s) field, enter the number of levels to download, or use the spinner buttons to increase or decrease the value in the Levels field. Alternatively, you can choose Get Entire Site to download every level (and subsequently every page) in the site.
5. Choose Stay On Same Path if you want Acrobat to download all pages along the path of the specified URL.
6. Choose Stay On Same Server if you want Acrobat to download only pages from the server of the specified URL and disregard links to URLs on another server.
7. Click the Create button to begin capturing the page(s). Acrobat opens the Download Status dialog box, which you can use to monitor download progress.

After the page downloads, you can invoke the command again to add additional pages to the document, or you can choose File | Save.

Tip   When you append a PDF document captured from a web page, you can modify the settings for the new pages by clicking the Settings button in the Add To PDF From Web Page dialog box. For more information on settings, refer to the upcoming section "Specify Web Page Conversion Settings."

When you append pages from another website to a captured web page, Acrobat creates a bookmark for the URL of the site. Captured pages from each site are listed under the site's URL bookmark.

Tip   Right-click a link to reveal a context menu with commands to open the link in a web browser, append the linked web page to the PDF, or open the link as a new PDF document.

Append All Links on a Page

After you download a web page, you can use any of the methods previously discussed to append other pages to the page, or you can download every page linked to the captured page by choosing View | Tools | Document Processing to open the Tools pane and then choosing Web Capture | Append All Links On Page. After you choose this command, Acrobat downloads the linked pages one at a time and displays the download progress in the Download Status dialog box. This operation may take a considerable amount of time if the page has several links.

After the linked pages are downloaded, you can view the downloaded pages by clicking a link in the main page or by opening the Bookmarks tab or Pages tab and then clicking a bookmark or thumbnail. You can apply the Append All Links On Page command on any of the newly downloaded pages to add additional pages to the document.

After you add all the desired pages to the document, you can disable web links by choosing View | Tools | Document Processing to open the Document Processing tab in the Tools pane and then choosing Remove All Links. This opens the Remove Web Links dialog box, with which you can specify how many pages of links to remove. After you apply this command, web links are visible in the document, but they will

How to...   ## Save a Web Search

If you use a web search engine to find web pages you want to save for reference, after you enter your query, launch Acrobat and choose File | Create | PDF From Web Page. Then enter the URL for the search engine's results page. After Acrobat downloads the page, you can append the document with the web pages from the results of your search by clicking the links in the results page. Download additional web pages by clicking other links. After you download all the pages you want to save, you can delete the initial search page by clicking its thumbnail and then choosing Document | Delete Pages. If your search returns pages of URLs, you can save the PDF document and open the document at a later date to peruse the desired URLs at your leisure.

no longer function as links to URLs. Links to other downloaded web pages will still be functional, however, and open the proper document page when clicked. When you remove web links, you reduce the size of the PDF file.

Specify Web Page Conversion Settings

You can modify the conversion settings used to capture web pages and convert them to PDF format. When you modify these settings, this is a global action that applies to future web pages you capture until you modify the settings again. To modify web capture conversion settings, do the following:

1. Choose File | Create | PDF From Web Page to open the Create PDF From Web Page dialog box, shown previously.
2. In the Create PDF From Web Page dialog box, click the Settings button to open the Web Page Conversion Settings dialog box, shown next. You can modify parameters for General options and Page Layout options, as detailed in the following sections.

Modify General Conversion Settings

When you open the Web Page Conversion Settings dialog box, the General tab is selected by default, as shown. The supported file types Acrobat can convert to PDF are listed in the File Type Settings window. You can modify settings for two file types—HTML and Plain Text—as described in the next section, "Modify HTML Display Settings."

The following are the options you can modify in the PDF Settings area:

- **Create Bookmarks**   Choose this option to have Acrobat generate a new bookmark for each additional page you capture. This option is checked by default.
- **Create PDF Tags**   Choose this option to have Acrobat create a document structure that conforms to the layout of the HTML document. If you check this option, Acrobat adds bookmarks for HTML items, such as paragraphs, lists, tables, and so on. The tagged document can be reflowed for easier reading on devices with smaller viewing areas. For more information on tagged documents, refer to the section "About Tagged Documents" in Chapter 11.
- **Place Headers And Footers On New Page**   Check this option to have Acrobat add a new header and footer to each captured web page. The header shows the web page title as it appears in the browser, and the footer displays the web page URL, plus the date and time the file was downloaded. If the URL is exceptionally long, the footer may be truncated to allow room for the page number.

To save the settings, click OK, which closes the Web Page Conversion Settings dialog box and returns you to the Create PDF From Web Page dialog box.

Modify HTML Display Settings

When you capture a web page as a PDF, you can modify the look of the captured page by changing the HTML display settings. You can modify font style, font color, and other parameters of the converted page, such as background color and table cell colors. To modify the display characteristics of captured web pages, do the following:

1. Open the Web Page Conversion Settings dialog box as outlined previously.
2. In the File Type window, click HTML to activate the Settings button.
3. Click the Settings button to open the HTML Conversion Settings dialog box as shown here.
4. In the Input Encoding area, accept the Default Encoding option or click the drop-down arrow and then choose the appropriate encoding system from the drop-down menu.
5. Choose whether to use the encoding specified in step 4 by clicking the desired radio

button. Your options are Always (which always uses the encoding, regardless of the encoding specified in the web page HTML) and When Page Doesn't Specify Encoding (which uses the encoding when the web page HTML doesn't specify encoding).

6. In the Language Specific Font Settings area, accept the default Language Script option, or click the drop-down arrow and choose the desired encoding language from the list.

7. Accept the default Body Text option, or click the drop-down arrow and choose the desired font from the list.

8. Accept the default Base Font Size (12 points), or click the drop-down arrow and choose the desired option from the list.

9. In the Default Colors section, you can modify the color of Text, Background, and Links, by clicking the color button to the right of an item to open the color picker. Choose a color for the item and then click OK to close the color picker and apply the change. Repeat as needed to change the color of other items.

10. If you click the Force These Settings For All Pages check box, the colors you specify in the previous step are applied to all pages you capture, regardless of the colors specified in the actual HTML document. If you don't choose this option, Acrobat applies the colors you specified in the previous step only to HTML documents that don't have colors specified in the document HTML code.

11. Click the Multimedia Content drop-down arrow and choose one of the following options:

    - **Disable Multimedia Capture**   Captures HTML and images, but doesn't capture multimedia content such as Flash movies.
    - **Embed Multimedia Content When Possible (Default)**   Embeds multimedia formats supported by Acrobat 9.
    - **Reference Multimedia Content By URL**   Creates a placeholder for the media linked to the URL from which you downloaded the web page. When you open the file, Acrobat plays the multimedia file by accessing the URL from which the page was captured, provided you are connected to the Internet. Otherwise, you only see a rectangular placeholder the same size as the multimedia content. This option creates a smaller file size, but it isn't recommended if you distribute the document to recipients who view the files on machines without Internet connections or with slow Internet connections. Also, the file won't play if the parent website removes the multimedia file or moves it to a different URL.

12. Click the Retain Page Background check box (the default option) to save an image background from the web page with the resulting PDF document.

13. Click the Convert Images check box (the default option) to have Acrobat include images from the captured web page. If you disable this option, Acrobat replaces the image with a colored border and the image Alt text, if specified, within the HTML document.

14. Click the Underline Links check box (the default option) to have Acrobat underline all text links when converting the document to PDF format, whether or not they are underlined in the HTML page.

15. Click OK to close the HTML Conversion Settings dialog box.

Modify Page Layout Options

The Page Layout tab of the Web Page Conversion Settings dialog box enables you to modify the size, margins, orientation, and scaling of the converted web pages. These options come in handy if you want to maintain the dimensions of a captured web page. For example, if you know each page in a website is configured to a certain size, say 760 × 420 pixels (a web browser maximized at an 800 × 600 desktop resolution), you can change the default Acrobat document size (8 ½ × 11 inches) to match. The following steps describe how to modify the page layout of a captured web page:

 The default unit of measure for Acrobat is inches. When you capture web pages, you may find it helpful to convert the unit of measure to points by choosing Edit | Preferences (Macintosh), and in the Units and Guides section, choosing Points.

1. Open the Web Page Conversion Settings dialog box as outlined previously.
2. Click the Page Layout tab, shown next.

Web Page Conversion Settings

General | Page Layout

Size
Page Size: Letter
Width: 8.5 in   Height: 11 in

Margins
Top: 0.361 in   Bottom: 0.5 in
Left: 0.14 in   Right: 0.14 in

Orientation
⦿ Portrait   ◯ Landscape

Scaling
☑ Scale Wide Contents to fit page
   ☑ Switch to landscape if scaled smaller than (%)   70

Help   Defaults   OK   Cancel

3. Click the Page Size drop-down arrow and choose an option. When you select a preset page size, the values in the Width and Height fields change to reflect your choice. Alternatively, select Custom from the Page Size drop-down menu and specify the page size by entering values in the Width and Height fields or by clicking the spinner buttons to change the values.
4. In the Margins area, accept the defaults or enter your own values in the Top, Bottom, Left, and Right fields.

Tip If the web page you're capturing has no margins, you can duplicate this when you capture the page by entering 0 for each margin setting on the Page Layout tab of the Web Page Conversion Settings dialog box.

5. In the Orientation area, choose Portrait (the default) or Landscape.
6. In the Scaling area, you can modify the following options:
   - **Scale Wide Contents To Fit Page** Check this box to have Acrobat resize the contents of a web page that exceeds the width of the screen to fit the page.
   - **Switch To Landscape If Scaled Smaller Than [ ] %** Accept the default value (70 percent) or enter a value of your own in this field. Acrobat automatically switches the page layout from Portrait to Landscape if it's necessary to scale the page to a value lower than specified.
7. Click OK to apply the settings and close the Web Page Conversion Settings

dialog box.

How to... Capture Web Pages from Internet Explorer

If you have Internet Explorer (IE) installed on your computer, the Acrobat install utility adds a button to IE that enables you to capture a web page as a PDF document. After capturing a web page in this manner, you can append other web pages to the document or refresh it as outlined previously. To capture a web page from within IE, click the Convert Current Web Page To An Adobe PDF File button, as shown here. This feature is also a wonderful way to create a PDF of a transaction at a secure website. The fact that the page is already open in the browser means the conversion is almost instantaneous. If you were to choose Create | PDF From Web Page and enter a secure link, the conversion would slow down to a crawl because the website would require authentication before opening the secure page. You can also choose commands from a drop-down menu by clicking the drop-down arrow to the right of the icon. These options enable you to convert the web page to a PDF, add the web page to an existing PDF, print the web page, or send it via e-mail. There is also an option to view the resulting PDF in Acrobat, which is selected by default, and an option to open the Web Page Conversion Settings dialog box discussed previously.

Another powerful option is the ability to select a portion of the web page and convert the selection to PDF. Click Select and then move your cursor over the area on the HTML page you want to convert to PDF. As you move your cursor, a red bounding box appears around an area. When the bounding box encompasses the area you want to convert to PDF, click inside the box and then click Convert to open the Convert Web Page To Adobe PDF dialog box. Enter a name for the file and click Save to complete the conversion process.

Use the Web Capture Feature

After you use the Web Capture feature a few times, you begin to see how useful it is. You can use the Create PDF From Web Page command to capture a web page with product specifications. If you're contemplating a major purchase, you can download the product specifications of every product you're considering and then compare them at your leisure, without having to wait for the web pages to download or perhaps being bumped off the Internet during peak traffic.

If you use the Internet for research, capturing web pages is a great way to build a reference library. After you save several (or several hundred) web pages as PDF documents, you can use the Full Text Index with Searchable Catalog command to build a searchable index. Building a searchable index is covered in Chapter 15.

Summary

In this chapter, you learned how to create PDF documents by capturing them with your scanner, and from web pages. In the next chapter, you will learn how to create navigation for your PDF documents.

6

Create Navigation for PDF Documents

HOW TO...

- Create bookmarks
- Edit bookmarks
- Use thumbnails
- Create links
- Create a navigation menu

When you create a PDF document within an authoring application, navigation devices are added to the document. PDF documents have two types of automatically created navigation devices: bookmarks and page thumbnails. Bookmarks and page thumbnails have their own panels in the Navigation pane.

When you create a PDF document, one thumbnail is created for each page. Viewers of your PDF document can navigate to a specific page of the document by clicking its thumbnail. Alternatively, for a single-page document, they can navigate to a specific part of the page, as you learn in this chapter. Bookmarks, on the other hand, may or may not be created, depending on the method you used to create the PDF document. If, for example, you use Acrobat PDFMaker (the Adobe Acrobat plug-in for Microsoft Office applications) with its default settings to create a PDF file from a Microsoft Word document in Windows that contains heading styles, a bookmark appears for each heading style used in the document. If you use the Word Print command and choose Adobe PDF to create the PDF document, no bookmarks are created. To navigate to a bookmark within a document, viewers just click its name in the Bookmarks panel of the Navigation pane. For more information on the Navigation pane, refer to Chapter 2.

After you open a PDF file in Acrobat, you can modify bookmarks and thumbnails, as well as create other navigation devices, such as text links or buttons. After you create a link (also known as a hotspot), you can assign an action to it that determines what occurs when the link is activated with a mouse click. You can also add actions to bookmarks and links, and assign to an individual page one or more actions that occur when the page opens or closes.

Use the Bookmarks Panel

In Adobe Reader, you use the Bookmarks panel to navigate to bookmark destinations. In Acrobat, you also use the Bookmarks panel to navigate to a bookmark within the document, as well as to edit existing bookmarks and add new ones. The Bookmarks panel is part of the Navigation pane. To open the Bookmarks panel, click the Bookmarks icon. Figure 6-1 shows the Bookmarks panel for a PDF document.

About the Bookmarks Panel Toolbar

Bookmarks are an important part of any multipage PDF document. Without bookmarks, viewers of your PDF files would have a hard time navigating to the parts of the document they want to view. When you create bookmarks, edit bookmarks, or

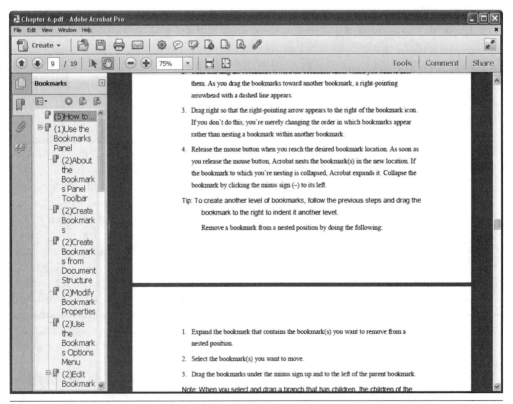

FIGURE 6-1 In Acrobat, you use the Bookmarks panel to navigate to, create, and edit bookmarks.

use bookmarks to navigate within a document, you can use the Bookmarks panel toolbar to streamline your work.

The Bookmarks panel toolbar contains three tool icons, an Options menu icon, and a Collapse icon, as shown here.

The Collapse icon is in the upper-right corner of the panel. Below the Collapse icon, you find the Options menu icon and three tool icons. Their functionality is as follows:

- **Collapse**   Click this icon to close the Bookmarks panel.
- **Options**   Click the text icon to open the Bookmarks panel Options menu.
- **Delete Selected Bookmarks**   Click this icon to delete selected bookmarks.
- **New Bookmark**   Click this icon to create a new bookmark. Specific instructions for creating bookmarks are presented in the upcoming section, "Create Bookmarks."
- **Expand Current Bookmark**   Click this icon to expand the currently selected bookmark, which enables you to view bookmarks nested within a bookmark.

Create Bookmarks

A bookmark is a text link in the Bookmarks panel of the Navigation pane that viewers of your PDF document can use to navigate to a specific part of the document. If the bookmarks in the document are created from an authoring application plug-in, each bookmark is linked to a specific part of a document, such as a heading or, in the case of a document composed of captured web pages, a specific web page. You can also configure bookmarks to link to external PDF documents and other PDF files by modifying the action that occurs when the bookmark is clicked, as discussed in an upcoming section.

You can, however, create your own bookmarks to draw a viewer's attention to a specific place in the document. You can also use bookmarks to open other PDF documents or other files. To create a document bookmark, do the following:

1. Click the Bookmarks icon to open the Bookmarks panel.
2. Click the bookmark above the place where you want the new bookmark to appear. If you don't specify a place for the new bookmark, it's added at the bottom of the list.
3. Use the Hand tool, Viewing tools, or menu commands to navigate to the part of the document where you want the bookmark to link. Note that you can also use existing bookmarks and thumbnails to navigate to desired parts of the document.

Remember, you can also use a bookmark to link to a magnified view of a page to direct the reader's attention. You can magnify the page view by using the Zoom tool.

4. Click the New Bookmark icon (introduced in the previous section), or click the Options icon and choose New Bookmark from the Bookmarks Options menu. Either way, the new bookmark appears below the bookmark you selected when you clicked the icon. Acrobat gives the new bookmark the default name of Untitled, and the bookmark name is highlighted, indicating you can edit the default title.

5. Enter the desired name for the new bookmark and press ENTER or RETURN. When choosing a name for a bookmark, remember to choose a name that accurately reflects the contents of the bookmark. Your viewers will rely on the bookmark title to get an idea of what they can expect to find when they click the bookmark.

Note You will not be able to add a bookmark to a document that has security settings that prohibit editing of the document.

Create Bookmarks from the Document Structure

If the program used to create the PDF document didn't create bookmarks to your satisfaction, you can add additional bookmarks by using the method described in the preceding section, or you can automate the process by choosing certain elements from the document structure—such as headings—to create bookmarks. You can create bookmarks from the document structure only if you enabled the Enable Accessibility And Reflow With Tagged PDF option when choosing conversion settings in the authoring application from which you created the PDF. Note that not all applications have these conversion options. To create bookmarks from the document structure, do the following:

1. Open the document for which you want to create bookmarks.

2. In the Navigation pane, click the Bookmarks icon to open the Bookmarks panel.

3. Click the Options drop-down arrow and choose New Bookmarks From Structure to open the Structure Elements dialog box, shown here.

Structure Elements
Structure
H1
H2
H3
H4
H5
L
LBody
LI
P
Select All   Clear All
OK   Cancel

The New Bookmarks From Structure command is dimmed out if the document doesn't have elements that Acrobat can use to create bookmarks.

4. Click a structure element name to select it. To add additional structure elements, hold down SHIFT and click to add contiguous elements, or hold down CTRL (Windows) or CMD (Macintosh) and then click to add noncontiguous elements. To select all structure elements, click the Select All button.
5. Click OK. Acrobat scans the document and creates a bookmark for each selected structure element located. The bookmarks are untitled and nested in tree fashion. Click the plus sign (+) to the left of the top element to expand the first bookmark.

Modify Bookmark Properties

After you create a bookmark, you can modify it by changing its properties. You can modify the appearance of the bookmark, modify the view of the bookmark destination, and modify the action that occurs when a user clicks the bookmark. To change bookmark properties, follow these steps:

1. Click the bookmark whose properties you want to modify.
2. Click the Options drop-down arrow and choose Properties to open the Bookmark Properties dialog box, shown here. Alternatively, you can right-click a bookmark and choose Properties from the context menu.
3. When you open the Bookmark Properties dialog box, the Appearance tab is selected by default. You can modify the Appearance properties to change the look of the selected bookmark's text. Click the Style drop-down arrow and choose one of the following from the drop-down menu: Plain (the default), Bold, Italic, or Bold & Italic.
4. Click the Color swatch and choose a color from the pop-up palette. You can choose one of the preset colors or click Other Color to create a custom color from the color picker.

You can direct a reader's attention to important bookmarks by changing the bookmark's text style and color.

5. Click the Actions tab, and the currently selected action for the bookmark is displayed, as shown here. If the bookmark was created in an authoring application, the action shown in the Actions area is usually Go To A Page In This Document. To select a different action, click the Select Action drop-down arrow and choose an option from the drop-down menu. The other available actions are discussed in detail in Chapter 7.

Bookmark Properties

Appearance | **Actions**

Add an Action

Select Action: | Execute a menu item

Add...

Actions

⊟ Go to a page in this document
Page: 2
Zoom level: Fit Page

Up | Down | Edit | Delete

OK | Cancel

6. Click Edit to open the Go To A Page In This Document dialog box.
7. Enter the number of the page you want to open when the bookmark is clicked.
8. Click the Zoom drop-down arrow and choose an option from the drop-down menu. For more information on the magnification options, refer to the section "Change Bookmark Zoom Settings."
9. Click OK to close the Go To A Page In This Document dialog box, and then click Close to exit the Bookmark Properties dialog box and apply your changes.

You can change the text size of all bookmarks by selecting one or more bookmarks and then choosing an option from the Text Size submenu of the Bookmark panel's options menu. Your options are Small, Medium, and Large.

To change the style of an individual bookmark, select it and then choose Properties from the Bookmark panel's options menu or context menu. This opens the Bookmark Properties dialog box from which you can change the font style from Plain to Bold, Italic, or Bold & Italic, and change the color of the bookmark text.

Use the Bookmarks Options Menu

You use the Bookmarks Options menu to perform functions associated with bookmarks. You can use commands from this menu to modify bookmarks, navigate to bookmarks, and maintain the Bookmarks panel. To do so, follow these steps:

1. To open the Bookmarks Options menu, click Bookmarks in the Navigation pane to open the Bookmarks panel and then click the Options icon.
2. After you open the Bookmarks Options menu, click the menu command you want Acrobat to perform. Some of the commands in this menu were already presented; others will do the same job as their toolbar counterparts. For example, to expand a bookmark, you can click the plus sign next to a collapsed bookmark or choose the Expand Current Bookmark command from the Bookmarks Options menu. Detailed information about other relevant Bookmarks Options menu commands are discussed in upcoming sections.

Tip If you're viewing a document with long bookmarks that aren't completely visible in the Bookmarks panel, choose Wrap Long Bookmarks from the Bookmarks Options menu.

Edit Bookmarks

You can edit existing bookmarks by changing the bookmark destination, renaming the bookmarks, deleting selected bookmarks, and rearranging the hierarchy of bookmarks. When you add new bookmarks to a document, you can specify the bookmark destination and view magnification. At times, though, it may be preferable to lay out the document structure by creating bookmarks first and then modifying the destination and view of the bookmarks later. You can use the Bookmarks panel toolbar and Options menu to edit bookmarks. You can also right-click within the Bookmarks panel to choose a command from the Bookmarks panel context menu, which is a watered-down, but still useful, version of the Bookmarks Options menu.

Change a Bookmark Destination

You can change the destination of a bookmark, change its zoom, or change both. By modifying the view of a bookmark, you call attention to a specific part of the document. To modify a bookmark destination, follow these steps:

1. In the Bookmarks panel, select the bookmark whose destination you want to modify.
2. In the Document pane, change to the location you want the bookmark to link to by using the Hand tool, navigation tools, or menu commands. Alternatively, you can click a thumbnail in the Pages panel to navigate to a page.
3. Change the zoom of the document by using the viewing tools or menu commands.
4. Choose Set Bookmark Destination from the Bookmarks Options menu. Alternatively, you can right-click and choose Set Destination from the context menu. After you choose this option, a dialog box appears asking you if you really want to change the bookmark location.
5. Click Yes to change the bookmark destination and close the dialog box.

Note When you combine files such as images to create a PDF, you cannot change the destination of a bookmark created by Acrobat. You can, however, change the destination of a bookmark you manually created.

Rename a Bookmark

Another edit you may need to perform is to rename a bookmark. Follow these steps to change a bookmark name:

1. Select the bookmark and then click inside the text box to select the bookmark text.
2. Enter a new name for the bookmark and then press ENTER or RETURN.

Alternatively, you can do the following:

1. Select the bookmark and then choose Rename Bookmark from the Bookmarks Options menu to select the bookmark text.
2. Enter a new name for the bookmark and then press ENTER or RETURN.

Delete a Bookmark

You can delete any bookmark. When you delete a bookmark, you don't change the content of the document; instead, you merely remove a link. If you created a PDF document that has several heading levels, you may want to consider deleting a few bookmarks to simplify navigation.

Caution There is no warning before the bookmark is deleted. If you delete a bookmark in error, choose Edit | Undo Delete Bookmark or press CTRL-Z (Windows) or CMD-Z (Macintosh) immediately after deleting the bookmark.

1. Select the bookmark. To add contiguous bookmarks to the selection, press SHIFT and click the bookmark(s) you want to add to the selection. To add noncontiguous bookmarks to the selection, press CTRL (Windows) or CMD (Macintosh) and then click the bookmark(s) you want to add to the selection.
2. Choose Edit | Delete, press DELETE, or click the Delete Selected Bookmarks icon (looks like a trash can). Alternatively, you can choose Delete Selected Bookmarks from the Options menu.

Arrange Bookmarks

When you create a PDF document, bookmarks are created in descending order from the first page of the document to the last. Acrobat nests bookmarks when you convert a document with multiple heading levels or if you use the New Bookmarks From Structure command. You can create your own bookmark nests to organize a cluttered Bookmarks panel. Here's how to nest a bookmark or group of bookmarks under another bookmark:

1. Select the bookmark(s) you want to nest. You can select contiguous (SHIFT-click) or noncontiguous (CTRL-click for Windows or CMD-click for Macintosh) bookmarks.
2. Click and drag the bookmarks toward the bookmark under which you want to nest them. As you drag the bookmarks toward another bookmark, a right-pointing arrowhead with a dashed line appears.
3. Drag right so that the right-pointing arrow appears underneath the bookmark with which you want to nest the selected bookmark. If you don't do this, you're merely changing the order in which bookmarks appear rather than nesting a bookmark within another bookmark.
4. Release the mouse button when you reach the desired bookmark location. As soon as you release the mouse button, Acrobat nests the bookmark(s) in the new location. If the bookmark to which you're nesting is collapsed, Acrobat expands it. Collapse the bookmark by clicking the minus sign (–) to its left (Windows) or the triangle to its left (Macintosh).

To create another level of bookmarks, follow the previous steps and drag the bookmark to the right to indent it another level.

You can remove a bookmark from a nested position by doing the following:

1. Expand the bookmark that contains the bookmark you want to remove from a nested position.
2. Select the bookmark you want to move.
3. Drag the bookmark under the minus sign up and to the left of the parent bookmark. On the Macintosh version of Acrobat, nested bookmarks are noted by a left-pointing triangle.

Note When you select and drag a branch that has children, the children of the parent are moved as well, maintaining the structure of the branch.

4. Release the mouse button. Acrobat moves the bookmark out of a nested position.

Change Bookmark Zoom Settings

When you create or edit a bookmark, you can control the magnification setting of the bookmark destination. You can change magnification in the Zoom field of the Go To A Page In This Document dialog box, which can be accessed as follows:

1. Select the bookmark from within the Bookmarks panel whose zoom settings you want to modify.
2. Right-click the bookmark and choose Properties from the context menu. After you choose this command, the applicable Properties dialog box appears with the previously used tab displayed. If it isn't already displayed, click the Actions tab.

3. Select the Go To A Page In This Document action from the list of actions assigned to the bookmark.
4. Click Edit to open the Go To A Page In This Document dialog box.
5. Click the Zoom drop-down arrow and choose one of the following options:
   - **Fit Page**   Sizes the visible contents of the bookmark or link destination to fit the Document pane.
   - **Actual Size**   Displays a selected link or bookmark destination at 100-percent magnification, the original size of the document.
   - **Fit Width**   Zooms a selected link or bookmark destination to the current width of the Document pane. If you choose this option, images on the page may be pixelated. An image becomes pixelated when it is enlarged enough to make the individual pixels appear as square blocks of color. At normal magnification, pixels are blended so they aren't visible.
   - **Fit Visible**   Zooms a selected link or bookmark destination so all visible elements on the page resize to the current width of the Document pane. Note that this view will differ at different monitor resolutions.
   - **Inherit Zoom**   Displays a selected link or bookmark destination at the viewer-selected magnification level.
6. Click OK to close the Go To A Page In This Document dialog box, and then click Close to apply the zoom settings to the bookmark or link. The new zoom settings will be applied the next time the bookmark is clicked.

Use the Pages Panel

When you convert a file to PDF format and open the document in Acrobat, a thumbnail for each page is automatically generated. Thumbnails are neatly arranged by page order in the Pages panel, which resides in the Navigation pane. You can use thumbnails as navigation devices when reading a document, as well as to reorder pages, a technique discussed in Chapter 8. Thumbnails are also used to print and change the magnification of pages. To access the Pages panel, click the Pages icon on the left side of the Navigation pane. If the Navigation pane is open, but another pane

How to... ## Change Page Magnification with Thumbnails

When you select a thumbnail, a black border appears, which signifies the current view of the page. You can change page magnification by clicking and dragging the black border's lower-right corner. After you change the page magnification, the shape and size of the black rectangle changes to reflect the current page view. Move your cursor toward any rectangle border. When your cursor becomes an open hand, click and drag to pan to a different view. You may not see the cursor immediately or if you're not exactly over the right spot. However, once you get the hang of it, you'll be able to change page views as described here.

FIGURE 6-2 Use page thumbnails to navigate and edit a PDF document.

is displayed, click the Pages icon to open the panel. Figure 6-2 shows the Pages panel with the default thumbnail size.

Use the Pages Panel Options Menu

The Pages panel has a menu you can use to perform tasks, such as edit pages, embed thumbnails or remove embedded thumbnails, and change the size of thumbnails. In upcoming sections, you learn how to use the commands that pertain to editing thumbnails. In Chapter 8, you learn how to use thumbnails to edit and reorder document pages.

To open the Pages Options menu, open the Pages panel and then click the Options icon. Alternatively, with no thumbnail selected, you can right-click within the Pages panel to open a context menu. The Pages panel context menu is a carbon copy of the Pages Options menu. The context menu is handy when you need to access its commands quickly.

Create Thumbnails

When you create a PDF document in an authoring application or by using the Acrobat PDFMaker plug-in, you can modify a conversion setting to embed thumbnails. Embedded thumbnails increase the file size of the published PDF document by approximately 2KB or more per thumbnail for a page with images; thumbnails for pages with text only are slightly smaller. The actual size of the thumbnail varies, depending on the amount of graphics in the page from which the thumbnail is generated. An embedded thumbnail for a page with text only is about 0.5KB.

When you create a document without embedded thumbnails, Acrobat creates them dynamically when you open the Pages panel. This can take several seconds for a large document. You can choose to embed thumbnails to circumvent the redraw every time you open the panel. You can easily remove embedded thumbnails in the future, if desired.

To embed all thumbnails within a document, follow these steps:

1. Open the Pages panel as outlined previously.
2. Open the Pages Options menu and choose Embed All Page Thumbnails. Alternatively, you can choose the Embed All Page Thumbnails command from the Pages panel context menu.

Follow these steps to remove embedded thumbnails from a document:

1. Open the Pages panel.
2. Open the Pages Options menu and choose Remove Embedded Page Thumbnails. Alternatively, you can right-click (Windows) or CTRL-click (Macintosh) and choose Remove Embedded Page Thumbnails from the context menu.

Note After you remove thumbnails from a document, Acrobat creates them on the fly whenever the Pages panel is opened. As mentioned previously, this may take considerable time with a lengthy document. As a rule, you should remove embedded thumbnails only when the file size of the published PDF document is a factor.

Resize Thumbnails

When you open the Pages panel, all thumbnails are displayed at default size. Unless you resize the width of the Navigation pane, the thumbnails are displayed in a single column. If you prefer, you can display more thumbnails in the Navigation pane by choosing Reduce Page Thumbnails from the Pages Options menu. After you choose this command, thumbnails are displayed at reduced magnification. To return thumbnails to their original size, or to the next highest level of magnification if you've reduced the size several times, choose Enlarge Page Thumbnails from the Pages Options menu.

You can use the Reduce Page Thumbnails or Enlarge Page Thumbnails command more than once to arrive at the optimum thumbnail size for your working preference.

Create Links

As you already learned, when you convert a document into PDF format, navigation devices in the form of thumbnails and bookmarks are created for you. You can, however, exceed the limitations of these rudimentary navigation devices by creating links.

When you create a link, you create an area in the document that, when a viewer pauses their cursor over the hotspot, the cursor icon becomes a hand with a pointing finger—the same thing that happens when you pause your cursor over a link on a web page. You can create links for text or images in a PDF document or create any other kind of link anywhere in the document. The links you create can be visible or invisible.

Links give you tremendous flexibility. You can create links that change the view of a document, load another document, open a web page, load a multimedia element, and more. You can specify the appearance of a link as a visible or invisible rectangle, as well as specify the type of highlight that appears when a user's cursor hovers over the link. The first step in creating a link is to define the active area of the link, also known as a hotspot.

Create a Hotspot

As it relates to PDF documents, a *hotspot* is an active area of the document that, when clicked by a user, causes an action to occur. You create a hotspot with the Link tool, found in the Content panel of the Tools pane and on the Quick Tools toolbar. The Link tool looks like two interconnecting links of a chain. Use the Link tool to define the boundary of the hotspot as follows:

1. Click the Tools icon to open the Tools pane, click Content, and then choose the Link tool. After you select the tool and move your cursor into the Document pane, it becomes a crosshair. As long as the Link tool is selected, any other links in the document, even invisible ones, are displayed.

2. In the Document pane, click a spot to define one of the hotspot corners and then drag diagonally. As you drag, you see a bounding box, which displays the current area of the selection.

3. When the bounding box surrounds the area you want to define as a hotspot, release the mouse button. After you create the hotspot, the Create Link dialog box appears, as shown here.

4. In the Link Appearance area of the Create Link dialog box, click the Link Type drop-down arrow and choose one of the following options:
   - **Visible Rectangle**   This option creates a hotspot with a visible rectangle at its perimeter.
   - **Invisible Rectangle**   This option creates a hotspot that isn't visible. If you choose Invisible Rectangle, the Width, Color, and Style options aren't valid and are no longer displayed.
5. Click the Highlight Style drop-down arrow and choose one of the following options to determine how the link is highlighted when users click it:
   - **None**   No highlight appears when the link is clicked.
   - **Invert**   The link is highlighted in black when clicked.
   - **Outline**   The link outline color changes when clicked.
   - **Inset**   A shadow appears when the link is clicked. This effect is similar to a web page button that appears to recess into the page when clicked.
6. If you chose Visible Rectangle, click the Line Thickness drop-down arrow and choose Thin, Medium, or Thick. This option defines the thickness of the hotspot border.
7. Click the Line Style drop-down arrow and choose Solid, Dashed, or Underline. This option defines the line style for the hotspot border.
8. Click the Color swatch and choose the rectangle color from the pop-up palette. To choose a color other than the presets, click Other Color and then choose a color from the system color picker.
9. Choose one of the following options from the Link Action area to specify what happens when the link is clicked:
   - **Go To A Page View**   Enables you to specify which page will appear and at what zoom setting when the link is clicked.
   - **Open A File**   Loads a file when the link is clicked. If you choose this option, Acrobat creates a link to the file, including the absolute path of the file. Use this option when the document will be viewed only on the computer where the document is created or at a website to which you've also uploaded the file to be opened. You can also use this option when creating a PDF document that will be part of a CD presentation, as long as the file is also present on the CD and the relative path is the same.
   - **Open A Web Page**   Opens a web page when the link is clicked.
   - **Custom Link**   Lets you choose a custom action that will occur when the link is clicked.
10. Click Next. The dialog box that appears next depends on the option you selected in step 9. If you chose Open A File, the Select A File To Open dialog box appears, enabling you to select the document that opens when the link is clicked. The document is opened in the associated application. If you chose Open A Web Page, the Edit URL dialog box appears, enabling you to enter the URL of the web page that opens when the link is clicked. If you chose Custom Link, the Link Properties dialog box appears, enabling you to choose the action that executes when the link is clicked, as well as modify the appearance of the link. Custom

links are discussed in detail in Chapter 7. If you chose the default, Go To A Page View, the Create Go To View dialog box appears. The remaining steps are based on this choice.

11. Navigate to the desired page by using the Hand tool, scrolling with the scroll bars or clicking a page thumbnail.
12. Zoom to the desired magnification.
13. Click Set Link to close the Create Go To View dialog box.
14. Select the Hand tool and click the link to test it. If the link doesn't perform as you expected, you can edit the link by following the instructions in the upcoming section "Edit Links."

Did You Know?

You Can Create Links with the Select Tool

You can quickly create a link by selecting text or a graphic element, such as a logo or photo, with the Select tool. After selecting text or a graphic element with the tool, right-click, and then choose Create Link from the context menu. After the Create Link dialog box appears, follow the instructions starting at step 4 in the section "Create a Hotspot" to finish the process.

Edit Links

When the need arises, you can edit any property of a link. You can resize the link, change its destination, change the level of magnification, or change the appearance of the link. When you edit a link, the changes apply only to the selected link.

Change Link Properties

To change link properties, do the following:

1. Click the Tools icon, click Contents, and then select the Link tool. Alternatively, you can select the Link tool from the Quick Tools toolbar.
2. Double-click the link you want to edit, which opens the Link Properties dialog box. Alternatively, you can right-click the link and then choose Properties from the context menu.
3. Modify the Link Properties as described in the previous section, "Create a Hotspot."

Tip

After you edit a link and it's performing as you want it to, you can prevent inadvertently moving the link or otherwise editing it by right-clicking the link with the Link tool, choosing Properties from the context menu, and then clicking the Locked check box in the Link Properties dialog box.

Resize a Hotspot

When you use the Link tool to create a hotspot, the resulting hotspot may not be sized properly. It's better to make the hotspot a tad larger than needed, unless you have several hotspots in close proximity. You can change the size of a hotspot at any time, but you cannot resize a locked link. To resize a hotspot, follow these steps:

1. Click the Tools icon, click Contents, and then select the Link tool. Alternatively, you can select the Link tool from the Quick Tools toolbar.
2. Click the hotspot you want to resize. After you click the hotspot, eight handles in the form of solid blue rectangles appear on the hotspot perimeter. Click and drag any of the corner hotspots. Pressing SHIFT while you drag resizes the hotspot proportionately. Click the handle in the middle of the side of the hotspot and drag to resize the width of the hotspot. Click the handle in the middle of the top or bottom of the hotspot, and then drag to make the hotspot taller or shorter.

Delete a Link

If you decide a link is no longer needed, you can delete it from the document by doing the following:

1. Click the Tools icon, click Contents, and then select the Link tool. Alternatively, you can select the Link tool from the Quick Tools toolbar.
2. Select the link you want to delete and then choose Edit | Delete. Alternatively, select the link, right-click, and choose Edit | Delete from the context menu or simply press DELETE.

Tip   After you press DELETE, Acrobat does not display a warning dialog box asking you to confirm the action. If you delete a link in error, choose Edit | Undo or press CTRL-Z (Windows) or CMD-Z (Macintosh) before performing another task.

Create a Menu Using Links

When you create a PDF document, you can, of course, rely on the Acrobat built-in navigation devices: bookmarks and thumbnails. If your intended audience is unfamiliar with Adobe Reader, though, your document will be easier to navigate if you create a menu.

If you create a document in a word processing program, you can create a menu page as the first page of the document. On the menu page, list the major parts of the document you want your readers to be able to select by clicking links. Create the rest of the document, convert it to PDF by using the application's Print command, and then choose Adobe PDF as the printing device. Alternatively, if the application supports it, convert the document to PDF by using the application's Save As or Export command. If you're creating the document in Microsoft Word, you can access the Acrobat ribbon and then click the Create PDF button. Open the document in Acrobat and use the Link tool to create a link for each menu item. After you create the links for the menu page, choose File | Properties. In the Initial View section of the Document Properties dialog box, choose Page Only for the Navigation Tab option. Click OK to close the dialog box and then save the document. When your viewers open the document, the first thing they see is your menu page with the Navigation pane closed.

Summary

In this chapter, you learned how to work with bookmarks and page thumbnails, as well as how to create links. You learned how to use these objects as navigation devices and assign actions to these items to turn them into interactive devices. In the next chapter, you will learn how to work with other navigation elements and specify document Open options.

7

Create Interactive PDF Navigation

HOW TO...

- Use actions
- Add JavaScript to documents
- Create articles
- Use named destinations
- Modify Open options

In Chapter 6, you learned how to add navigation to your documents by using bookmarks, page thumbnails, and links. You can take PDF navigation to the next level when you use actions. Adding actions to a PDF document lets you open files, play media, navigate to websites, and more when a link or bookmark is clicked. You can assign multiple actions to a link or bookmark. You can also assign actions to page thumbnails to trigger an action when a page is opened or closed.

In this chapter, you find out how to work with actions. You learn how to add them to links, bookmarks, and page thumbnails. You also learn how to work with JavaScript. Acrobat features extensive JavaScript support. Another topic of discussion is the Article tool, which you use to create linked threads of text and graphics in different parts of the document. Article threads are much like magazine articles, where the topic of discussion begins on one page and is continued many pages later. You also learn how to add named destinations to your documents, which are also navigation devices. Toward the end of the chapter, you find out how to modify the view of a PDF document when it's opened.

Work with Actions

When you create a link or bookmark, the default action is Go To A Page View. However, Acrobat supplies you with a plethora of actions from which to choose that enable you to assign different actions to a link or bookmark, as well as add additional actions to these navigation items. You can also apply actions to form fields and individual pages. When you apply an action to a page, the action determines what the viewer sees or what happens when the page is opened or exited.

You set actions for bookmarks and links in their respective Properties dialog boxes within the Select Action field of the Actions tab. You can also add actions to individual pages of the document. For more information on page actions, refer to the upcoming section "Set a Page Action." To learn more about assigning actions to form fields, see Chapter 13. To add interactivity to a link, bookmark, form field, or page, choose from the following actions:

- **Execute A Menu Item** Use this action to execute a menu command. Even though you can choose any Acrobat command to execute as an action, the most logical choices would be to open another file, choose one of the navigation options from the Document menu, or choose one of the magnification options from the View menu.

Note If you distribute your document to users with Adobe Reader, make sure the menu command you choose is also an Adobe Reader menu command. For example, none of the commands to create a PDF is available with the Adobe Reader.

- **Go To A 3D/Multimedia View** Go To A 3D View switches to a view of a 3D file in the .U3D format, which is a 3D file you've embedded in the document. You can select which one of the 3D views are displayed when the action executes.
- **Go To A Page View** In most applicable dialog boxes, this is the default action. Use this action to advance to another page or view in the current document or another PDF file.
- **Import Form Data** Use this action to specify a file from which to import form data. The imported data is inserted in the active form. For more information on working with forms, see Chapter 13.
- **Multimedia Operation (Acrobat 9 and later)** This action can only be applied to Flash video (FLV file format) that is embedded in a document. The action enables you to assign a multimedia action to a video clip embedded in the page. Actions include Play, Pause, Rewind, Next Chapter Point, Previous Chapter Point, Seek to Time, Mute, Volume, or Custom.
- **Open A File** Use this action to open a file when the action is triggered. The opened file is viewed in its native application. Use this action only when the PDF file is viewed on the same machine on which the file was created, from a CD disc to which the file has been added, or from a website to which the file to be opened has been uploaded. The recipient of the PDF document needs the native software to view the file.
- **Open A Web Link** Use this action when you want to open a web page from a website. When you choose this action, you are prompted for the URL of the web link you want to open when the action executes.
- **Play A Sound** Use this action to play a sound file. If you add this action to a document, the document must be viewed on the machine used to create the PDF

file, or from a website from which the PDF file is to be opened and to which the sound file has both been uploaded.

- **Play Media (Acrobat 5 Compatible)**   Use this action to execute a QuickTime or AVI movie. To use this action, you must have a QuickTime or AVI movie within the document. For more information on adding movies to your PDF documents, see Chapter 15.
- **Play Media (Acrobat 6 And Later Compatible)**   Use this action to play any media that is Acrobat 6 and later compatible. To use this action, you must have the media embedded within the document. For more information on adding media that is Acrobat 6 and later compatible to your PDF documents, see Chapter 15.
- **Read An Article**   Use this action to read an article when the action is executed. After you choose this action, a dialog box appears with a list of articles in the document. For more information on creating articles, refer to the section "Create a Thread of Linked Articles."
- **Reset A Form**   Use this action to clear all previously entered data in a form.
- **Run A JavaScript**   Use this action to run a JavaScript. When you choose this option, you can create or edit a JavaScript from within the JavaScript Editor.
- **Set Layer Visibility**   Use this action to set the visibility for a layer in the document.
- **Show/Hide A Field**   Use this action to toggle the visibility of a form field in the document when the link is clicked.
- **Submit A Form**   Use this action with a button to submit data from a form to a URL.

Use Page Actions

You can make your PDF documents more interactive by having an action execute when a page opens or closes. For example, you can use an action to play a movie when a page opens and play a sound when a page closes.

Set a Page Action

You use the Page Properties dialog box to specify one or more actions that occur when a page opens or closes. If you choose multiple actions, you can edit the order in which the actions execute. To set a page action, follow these steps:

1. Choose the page to which you want to assign the action by selecting its thumbnail in the Pages panel of the Navigation pane.
2. Choose Page Properties from the Pages Options menu to open the Page Properties dialog box, and then click the Actions tab to reconfigure the Page Properties dialog box to add page actions, as shown next. Alternatively, you can right-click and choose Page Properties from the context menu and then click the Actions tab if it's not already open.

3. Click the Select Trigger drop-down arrow and choose one of the following:
   - **Page Open** Executes an action when a page loads.
   - **Page Close** Executes an action when a page closes.
4. Click the Select Action drop-down arrow and select an action from the drop-down menu, as shown here.

5. Click Add to add the action to the events that occur when the page opens or closes. This opens a dialog box for the selected action, in which you set the action's parameters.
6. After setting an action's parameters, click OK to apply the changes and exit the action's dialog box.
7. Repeat steps 4 through 6 to add additional actions to the list.
8. Click Close to exit the Page Properties dialog box.
9. Save the document.

The next time you open the document and select the page to which you applied the actions, they execute.

Edit Actions

The majority of time, when you assign actions to a bookmark, link, or page, they perform without a hitch. However, sometimes the actions don't execute in proper order, or you may decide to delete or add an action. When this occurs, you can easily edit actions by doing the following:

1. Select the bookmark, link, or page thumbnail to which you applied the actions.
2. Right-click and choose Properties from the context menu. The following illustration shows the Page Properties dialog box, as it appears when actions have been applied to a page. Notice the minus sign (or left-pointing triangle on a Macintosh computer) next to Page Open and Page Close. The minus sign on a Windows machine, or left-pointing triangle on a Macintosh computer, signifies that one or more actions occur when the page opens and when the page closes. If you assign actions to execute only when the page opens or when the page closes, there is no text for the other event.
3. In the Actions window, select the event you want to modify.
4. To add an action, select it from the Select Action drop-down menu and then click Add. This opens the selected action's dialog box. Set any parameters for the action, as outlined earlier in this chapter.
5. To delete an action, select it and then click Delete.

6. To edit an action, select the desired action and then click Edit. This opens the dialog box for the action, which enables you to modify the action to suit your document.
7. To rearrange the order in which actions execute, select an action and click Up or Down. If the action is at the top of the list, only the Down button will be available, and vice versa if the action is at the bottom of the list. If the action is in the middle of the list, both buttons are available. If only one action exists for a trigger, both buttons are dimmed out.
8. When you finish editing the actions for the bookmark, link, or page, click OK.

Use JavaScript Actions

You can add functionality and interactivity to your PDF document by creating JavaScript code to access database information, control document navigation, access information from the Internet, and more.

JavaScript is an object-oriented programming language. If you have designed web pages, you may be familiar with JavaScript. Each JavaScript object has associated methods and properties. Acrobat JavaScript uses standard JavaScript objects and has its own set of unique objects, such as the Bookmark object. Unfortunately, a detailed discussion of using JavaScript with Acrobat is beyond the scope of this book.

Create a JavaScript Action

You can use the JavaScript Action with form fields, bookmarks, and links, or you can create global JavaScript that can be used for an entire document. When you choose the JavaScript Action, you create the actual script in a text editor known as the JavaScript Editor. As previously mentioned, there are myriad uses for JavaScript with PDF documents. The following steps show how to create a link and use JavaScript to navigate to a specific page when a link is clicked:

1. Click the Tools icon, click Content, and then select the Link Tool. Alternatively, select the Link tool from the Quick Tools toolbar.
2. Create a link around the text or image that will trigger the JavaScript. This opens the Link Properties dialog box.
3. Click the Custom Link radio button and then click Next to open the Link Properties dialog box.
4. Click the Actions tab.
5. Click the Select Action drop-down arrow, choose Run A JavaScript from the drop-down menu, and then click Add. The JavaScript Editor opens.
6. Enter the JavaScript **this.pageNum = x**, where x is the page number you want displayed when the JavaScript executes. When you enter the page number for a document, always subtract one from the page number you want to open when the JavaScript executes. You need to do this because the JavaScript language,

like most other computer languages, begins indexing with the number 0, so page 1 is recognized as 0 in JavaScript. The illustration here shows JavaScript code to display page 4 when the link is clicked.

7. Click OK to exit the JavaScript Editor and then click OK to exit the Link Properties dialog box. When the link is clicked, the desired page is displayed.

Edit a JavaScript Action

When you create complex, multiline JavaScript code, it's easy to make a mistake. If you have Acrobat Pro or Acrobat Pro Extended, you can put the JavaScript Debugger on the case, but if you own Acrobat Standard, you have to unravel your own JavaScript errors. If you mistype a variable name or choose the wrong method for a JavaScript object, your script will fall flatter than a cake without enough baking powder. When this happens, you need to put on your thinking cap, or perhaps deerstalker cap, as you may have to do a bit of Sherlock Holmes–style deducting to figure out where your script went wrong.

To edit a JavaScript Action, select the object to which the JavaScript is assigned and open the Actions tab of the object's Properties dialog box. Select Run A JavaScript Action, click Edit to reopen the JavaScript Editor dialog box, and then examine the script. Make sure you have chosen the proper JavaScript object and the proper method of the object for the action you want to occur when the script executes. Note that many failed scripts are the result of typographical errors and not choosing the proper case for a JavaScript object. For example, if you refer to pageNum (proper syntax) as pagenum, your script will fail.

How to... Master JavaScript

JavaScript is a wonderful tool that you can use to make your PDF documents more interactive, but it does have a learning curve. You can find additional JavaScript information at http://partners.adobe.com/public/developer/pdf/topic_js.html. Here, you can download the Acrobat JavaScript Scripting Reference and the Acrobat JavaScript Scripting Guide. If you want to master JavaScript, consider investing in a good book to learn the proper syntax of this programming language. Two books to try are *How to Do Everything with JavaScript,* by Scott Duffy, and *JavaScript: The Complete Reference,* by Thomas Powell and Fritz Schneider, both published by McGraw-Hill.

Create a Thread of Linked Articles

You create articles to link blocks of text within a PDF file. If you're creating an e-book in magazine format (also known as an Ezine), an article that begins on page 23, for example, may be divided into sections, and the next section may begin on page 54. To make it easy for the reader to navigate from one part of the article to the next, you can define the block of the document that is the start of the article and then define the additional blocks of content that cover the rest of the article.

If you create an e-book for educational purposes, you can use articles to link chapter summaries together, thus making it easy for a student to skim through the book and locate desired information. An employee manual is another application that can benefit from articles. You create articles for pertinent information located in different parts of the document.

Create an Article

You define articles in a PDF document by using the Article tool to define the boundary of each block of content in the article. Note that an individual article can be a combination of text and graphics. The content area for different parts of the article are linked, and the viewer uses the Articles panel to easily navigate to each thread of the article. To create an article in a PDF document, do the following:

Add
Article Box
tool

1. Click the Tools icon, click Document Processing, and then select the Add Article Box tool (shown here).

Tip If you create a lot of articles, right-click the Add Article Box tool and choose Add To Quick Tools from the context menu. After you perform this menu command, the tool is easily accessible from the Quick Tools section of the toolbar.

2. Click and drag the Add Article Box tool around the area you want to define as the first thread of the article. As you drag the tool, a rectangular bounding box gives you a preview of the area you're selecting. When the bounding box surrounds the desired content, release the mouse button to have Acrobat define the first block of the article, as shown in the following illustration. Notice the article numbering system at the top of the article box. The 1-1 designates that article 1, block 1 has been created.

- Create a navigation menu   1-1

> When you create a PDF document within an authoring application, navigation devices are added to the document. PDF documents have two types of automatically created navigation devices: bookmarks and page thumbnails. Bookmarks and page thumbnails have their own panels in the Navigation pane.

3. After you create the first block of an article, your cursor changes to two lines forming a right angle around the Add Article Box tool icon, which means Acrobat is ready for you to define the next content area in the article. Navigate to the section of the document that contains the next portion of the article.

4. Click and drag the Add Article Box tool until it encompasses the next area of the article.

5. Continue in this manner until you define all blocks of content in the article, and then press ENTER or RETURN to open the Article Properties dialog box, shown here.

6. Enter the title, subject, and author of the article, plus any other keywords you want associated with the article, and then click OK to close the dialog box.

Article Properties

Title: Untitled

Subject:

Author:

Keywords:

[OK]   [Cancel]

Use the Articles Panel

After you create one or more articles, you can use the Articles panel to test your handiwork. Readers of your document also use the Articles panel to select an individual article to read. To open the Articles panel, shown here, right-click any icon in the Navigation pane and then choose Articles from the context menu.

Articles

Adding Links
Editing Links
My Article
PDF Navigation

To read an article, double-click its title, and Acrobat displays the first block of text in the article. After the first block of text is opened, your cursor becomes a hand with a down-pointing arrow in its palm. Click to navigate to the next thread in the article.

Note If you enable text selection for the Hand tool in Preferences, when reading an article, your cursor may fluctuate between an I-beam (which indicates you can select text) and the applicable icon for the article. To continue reading the article, wait until the article icon appears and then click to advance to the next thread in the article.

When you reach the last text block of the article, a line appears underneath the arrow, which signifies you reached the end of the article.

Add a Thread to an Article

After you review the article, you may find it necessary to add additional text blocks to the article. You can easily do this by following these steps:

1. Click the Tools icon, click Document Processing, and then select the Add Article Box tool. After you select the Add Article Box tool, Acrobat displays the bounding box of the first text block for each article in the PDF document.
2. Click the text block after which you want the new text block to appear. After you select the text block, a plus sign (+) appears in the lower-right corner of the box, as shown next.

> When you create a PDF document, one thumbnail is created for each page. Viewers of
> your PDF documents can navigate to a specific page of the document by clicking its
> thumbnail or, for a single-page document, navigate to a specific part of the page, as you
> learn in this chapter. Bookmarks, on the other hand, may or may not be created,
> depending on the method you used to create the PDF document. If, for example, you use
> Acrobat PDFMaker (the Adobe Acrobat plug-in for Microsoft Office applications) with

3. Click the plus sign and then navigate to the text block you want added to the article thread.
4. Click and drag to define the boundary of the box. When the bounding box encompasses the text, release the mouse button.
5. Add additional threads to the article or deselect the Add Article Box tool to finish editing the contents of the article. When you add threads to an article, Acrobat automatically renumbers the other threads in the order they appear in the article.
6. Press ENTER or RETURN when you finish modifying the article.

Delete an Article

After previewing the document, you may decide certain parts of an article thread are no longer needed. You can easily delete an entire article or article thread by doing the following:

1. Click the Tools icon, click Document Processing, and then select the Add Article Box tool to select the Add Article Box tool.
2. Click the article thread you want to delete. If you want to delete an entire article, click any thread in the article.
3. Right-click to open the Article context menu.

4. Choose Delete. Acrobat displays a dialog box asking if you want to delete the box or the entire article. Click Box to delete the article thread or click Article to delete the article. When you delete a thread, Acrobat renumbers the remaining threads in the article in their proper order.

Move or Resize an Article Box

When your article thread is viewed, Acrobat magnifies the view to fit the confines of the article box. If, after reviewing the document, you decide the position or size of an article box isn't right, you can move or resize it.

To move the article box, do the following:

1. Click the Tools icon, click Document Processing, and then select the Add Article Box tool.
2. Click the article box you want to move or resize.
3. Click inside the article box, or click a corner or side and drag to move or resize the box. After you move or begin resizing the box, Acrobat displays eight handles and the plus sign.
4. After displaying the handles, you can move the article thread by clicking inside the bounding box and dragging. When you click, your cursor becomes a filled arrowhead. As you drag the article box, a dashed bounding box gives you a preview of the current position of the box. When the article bounding box is in the desired location, release the mouse button.

To resize the article box, do one of the following:

1. Click one of the corner handles and drag to resize the entire article box. Hold down SHIFT to resize the box proportionately. Release the mouse button when the box is the desired size.
2. Click the handle in the middle on either side of the box and drag away from the box to make it wider or drag toward the center of the box to make it narrower. Release the mouse button when the box is the desired width.
3. Click the handle in the middle of either the top or bottom of the article box, and then drag up or down to change the height of the box.

Note When you grab a handle to change the width or height of the box, only the side corresponding to the handle you select is changed. The opposite side is unaffected.

Edit Article Properties

After you create an article, you can change the title or any other article properties by doing the following:

1. Click the Tools icon, click Document Processing, and then select the Add Article Box tool.

2. Click any thread of the article whose properties you want to modify.
3. Right-click and choose Properties from the context menu to display the Article Properties dialog box.
4. Modify the article properties as needed and then click OK.

When you create a document with articles, add an action on the first page of the document that invokes the View | Show/Hide | Navigation Panes | Articles command when the page opens. This displays the Articles panel in either Acrobat or the Adobe Reader, giving your document viewers a method to find the articles you added to the document.

Work with the Destinations Panel

When you create a complex PDF document, you may find it helpful to work with named destinations. A named destination links to a specific point in a document. When you work with multiple documents, as is often the case when creating a multimedia presentation, you can simplify cross-document navigation by adding a JavaScript action that links to a named destination. When you link to a named destination, the link remains active, even when pages are added or deleted from the target document.

You use the Destinations panel to create, display, and sort named destinations within a document. You also use the panel to rename destinations. To create the named destinations within a document, do the following:

1. Navigate to the document page you want added to the named destination list and set the magnification of the page.
2. Right-click any icon in the Navigation panel and choose Destinations from the context menu to open the Destinations panel.
3. Click the Create New Destination icon. Alternatively, you can right-click and choose New Destination from the context menu. After you create a new destination, it appears in the Destinations panel as Untitled.
4. Enter a name for the new destination. Give your destinations meaningful names that reflect their content. The image here shows two destinations after being renamed.

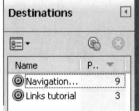

5. After creating several destinations, you can do the following:
   • To sort the destinations alphabetically, click the Name column title near the top of the panel.
   • To sort the destinations by page number, click the Page column title near the top of the panel.
   • To go to a named destination, double-click its name. Alternatively, you can right-click a destination and choose Go To Destination from the context menu.

- To delete named destinations, select them and click the Delete Selected Destinations icon or choose Delete from the context menu.
- To rename a destination, right-click the desired destination, choose Rename from the context menu, and enter a new name for the destination.
- To change the magnification of a destination, navigate to the destination, and then within the document use the Zoom tool to set the desired magnification. In the Destinations panel, right-click the destination title and choose Set Destination from the context menu.

6. Close the Destinations panel.

Summary

In this chapter, you learned how to enhance your navigation by assigning one or more actions to a link or bookmark. You discovered how to assign actions to a page that determine what occurs when a page opens or closes. You also learned how to create a thread of articles and how to work with named destinations. In the next chapter, you will find out how to edit PDF documents.

PART **III**

Edit and Optimize PDF Documents

8

The Basics of Editing PDF Documents

HOW TO...

- Edit visually with thumbnails
- Edit with menu commands
- Append PDF documents
- Add page transitions
- Touch up a PDF document

After you create a PDF document, you can easily edit it. Within Acrobat, you can add, delete, reorder, and renumber pages. You can also edit individual objects within the PDF document. You edit PDF documents by using panels, tools, and menu commands. Many of the edits you perform with Acrobat tools can also be accomplished using menu commands or by selecting commands from the appropriate panel Options menu or context menu. In this chapter, you learn how to edit PDF documents, as well as add pages to PDF documents. When you're editing a PDF document that's used for a presentation, you can create some interesting effects by applying page transitions, which are also discussed in this chapter.

Edit Visually with Page Thumbnails

Page thumbnails (also referred to as just thumbnails) are miniature images of each page in a PDF document. Each thumbnail is displayed with a page number beneath it. In previous chapters, you have seen thumbnails used as navigation devices. You can also use them to edit your documents. You can use thumbnails to insert pages, delete pages, and change the order of pages. Thumbnails are located on the Page Thumbnails pane, as shown in Figure 8-1.

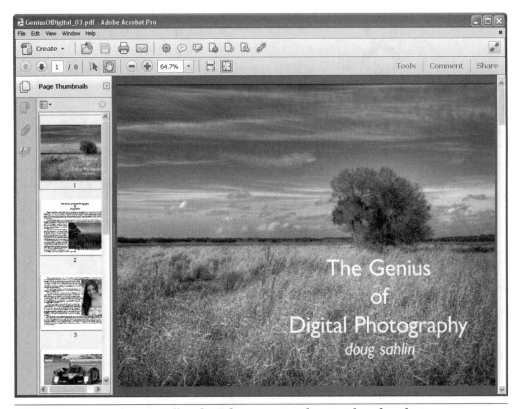

FIGURE 8-1 You can visually edit a document with page thumbnails.

The Page Thumbnails pane is part of the Navigation pane and can be opened by clicking the Pages icon or by choosing View | Show/ Hide | Navigation Panes | Page Thumbnails. The Pages Thumbnails pane has its own Options menu, a context menu, and the Delete Selected Pages tool.

Use the Page Thumbnails Pane Options Menu

You use the Page Thumbnails pane Options menu to access certain menu commands that enable you to edit a document and work with thumbnails. To open the Page Thumbnails pane Options menu, shown here, click the Options icon near the upper-left corner of the panel.

Insert Pages	▶
Extract Pages...	
Replace Pages...	
Delete Pages...	Shift+Ctrl+D
Crop Pages...	Shift+Ctrl+T
Rotate Pages...	Shift+Ctrl+R
Page Transitions...	
Number Pages...	
Print Pages...	Ctrl+P
Embed All Page Thumbnails	
Remove Embedded Page Thumbnails	
Reduce Page Thumbnails	
Enlarge Page Thumbnails	
Page Properties...	

Use the Pages Panel Context Menu

Many of the commands you use to edit PDF documents can be found on the Page Thumbnails pane context menu. To access the Page Thumbnails pane context menu, select a thumbnail and right-click. To access a context menu that contains menu commands to embed or change the size of thumbnails, place your cursor in the Page Thumbnails pane, without selecting a thumbnail, and then right-click.

Insert Pages

You can insert pages from within the Page Thumbnails pane. From within the pane, you click a thumbnail to navigate to a page and then insert pages before or after the selected page. You can insert any file type supported by Acrobat. If the document you select isn't a PDF document, it is converted to PDF and added as a page. To add one or more pages to your document, follow these steps:

1. Open the Page Thumbnails pane and click a thumbnail to navigate to the page before or after the place where the new pages will be inserted.
2. Choose Insert Pages | From File from the Page Thumbnails pane Options menu or context menu to open the Select File To Insert dialog box.
3. Click the Files Of Type drop-down arrow (Windows) or Show drop-down button (Macintosh) and select the type of document to insert.
4. Select the document(s) you want to insert and click Select to open the Insert Pages dialog box, shown here.
5. From the Location drop-down menu, choose Before or After.
6. In the Page section, select the page where you want the selected document inserted. You can insert the document before or after the first page, the last page, or the currently selected page in the PDF document you're editing. Alternatively, you can enter the specific page where you want the file inserted.
7. Click OK. Acrobat inserts the selected documents in the location specified and creates a thumbnail for each new page.

You can also add pages to a PDF document by copying content from an application to the system clipboard and then choosing Insert Pages | From Clipboard from the Pages Options menu or from the Pages context menu. For example, you can copy part of a Word document or a selection of an image file in Photoshop or Photoshop Elements to the clipboard and insert the selection as a page.

Delete Pages

You can also use page thumbnails to delete one or more pages. To delete pages from within the Page Thumbnails pane, do one of the following:

- To delete a single page, click its thumbnail and then click the Delete Selected Pages button. Acrobat displays a warning dialog box asking you to confirm the deletion. Click OK to delete the page or click Cancel to stop the operation.
- To delete contiguous pages, click a thumbnail that corresponds to a page you want to delete and then, while pressing SHIFT, click contiguous thumbnails to add them to the selection. When you finish selecting thumbnails, click the Delete Selected Pages button. Click OK to close the warning dialog box and delete the pages.
- To delete noncontiguous pages, click a thumbnail that corresponds to a page you want to delete and then, while pressing CTRL (Windows) or CMD (Macintosh), click additional thumbnails to add them to the selection. Click the Delete Selected Pages button to delete the pages from the document. Click OK to accept the deletion of the pages.

You can also delete pages by selecting contiguous thumbnails and choosing Delete Pages from the Page Thumbnails pane Options menu or context menu. When you choose this command, Acrobat displays the dialog box shown here, which gives you the opportunity to change the pages that will be deleted when you execute the action by clicking the From radio button and then entering the first and last page you want to delete. Click OK to complete the deletion.

You can also delete pages by selecting them and then pressing DELETE. This alternative circumvents the Delete Pages dialog box, but it displays a dialog box asking you to confirm deletion.

Drag-and-Drop Editing

The Page Thumbnails pane not only gives you a visual representation of each page in your document, but also enables you to edit the document by dragging and dropping page thumbnails. You can use the Page Thumbnails pane to change the order in which document pages display and to import pages from other documents.

Reorder Document Pages

You can use thumbnails to change the order in which pages appear in a PDF document. To move a single page or a selection of pages to a new position in the document, select them and then drag and drop them to a new location. To change the order of document pages, follow these steps:

1. Open the Page Thumbnails pane and select the page thumbnail that corresponds to the page you want to move. You can move more than one page at a time by selecting contiguous or noncontiguous thumbnails, as discussed previously.

Tip To view several thumbnails at once, choose Reduce Page Thumbnails from the Page Thumbnails pane Options menu or context menu. You can also display more thumbnails by clicking and dragging to the right the vertical border between the Navigation pane and the Document pane.

2. Drag the selected thumbnails up or down. As you drag the thumbnails, your cursor becomes a filled arrow attached to a document, and a solid blue line appears to indicate the current position of the thumbnail(s) you are moving, as shown here. If the Navigation pane is sized so that more than one column of thumbnails is visible, the blue line appears to the side of the thumbnail where the selection would be placed.
3. Release the mouse button when the selected thumbnails are where you want them. Acrobat moves the selected pages to their new location and renumbers the thumbnails.

Copy Pages from Other Documents

If you have more than one document open, you can use the Page Thumbnails pane to copy pages from one document to another. Copying pages is an excellent way to build a document when working with a team of PDF authors. To copy pages from one document to another, follow these steps:

1. Open the source and target document(s).
2. Choose Window | Tile and then choose Vertically or Horizontally. Alternatively, you can choose Cascading, but you will have to rearrange the documents so that each document's Page Thumbnails pane is visible.
3. If they aren't already visible, open the Page Thumbnails pane of each document by choosing View | Show/Hide | Navigation Panes | Page Thumbnails while the respective document is selected.
4. On the Page Thumbnails pane of the source document, select the thumbnail for the page you want to copy. You can select more than one thumbnail if necessary.

5. Drag the selected thumbnails from the Page Thumbnails pane of the source document to the Page Thumbnails pane of the target document.
6. As your cursor moves into the Page Thumbnails pane of the target document, the cursor becomes an angled arrow attached to a document with a plus sign (+) in it.
7. On the Page Thumbnails pane of the target document, drag the thumbnails to the desired position and release the mouse button. After you release the mouse button, Acrobat copies the selected pages to the target document and then creates numbered thumbnails for the copied pages.

Tip Hold the CTRL-SHIFT (Windows) or CMD-SHIFT (Macintosh) keys while dragging the thumbnail to permanently move the page from the source document to the target document. A warning dialog box appears asking you if you want to delete the page from the source document. Click OK to permanently move the page to the target document.

Edit from the Pages Pane

Many of the menu commands discussed in the following sections are exact copies of Page Thumbnails pane Options menu commands and Page Thumbnails pane context menu commands. When you use these commands in the Page Thumbnails pane, you work with a single thumbnail or selection of thumbnails. When you use a command from the Pages pane, you can specify any page in the document. The previous sections dealt with using editing commands in a specific manner within the Page Thumbnails pane. The following sections show you how to use commands from the Pages pane to edit selected pages within your documents.

Insert Pages

You can add existing documents to any PDF document by using a command from the Insert Pages section of the Pages pane. From the Insert Pages section, you can choose the Insert From File command and specify the exact location within the document where the pages are to be added. You can insert an existing PDF document or any file type supported by Acrobat. To append an existing PDF document by using the Insert Pages command, follow these steps:

1. Open the PDF document to which you want to add pages.
2. Navigate to the document page before or after the place where you want to insert the pages. This step is optional—you can specify the exact location to add the pages in the Insert Pages dialog box.
3. Click the Tools icon, click Pages, and then choose Insert Pages | From File to open the Select File To Insert dialog box.
4. Choose the file(s) you want to insert and then click Select to open the Insert Pages dialog box.

5. From the Location drop-down menu, choose After or Before.
6. In the Page section, the Page radio button is selected by default with the page currently being viewed listed in the Page field. You can change this by choosing First or Last, or by entering a different page number in the Page field.
7. Click OK. Acrobat inserts the selected pages at the specified location and creates a thumbnail for each added page.

 Choose More Insert Options from the Insert Pages section of the Pages pane and you can choose a menu option to insert a page from a scanner, add content from a web page, or insert a blank page.

Delete Pages

You can modify a PDF document by deleting unwanted pages. To do this, you use the Delete command from the Pages section of the Tools pane. This command enables you to delete a single page, a range of pages, or selected pages. To remove pages from a PDF document, follow these steps:

1. Open the document from which you want to remove pages.
2. Select the pages you want to delete by clicking their thumbnails in the Page Thumbnails pane. This step is optional unless you want to delete noncontiguous pages. You can specify a range of pages you want to delete after invoking the command.
3. Click the Tools icon, click Pages, and then choose Delete to open the Delete Pages dialog box, shown previously.
4. If you selected the pages to delete, click OK. Otherwise, enter the range of pages to delete and then click OK. After you click OK, Acrobat displays a warning dialog box, asking you to confirm that you want the pages deleted.
5. Click OK. Acrobat deletes the specified pages and their thumbnails and then renumbers the remaining thumbnails.

Replace Pages

You can update a document by replacing a page or a selection of pages. This option is useful when you have a multipage PDF document that needs only minor revisions. Create the pages you need to replace in an authoring application, save them, and then choose the Replace command from the Pages section of the Tools pane. You can replace pages with any existing file of a type supported by Acrobat. You can also replace a specific number of pages in one document with the same number of pages from another document. To replace pages in a PDF document, follow these steps:

1. Open the document that contains the pages you want to replace.
2. Open the Page Thumbnails pane by clicking the Pages icon in the Navigation pane or by choosing View | Show/Hide | Navigation Panes | Page Thumbnails.

3. Click the thumbnails that correspond to the pages you want to replace. Note that you can only select contiguous thumbnails. If you select noncontiguous thumbnails, Acrobat will replace a range of pages from the first selected thumbnail to the last.

4. Click the Tools icon, click Pages, and then choose Replace to open the Select File With New Pages dialog box.

5. Locate the file with the pages that will replace the selected ones and click Select to open the Replace Pages dialog box.

6. If you already selected the pages you want to replace, go to step 7. Otherwise, in the Replace Pages field of the Original section, enter the number of the first page you want replaced and then, in the To field, enter the number of the last page you want replaced.

7. In the With Pages field of the Replacement section, enter the number of the first replacement page of the file you selected. Acrobat automatically calculates the ending page, based on the number of pages selected in the original document. If you don't specify a page number, Acrobat will replace the first specified page in the target document with the first page of the replacement document.

8. Click OK. Acrobat replaces the pages and generates thumbnails for the new pages.

Extract Pages

You can extract pages from an existing PDF document and use them as the basis for a new PDF document. When you extract pages, you can preserve the extracted pages in the original document or delete them. To extract pages from a PDF document, follow these steps:

1. Open the PDF document that contains the pages you want to extract.

2. Open the Page Thumbnails pane by clicking the Pages icon in the Navigation pane or by choosing View | Show/Hide | Navigation Panes | Page Thumbnails.

3. Click the thumbnails that correspond to the pages you want to extract. Alternatively, you can enter the range of pages to extract in the Extract Pages dialog box. Note that if you select noncontiguous pages, Acrobat extracts a range of pages from the first selected page to the last.

4. Click Tools, click Pages, and then select Extract to open the Extract Pages dialog box, as shown here.

5. If you already selected thumbnails, go to step 6. Otherwise, specify a range of pages by entering page numbers in the From and To fields.

6. Check the Delete Pages After Extracting check box to have Acrobat delete the pages from the original document when they're extracted.

7. Check the Extract Pages As Separate Files check box to create one PDF document for each page extracted.
8. Click OK to extract the pages. If a single document is being created, Acrobat opens the extracted pages as a new document.

> **Note** If you check the Extract Pages As Separate Files check box, the Browse For Folder dialog box appears, prompting you for a folder in which to save the extracted pages. After you select the desired folder, click OK, and Acrobat creates a PDF file for each extracted page, but it doesn't open the new documents in Acrobat. The extracted pages inherit the filename of the document from which they were extracted, followed by the page number.

9. Choose File | Save As and then specify a filename and location where you want the extracted pages saved.

Split a Document

When you've got a document that's getting large and you want to display it on the Internet or send it via e-mail, you can easily split the document into byte-size pieces using the Split Document command. You can split the document using file size as an attribute or the number of pages. To split a document, follow these steps:

1. Open the document you want to split.
2. Click Tools, click Pages, and then choose Split Document to open the Split Document dialog box, shown next.

3. Choose the manner in which you want to split the document. Your choices are Number Of Pages, File Size, and Top-Level Bookmarks.
4. If you choose Number Of Pages, enter the number of pages for each resulting document. If you choose File Size, enter the file size for each resulting document.

5. Click Output Options to open the dialog box shown here.

6. In the Target Folder section, choose The Same Folder Selected At Start or A Folder On My Computer. If you choose A Folder On My Computer, the Browse button appears. Click the button and navigate to the desired folder, or create a new folder in which to store the files.

7. Choose one of the following File Name options:

   - **Use Bookmark Names For File Names**   This option becomes available when you choose to split the document by top-level bookmarks.

   - **Add Label And Number Before Original Name**   Adds a label and number as a prefix to the original filename.

   - **Add Label and Number After Original Name**   Adds a label and number as a suffix to the original filename.

8. Accept the default method of identifying the new files with a label. The default label name is Part. You can change this by entering a different label in the text field.

9. Accept the default option of separating the original filename from the label. The default separator is an underscore. If desired, enter a different separator in the text field.

10. The option of not overwriting original files is selected by default. If you deselect this option and save the resulting files in the original folder, you run the risk of overwriting the original.

11. Click OK to exit the Output Options dialog box.

12. If you want to split multiple documents, click Apply To Multiple to open the Split Documents dialog box, shown here.

13. Choose one of the following options from the Add Files drop-down list: Add Files, Add Folders, or Add Open Files. After you select one of these options, a new dialog box appears that enables you to choose the files you want to add, choose the

folders you want to add, or choose the open documents you want to add to the list of documents to split.

Note   If you add a file in error, click the file to select it and then click Remove.

14. Click OK to split the selected documents.

Crop Pages

If you create a PDF document and you find one or more of the document pages has excessive margins, you can trim (crop) the pages. You can also use this command to crop extraneous material from a PDF document, such as a banner in a PDF document created from a web page. You crop pages by using a menu command.

To crop pages using the menu command, follow these steps:

1. Open the document whose pages you want to crop. Select a range of pages to crop by clicking thumbnails in the Page Thumbnails pane. Alternatively, you can select the range of pages to crop after you open the Crop Pages dialog box.
2. Click Tools, click Pages, and then choose Crop.
3. Click inside the document and then drag diagonally to select the area to which the page is to be cropped and then double-click to open the Set Page Boxes dialog box, as shown in Figure 8-2.
4. Accept the default Show All Boxes option. This option shows each crop box on the thumbnail in the right side of the dialog box. If you deselect this option, only the box selected from the Crop Options drop-down menu is shown.
5. Select one of the following crop options:
   - **CropBox**   Choose this option, the default, to crop the page(s) to the dimensions you specify.
   - **ArtBox**   Choose this option to specify the relevant content of the page(s), including white space you want included in the finished document.
   - **TrimBox**   Choose this option to specify the size of the page(s) after applying the command.
   - **BleedBox**   Choose this option to specify the clipping path when the page is printed by a service center. This option allows for paper trimming and folding. Note that printer marks may fall outside the specified bleed area.
6. Select a unit of measure from the Units drop-down menu. In most instances, the default unit of measure is the same as the unit of measure for the document.
7. Click the Constrain Proportions check box to crop the document proportionately to its original aspect ratio.
8. In the Margin Controls area, enter a value to crop in any or all of the following fields: Top, Bottom, Left, and Right. For example, to crop one inch from the top margin, enter **1** in the Top field. Alternatively, you can click the spinner buttons to select a value. Press SHIFT while clicking a spinner button to make the

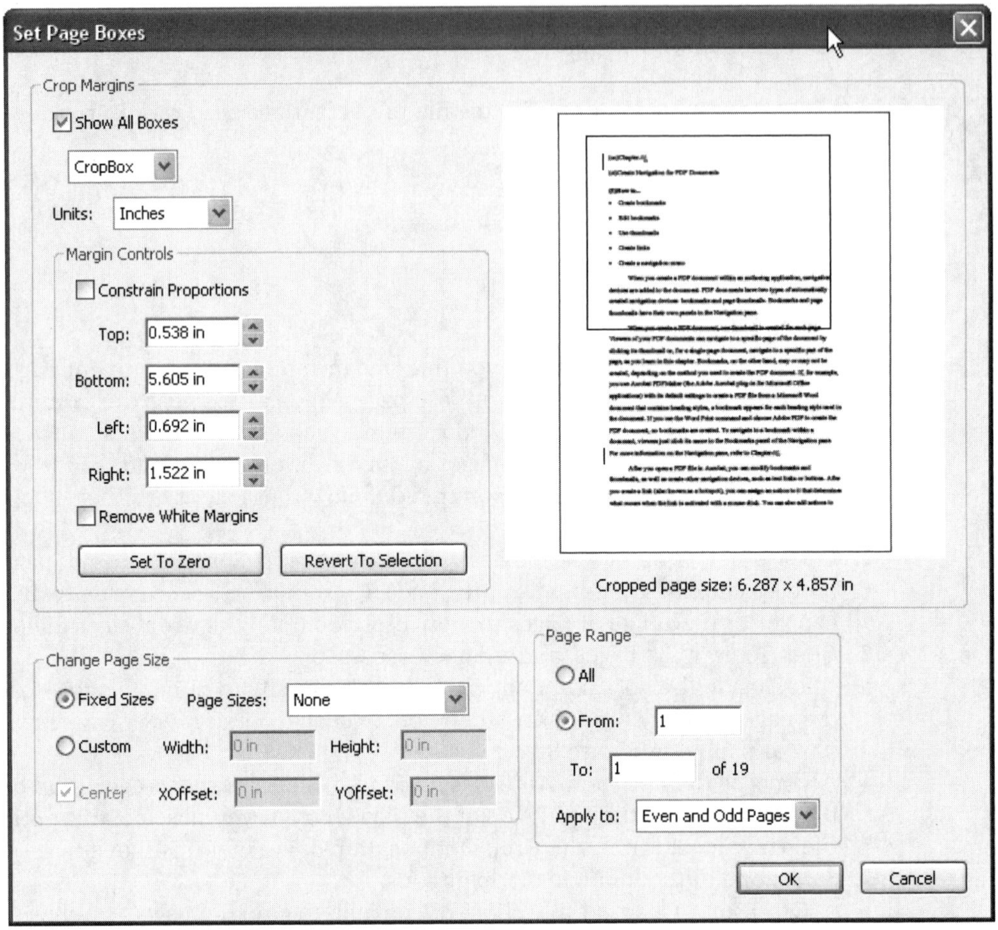

FIGURE 8-2   The Set Page Boxes dialog box holds all the options you need to
precisely crop a document.

values change in greater increments. As you modify the margin values, a black
rectangle around the thumbnail on the right side of the Crop Margins section
changes to reflect the size of the page with the modified margin settings. If you
choose the Constrain Proportions options, Acrobat updates the other fields so
that the document is cropped to its original aspect ratio.

9. Click the Remove White Margins check box to crop the side margins to the
   document contents, thus eliminating a white border.
10. Click Set To Zero to reset the margin values to zero.
11. Click Revert To Selection to reset the margins to the previous cropping rectangle.
    This button resets the margins to zero unless you use the Crop tool to define the
    cropping rectangle and then modify one of the margins.

Tip

To crop a document to a given page size, open the Set Page Boxes dialog box and, in the Change Page Size area, click the Fixed Sizes radio button. Then, click the Page Sizes arrow and choose an option from the drop-down menu. Alternatively, click the Custom radio button and enter values in the Width and Height fields. This option doesn't change the physical dimensions of the page content, but adds white space around the existing content.

12. In the Change Page Size area, choose one of the following:
    - **Fixed Sizes**   Choose this option and select the desired size from the Page Sizes drop-down list.
    - **Custom**   Choose this option and then enter the desired values in the Width and Height fields. If you choose the Center option, Acrobat supplies the values for the xOffset and yOffset fields. Deselect this option to enter your own values in the fields.
13. In the Page Range area, choose one of the following:
    - **All**   Choose All to have Acrobat crop all pages to the specified size.
    - **From**   Choose From to have Acrobat crop to a range of pages that you specify. Enter a value in the From and To fields to specify the first and last pages to crop. This field is filled in by default when you select a page or range of pages in the Page Thumbnails pane.
14. From the Apply To drop-down menu, choose one of these: Even And Odd Pages, Odd Pages Only, or Even Pages Only.
15. Click OK. Acrobat crops the page(s) to the sizes you specified.

How to...   ## Restore Keyboard Shortcuts

By default, keyboard shortcuts are not enabled for Acrobat X Pro. If you like the convenience of keyboard shortcuts, you can restore them by choosing Edit | Preferences to open the Preferences dialog box. If you run Acrobat on a Macintosh computer, choose Acrobat | Preferences. Click General in the left-hand window to open the General section of the dialog box, and then enable the Use Single-Key Accelerators To Access Tools option. Click OK to exit the dialog box. Exit Acrobat and relaunch the application to apply the new preference. After you enable this preference option, each tool's keyboard shortcut is displayed in a Tooltip when your cursor is over the tool. After a while, the shortcuts for the tools you commonly use will become second nature and you'll be able to quickly access a tool by pressing the proper key.

Rotate Pages

When you create a PDF document by combining several documents, you often end up with different page sizes and orientations. For example, when you combine files to create a multipage PDF document, you may end up combining documents with both landscape and portrait orientation. When this happens, you can rotate pages as needed by following these steps:

1. Open the document whose pages you want to rotate.
2. To select specific pages, open the Page Thumbnails pane and select the thumbnails for the pages you want to rotate. You can select noncontiguous pages to rotate. Alternatively, you can navigate to a specific page or specify a range of pages in the Rotate Pages dialog box.
3. Click Tools, click Pages, and then click Rotate to open the Rotate Pages dialog box.
4. Choose one of the following options from the Direction drop-down menu: Counterclockwise 90 Degrees, Clockwise 90 Degrees, or 180 Degrees.
5. In the Page Range section, choose one of the following options:
   - **All**   Choose this option, and Acrobat rotates all pages in the direction specified.
   - **Selection**   This option is available if you selected pages by clicking their thumbnails. Otherwise, it's dimmed out. By default, Acrobat chooses the Pages option when you select noncontiguous thumbnails in the Page Thumbnails pane. When you select this option, Acrobat rotates the selected pages instead of the range of pages from the first selected thumbnail to the last.
   - **Pages**   This option is available if you navigate to a specific page or multiple contiguous thumbnails in the Page Thumbnails pane before invoking the Rotate Pages command. You can accept the page range (the page you navigated to) or modify the range by entering page numbers in the From and To fields.
6. Click the top Rotate drop-down arrow and choose one of the following: Even And Odd Pages, Even Pages Only, or Odd Pages Only.
7. Click the bottom Rotate drop-down arrow and choose one of these options: Landscape Pages, Portrait Pages, or Pages Of Any Orientation.
8. Click OK. Acrobat rotates the specified pages to the desired orientation.

How to... **Combine Two PDF Documents**

You can combine two PDF documents by opening one PDF document and then navigating to the page where you want to add another document. Click Tools, click Pages, and then choose Insert From File. Select the PDF file and then choose the proper option to insert the new PDF file before or after the first, last, or current page of the currently open PDF document.

Number Pages

When you create a PDF document, Acrobat automatically numbers the pages. When you add pages, move pages, or delete pages, Acrobat updates the page numbers to reflect the order in which the pages appear. Acrobat uses a default integer numbering system, starting with 1 for the first page of the document, and so on. If you create a document such as an e-book and would like to include a title page, copyright pages, or similar front matter pages, you can modify the numbering style by following these steps:

1. On the Page Thumbnails pane, select the thumbnails of the pages you want to renumber. Alternatively, you can specify a range of pages to renumber in the Page Numbering dialog box.

2. Click the Options icon to open the Page Thumbnails pane Options menu and then choose Number Pages to display the Page Numbering dialog box, shown here.

3. In the Pages area, choose one of the following options:
   - **All**   Choose this option to have all pages renumbered.
   - **Selected**   This option is available and selected by default when you create a selection of pages by clicking their thumbnails.
   - **From [ ] To [ ]**   Choose this option to renumber a range of pages. To specify the range of pages you want to renumber, enter the desired page numbers in the From and To fields.

4. In the Numbering area, choose an option from the Style drop-down menu. After you choose a style, a preview appears in the Sample section at the bottom of the dialog box. You can renumber selected pages using any of these styles:
   - **None**   No page numbers appear below the thumbnails you selected for renumbering. However, the document page number information is still displayed in the Page Navigation toolbar.
   - **1, 2, 3**   Use this style for the pages that comprise the content of a document or e-book.
   - **i, ii, iii**   Use this style to display the selected pages as lowercase Roman numerals.
   - **I, II, III**   Use this style to display the selected pages as uppercase Roman numerals.
   - **a, b, c**   Use this style to display the selected pages as lowercase letters.
   - **A, B, C**   Use this style to display the selected pages as capital letters.

5. In the Numbering area, choose one of the following options:
   - **Begin New Section** Choose this option to begin a new numbering sequence. Click the Style drop-down arrow and choose an option. To add a prefix to the page numbers, enter the desired prefix in the Prefix field. In the Start field, enter the beginning value for the new page sequence.
   - **Extend Numbering Used In Preceding Section To Selected Pages** Choose this option to have Acrobat renumber the selected pages using the same sequence as the preceding pages, numbering the first selected page with the next page number in the sequence.
6. If desired, enter text in the Prefix window to add a prefix to the page number.
7. Click OK to renumber the selected pages.

Add Page Transitions

If you're creating a PDF document as part of a presentation, you can add a bit of panache by adding a transition between pages. When you add a transition, the PDF document looks similar to a PowerPoint presentation or a slideshow. Transitions are only displayed when the document is viewed in Full Screen mode. You can set a document to display in Full Screen mode by setting Window Options in the Initial view section of the Document Properties dialog box. To add transitions between pages, follow these steps:

 Some of the more complex PowerPoint animation effects aren't supported in Acrobat and, therefore, won't be rendered as animations when a PowerPoint presentation is converted to PDF. Unsupported animation appears as a static image in the converted PDF.

1. Click Tools, click Document Processing, and then click Page Transitions to open the Set Transitions dialog box.
2. Click the Transition drop-down arrow and choose one of the presets from the drop-down menu. The effects are similar to those found in PowerPoint and other presentation programs.

Tip If you choose Random Transition from the Transition drop-down menu, Acrobat randomly chooses a different effect every time the viewer navigates to a different page.

3. If available for the selected transition, click the Direction drop-down arrow and choose the direction from which the transition begins.
4. Click the Speed drop-down arrow and choose one of the following: Fast, Medium, or Slow.
5. Click the Auto Flip check box to turn the pages automatically. When you choose this option, the After [ ] Seconds field becomes available. Enter a value for the number of seconds you'd like each page displayed, or choose a preset from the drop-down menu.

6. In the Page Range area, choose one of the following options:
   - **All Pages In Document**   Applies the selected transition to all pages in the document.
   - **Pages Selected In Pages Panel**   Applies the selected transition to the pages corresponding to the thumbnails you selected from the Page Thumbnails pane. This option is dimmed out if no thumbnails are selected.
   - **Pages Range**   Applies the selected transition to a range of pages. When you choose this option, enter values in the From and To fields to specify the page range.
7. Click OK to apply the transition to the selected pages.
8. Save the document.

 Even though Acrobat provides an option for a random selection of transitions, when you're creating a presentation, a good idea is to stick with one transition type for the entire presentation. Mixing transitions can be jarring and looks unprofessional.

Touch Up a PDF Document

As you know, PDF documents originate in authoring applications, where you convert them to the PDF format by using the authoring application plug-in, by using an Export command, or by using the application's Print command and then choosing Adobe PDF as the printing device. The converted document retains the look and feel of the original. When you open the document in Acrobat, you can add interactivity to the document, but you cannot perform wholesale edits to the document. You can, however, perform minor edits by using the TouchUp tools. You can also touch up the order of a tagged PDF document.

Touch Up Text

You use the TouchUp Text tool to perform minor edits to text within a PDF document. You can use the tool to change a word or letter, to copy a line of text to the clipboard, to fit text within an existing selection, and more.

Edit Text

When you choose the Edit Document Text command in the Content section of the Tools pane, you can select text within a PDF document and delete or replace the text. To edit text with the TouchUp Text tool, follow these steps:

1. Click Tools, click Content, and then choose Edit Document Text. After you select the tool, Acrobat loads the system fonts. This may take a few seconds, depending on the number of fonts you have installed on your system.

Note When you attempt to edit a document with a font type that isn't loaded on your machine and not embedded in the document, Acrobat attempts to re-create the font using the built-in Multiple Master fonts. If the font cannot be re-created, it's displayed as your system's default serif or sans serif font.

2. Click a block of text to select it. Click the sentence or paragraph you want to edit, and Acrobat selects all text on the page. After you select the text, Acrobat places a bounding box around the text block, as shown here, and your cursor becomes an I-beam.

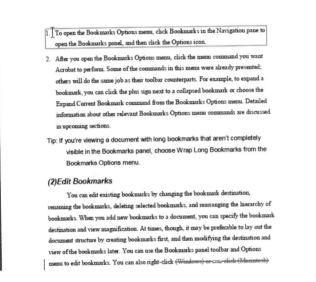

3. To change a letter or a word in a text selection, select the letter or word you want to change. As you move your cursor over the text, your selection is highlighted. Release the mouse button after you select the characters you want to change.

4. Enter new text. Acrobat applies the edit to the selected text. If the embedded font isn't installed on your system, Acrobat displays a warning dialog box to this effect. Click Yes to remove font embedding. If the unembedded single-byte font isn't present in your system encoding, you receive an error message saying you cannot edit the font.

Caution Even though a font may be present in your system, legally you must own a licensed version of the actual font or have it installed on your system to change the text.

Change Text Appearance

After you select a block of text with the TouchUp Text tool, you can change the font style, font size, font color, and more. To change text appearance, follow these steps:

1. Invoke the Edit Document Text command, as outlined previously.
2. Click a block of text to select it.
3. Click and drag to select a single character, word, or the entire line of text.
4. Right-click and choose Properties from the context menu to open the TouchUp Properties dialog box, shown next. The dialog box gives you information about the original font, the editing font (if the original font isn't installed on the system), and permissions as to whether or not the font can be embedded.

Note As you change text parameters in the dialog box, the text updates in real time. If the dialog box covers the text, click and drag the dialog box title bar to move the dialog box to a new location.

5. To change the font face, choose a font face from the Font drop-down menu.
6. If a licensed version of the font you chose is present on your system, you will see Can Embed Font to the right of the Permissions field. If you choose to embed the font, you have two options:
   - **Embed** Embeds the entire font set, even characters not used in the selected text.
   - **Subset** Embeds a subset of the font type to cover all characters used in the text selection. If another party attempts to edit the document, they won't be able to access characters that aren't part of the subset.
7. To change the font size, choose a size from the Font Size drop-down menu.

Note If you use Acrobat on a computer with limited processing power, Acrobat may take a while to render your font changes, especially when you significantly enlarge the font size or make changes within large blocks of text.

8. To change spacing between the characters of the selected text, choose a value from the Character Spacing drop-down menu. Alternatively, you can enter a value between –1 and 2 points.

9. To change spacing between selected words, choose a value from the Word Spacing drop-down menu. Alternatively, you can enter a value between –1 and 2 points.

10. To change the horizontal scale of the selected text, choose a value (percentage) from the Horizontal Scaling drop-down menu. This option changes the proportion between the width and height of the selected text.

11. To change the font fill color, click the Fill button and choose a color from the pop-up palette. Alternatively, you can choose a color not listed on the palette by clicking the Other Color icon and choosing a color from the system color picker. To display only an outline around the selected text, click the No Color icon.

12. To change the font stroke (outline) color, click the Stroke button and choose a color from the pop-up palette. Alternatively, you can click the Other Color icon and choose a color from the system color picker. To display the text with no stroke, click the No Stroke icon.

Note If you choose No Stroke and No Fill, the selected text won't be visible.

13. Accept the default Stroke Width, or choose a different value from the drop-down menu. This option determines the width of the outline around the selected letters.

14. To change the baseline shift of the selected text, choose a value from the Baseline Offset drop-down menu. Alternatively, you can enter a value between –4 points and 14 points. This option determines where the text appears in relation to the baseline. For example, if you select one word from a sentence and increase the baseline shift, the word appears above (positive value) or below (negative value) the other words in the sentence.

15. Click Close to exit the dialog box.

Tip If you do extensive modifications to a document and it isn't turning out as you planned, you can eliminate all your modifications by choosing File | Revert. When you choose this command, Acrobat reverts to the last saved version of the document.

Tip The Color tab of the TouchUp Properties dialog box enables you to convert the current color space to a different color space.

Look Up the Meaning of a Word

If you're connected to the Internet while working in Acrobat, you can look up the meaning of any word in a text object. Acrobat Pro X has a powerful option that's equivalent to having a dictionary on demand. To look up the meaning of a word, access the Select tool and select the word for which you want to find the meaning. Right-click and then choose Look Up [selected word], where [selected word] is the word you highlighted with the Select tool. After you select the command, Acrobat launches your web browser and the meaning for your selected word is displayed.

Edit an Object

You use the Edit Object command to perform minor edits to an image, or to edit the image in a supported external image editor. When you select this menu command, the context menu (described in the next section) has several commands that let you perform other tasks with embedded graphics. You can use the Edit Object command to delete, move, or remove an object by performing the following steps:

1. Click Tools, click Content, and then choose Edit Object.
2. Click the object you want to edit. You can select graphic images or entire blocks of text after invoking this command. To select more than one object, select the first object and then click additional objects while pressing SHIFT. After selecting the object(s), do one of the following:
   - Drag the object to a new location.
   - Delete the object by choosing Edit | Delete, or by choosing Delete from the context menu.

Use the Edit Object Command Context Menu

When you use the Edit Object command to edit a document, you have additional options available through its context menu. Select an object with the tool and then right-click to open the context menu.

The available context menu commands vary, depending on previous actions you performed with the command. The following list includes all the tasks you can perform from the Edit Object context menu, shown here. Most of the commands are similar to those found

Cut
Copy
Delete
Select All
Select None
Place Image...
Set Clip
Flip Horizontal
Flip Vertical
Rotate Clockwise
Rotate Counterclockwise
Rotate Selection
Create Artifact...
Find...
Edit Image...
Show Metadata...
Properties...

in many image-editing and word processing applications. The following explains the commands specific to Acrobat:

- **Place Image** Displays the Open dialog box, which enables you to select an image and place it in the document.
- **Delete Clip** This option becomes available when you select an object that has an associated clipping region. Selecting this option deletes any objects clipping the selected objects. For example, if you modify the size of a text object and some of the characters are clipped, choosing this command reveals the clipped text.
- **Set Clip** Sets the clipping region for the selected objects.
- **Create Artifact** Adds an artifact to the selected object. Artifacts are used as elements in tagged documents.
- **Remove Artifact** Removes an unwanted artifact from a PDF file.
- **Find** Launches the Find Element dialog box, enabling you to search for a document element such as an artifact, unmarked link, and so on.
- **Edit Image** Launches the supported image-editing application. To specify an external editor, choose Edit | Preferences | General (Windows) or Acrobat | Preferences | TouchUp (Macintosh) and click the Choose Image Editor. You can then choose Photoshop or Photoshop Elements as the application to use for editing images or illustrations from within Acrobat.

Note Although you can choose another image editor from within the Preferences dialog box, at press time, only Photoshop and Photoshop Elements have the capability to edit an image within a PDF document. If you attempt to do this after specifying a different image editor in Preferences, the image-editing application displays a warning dialog box stating the file type isn't supported.

- **Edit Object** Launches the supported illustration-editing application. To specify an external editor, choose Edit | Preferences | TouchUp (Windows) or Acrobat | Preferences | TouchUp and Choose Page | Object Editor. You can then choose Adobe Illustrator as the application you will use to edit graphic objects selected with the TouchUp Object tool.
- **Show Metadata** Opens a dialog box that displays any metadata, such as the author, keywords, and copyright notice, that was embedded with the image.
- **Properties** Opens the Properties dialog box, which supplies information about the selected object.

Summary

In this chapter, you learned how to edit your PDF documents by adding pages, deleting pages, and extracting pages. You discovered how to accomplish these tasks using the Page Thumbnails pane, menu commands, and tools. And you learned how to remove unwanted elements from pages with the Crop tool and the Crop Pages menu commands. If you create PDF documents for presentations, you now know how to add a touch of professionalism by using page transitions. In the next chapter, you will learn how to review and add comments to PDF documents.

9

Review PDF Documents

HOW TO...

- Use the Comments List
- Add comments
- Use the Sticky Note tool
- Add audio comments
- Use the File Attachment tool
- Use the Attachments panel

When you use Acrobat in a corporate environment, you can share information with colleagues in faraway locales. You can send documents via e-mail or corporate intranet for review and approval. Team members or clients can mark up the PDF document with audio comments, notes, highlighted phrases, shapes to highlight items, text boxes, and more. Have you ever sent out an original document for review and had a team member alter the original by adding comments to the text or modifying the formulas of a spreadsheet? If so, you will appreciate how easy it is to create a PDF document from the original, and to use the copy to share and receive comments with colleagues using the Acrobat annotation tools.

When you mark up a document, you often need to identify the object you want modified, and then create a note or other annotation to reflect the desired change. You can use shapes to identify the object, highlight the object, or point to the object with an arrow, a straight line, a callout, or a squiggly line drawn with the Draw Free Form tool. In this chapter, you will learn how to use the annotation tools to mark up a document, add comments to a document, and more.

Initiate an E-Mail Review

If you created a PDF document that you want other colleagues to review, you can easily seek their input by initiating an e-mail review. When you start an e-mail review and send the document to selected reviewers, Acrobat sends a Forms Data Format

(FDF) file that contains setup and configuration information, as well as a copy of the PDF document you want reviewed. Your reviewers can open the e-mail file attachment, which opens the document in Acrobat 6 or later or Adobe Reader 7.0 or later. To initiate an e-mail review, follow these steps:

1. Open the document you want to send for review.
2. Click Comment, click Review, and then choose Send For Email Review. Acrobat displays the Identity Setup dialog box, shown next.

Note   The Identity Setup dialog box appears the first time you send any PDF document for an e-mail review. The information you enter is stored and automatically sent for each additional e-mail review you initiate. You can change your identity information at any time in the future by opening the Identity section in Preferences and then making the desired changes.

3. Enter your information in the Identity Setup dialog box and then click Complete to display the first page (Getting Started) of the Send By Email For Review Wizard. If you currently have a document open, its filename is displayed in the Specify A PDF File To Send By Email For Review field, as shown in the illustration at the top of the next page. You can send a different PDF document for review by clicking the Browse button, which displays the Open dialog box and enables you to navigate to the file you want to send.
4. Click Next to open the Invite Reviewers page of the Send By Email For Review Wizard, which is shown in the illustration at the bottom of the next page.
5. Enter the e-mail addresses of your reviewers in the Invite Reviewers field. Separate each e-mail address with a comma. Alternatively, you can click the Address Book button and choose recipient e-mail addresses from your e-mail address book.

Getting Started

Steps:
→ Getting Started
Invite Reviewers
Preview Invitation

Getting Started: Initiating an Email-Based Review

Acrobat X lets you send PDF files by email for review and helps you manage the comments you receive back.

- Recipients of the file are told how to review it and how to send their comments back to you.
- Anyone with Adobe Acrobat 6 or Adobe Reader 7, or later, can review your PDF file.

Specify a PDF file to Send by Email for Review:

Chapter 6.pdf   Browse...

Cancel   < Previous   Next >

Invite Reviewers

Steps:
Getting Started
→ Invite Reviewers
Preview Invitation

Invite Reviewers

Enter an email address for each person whom you would like to invite to review this PDF file.

Address Book

Cancel   < Previous   Next >

6. Click the Next button to display the Preview Invitation dialog box, shown next.

7. Accept the default Invitation Message Subject title or enter a different title.
8. Accept the default Invitation Message or modify it with additional information. The default message gives reviewers detailed instructions on how to conduct the review and return their comments to you.
9. Click Send Invitation. Acrobat sends the document for review and displays a message to that effect. If your e-mail application isn't set up to automatically send messages, Acrobat puts the e-mail message and attachment in the outbox of your e-mail application. You will then have to manually send the review invitation from your e-mail application.
10. The Outgoing Message Notification dialog box appears, which tells you the message has been passed to your default e-mail application. The dialog box also notes that if your e-mail application is not set up to automatically send mail, you will have to send it manually from the application's outbox. You can prevent this dialog box from reappearing by clicking the Don't Show Again check box.
11. Click OK to exit the Outgoing Message Notification dialog box.

You receive comments from your reviewers as FDF files attached to e-mail messages (reviewers won't be able to see the original document with comments from all reviewers unless you send the document with comments for another review). When you open the file, Acrobat opens the original file you sent for review and adds the reviewers' comments. You can keep track of your reviews by using the Tracker, as discussed in the next section, "Use the Tracker."

In addition to e-mail-based reviews, you can also launch shared reviews and browser-based reviews. For more information, see Chapter 12.

Most people use a spam blocker to cut down on unwanted messages. Make sure the default Acrobat subject line doesn't put your recipient's spam blockers on full alert. After sending a review, make sure your intended recipients have received it. If the message has ended up in the spam folder, modify the subject line for future reviews.

Use the Tracker

You use the Tracker to keep tabs on the documents you send out for review. When you use the Tracker, it appears in a floating window that you can maximize. To use the Tracker, follow these steps:

1. Click Comment, click Review, then choose Track Reviews. The Tracker opens, as shown in Figure 9-1. In the left pane, you see a list of the documents you've sent for review. When you click a document title, information about the review appears in the right pane of the dialog box.

If you're participating in e-mail reviews instituted by other parties, they appear in the Joined section of the Tracker.

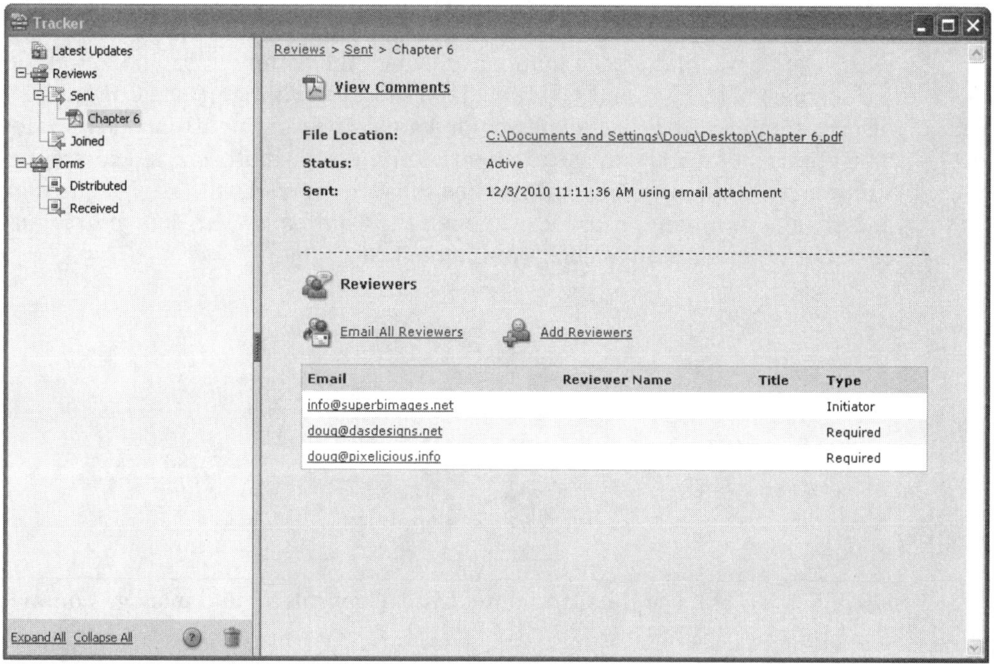

FIGURE 9-1   You use the Tracker to manage browser- and e-mail-based reviews.

2. Select a review in the left pane to display the following information in the right pane:
   - **View Comments** Click this option to open the document in the Document pane and review all comments submitted by reviewers.
   - **File Location** Displays the path to the document and also acts as a link to the document. Click the link to open the document in the Document pane.
   - **Status** Displays the status of the review.
   - **Sent** Displays the date and time you initiated the review.
   - **Reviewers** Displays the e-mail address of each reviewer. Click the e-mail address to open your default e-mail application and send a message to the reviewer.
3. You can manage a review by clicking one of the following buttons above the reviewers' e-mail addresses:
   - **Email All Reviewers** Launches your e-mail application with the subject and the e-mail addresses of your reviewers already entered. Fill in the Subject field and add the desired message.
   - **Add Reviewers** Launches the Send By Email For Review Wizard. Follow the prompts to add additional reviewers, as outlined previously in the section "Initiate an E-Mail Review."

Use the Comments List

When you open a document with comments, each comment is noted in the Comments List, which is found in the Comment panel. The Comments List shows each comment and the page number on which the comment can be found. Comments are segregated by type and reviewer name. You can configure the Comments List to display comments by type, reviewer, or status. The Comments List has two tools and an Options menu you can use to import comments, export selected comments, and summarize comments. You can also use the Comments List to navigate to comments and change comment properties. To open the Comments List, shown in Figure 9-2, click Comments and then click Comments List.

FIGURE 9-2 You use the Comments List to navigate to and manage comments.

Navigate to a Comment

The Comments List is similar to the Comments panel that you found in Acrobat 9, but is now housed in the Panes panel on the right side of the interface. A comment is noted by its icon type and the name of the reviewer. If a document is annotated with an attached file, it is referred to by a paper-clip icon. The attachment's filename is listed in the Attachments panel. A down arrow appears to the right of the comment author. When the icon is clicked, you can choose from a menu that gives you options on how to respond to the comment. These options will be covered in future sections. To navigate to a comment in the document, click the comment icon or the comment title.

Use the Comments List Options Menu

You use the Comments List Options menu to perform various tasks related to comments, such as importing comments, exporting comments, summarizing comments, and so on. To open the Comments List Options menu, shown here, click the Options icon near the upper-right corner of the panel.

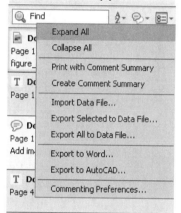

Use the Comments List Menu

When you select a comment in the Comments List, you can access a menu (shown here) for that comment by clicking the down arrow to the right of the author's name. Within the menu, you can find commands to expand all comments, set the status of the comment, reply to the comment, delete the comment, add a checkmark to show you've viewed the comment, or view its properties.

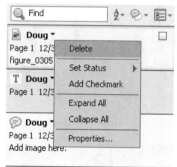

Set Comment Status

When you receive a document with comments from several reviewers, you can set the status of the comment to indicate your disposition to other reviewers regarding a particular comment. The default comment status is None, which changes as

soon as a reviewer responds to a comment by setting its status. To set the status of a comment, follow these steps:

1. Select the comment whose status you want to change.
2. Click the down arrow to reveal the comment, choose Set Status to reveal the Set Status menu, and then choose one of the following options: None, Accepted, Cancelled, Completed, or Rejected.

> **Note** You can mark comments with a checkmark by selecting a comment, clicking the down arrow next to the author's name, and then choosing Add Checkmark from the menu. Marking a comment in this manner is your reminder that you've already reviewed the comment. When you mark comments in this manner, the checkmarks are saved with your copy of the document, but other reviewers won't be able to see them.

Use the Filter Comments Menu

When you're reviewing a PDF document with multiple comments, you can decide which comments are displayed and which comments are not. For example, you can choose to show only comments created by a certain reviewer, or show only comments created with the Sticky Note tool. To specify which comments are displayed, follow these steps:

1. Click Comment and then click Comments List to open the Comments List.
2. Click the Show icon and choose one of the following options from the pop-up menu:
   - **Show All Comments** Displays all comments in the document and Comments List.
   - **Hide All Comments** Hides all comments in the document and in the Comments List. After you invoke this command, the Show All Comments command appears on the pop-up menu. Choose the Show All Comments command to display comments again.
   - **Type** Displays a drop-down menu with a list of all comment types. Select a comment type, and only comments of that type are displayed in the document and Comments List. You can select more than one comment type.
   - **Reviewer** Displays a drop-down menu listing all reviewers. Select one or more reviewers whose comments you want to display, or select All.
   - **Status** Displays all status types assigned to comments in the list. Select one or more comment status types you want to display, or select All.

Sort Comments

By default, Acrobat sorts all comments by the number of the page on which they appear. You can, however, change the way Acrobat sorts comments. For example, if you work with a team of authors on a document, you can sort comments by author. To change the way in which comments in the document are sorted, follow these steps:

1. Click Comment and then click Comments List.

2. Click the Sort By icon and, from the drop-down menu, choose one of the following:
   - **Type**   Acrobat sorts the comments by type. When you choose this option, Acrobat creates one heading in the Comments panel for each type of comment used in the document.
   - **Page (Default)**   Acrobat creates a heading for each page with comments.
   - **Author**   Acrobat creates a heading for each author who added comments to the document.
   - **Date**   Acrobat sorts comments by date, creating a heading for each date on which a comment was created. Acrobat displays the earliest date at the top of the panel. Dates are displayed numerically in the default format specified by the operating system (OS).
   - **Checkmark Status**   Choose this option, and comments to which you have added checkmarks appear at the top of the list.
   - **Status By Person**   Choose this option, and comments are sorted by the name of the author.

Search Comments

When you're reviewing a document with multiple comments, you can search for specific information by entering a word or phrase in a field. To search comments, follow these steps:

1. Click Comment and then click Comments List to open the Comments List.
2. In the Search field, enter the word or phrase you want to find within the document's comments. If the word or phrase you entered is included in one or more comments, they are displayed in the Comments List and in the document.
3. After searching comments, choose Show All Comments from the Filter Comments menu.

Tip   To print a copy of all comments in a document, choose Print with Comment Summary from the Comments List Options menu. This opens the Print menu from which you can choose the device to which you want the comments printed. Alternatively, you can choose Create Comment Summary from the Comments List Options menu to create a PDF summary of all comments in the document.

Delete Comments

When a comment has outlived its usefulness, you can delete it. When you delete comments, you decrease the file size of the document and eliminate having to deal with comments that are no longer relevant. Here's how to delete a comment:

1. Click Comment and then click Comments List to open the Comments List.
2. Click the down arrow to the right of the author of the comment you want to delete and then choose Delete from the menu.

If you delete a comment you did not author, a warning dialog box appears to that effect. Click OK to delete the other reviewer's comment, or press CTRL-Z (Windows) or CMD-Z (Macintosh) to undo the deletion.

Modify Comments

You can modify the appearance of comments, such as the color, and change the author and subject information. You can also change the default icon used to display a comment created with the Sticky Note tool. However, the icons for many of the other annotation methods are set by default. To modify a comment, follow these steps:

1. Click Comment and then click Comments List to open the Comments List.
2. Select the comment you want to modify.
3. Click the down arrow to the right of the author of the comment you want to modify and then choose Properties from the menu to open the Properties dialog box. Note that the dialog box name varies to reflect the comment type you select. The following illustration shows the Sticky Note Properties dialog box.

4. Modify the comment as desired. From within the Appearance tab, you can change the icon displayed with the comment. The General tab enables you to change the author of the comment and the subject. The Review History tab displays the Review History of the comment. In addition, you can choose from two check boxes: The first enables you to lock a comment, which prevents it from being moved; the second makes the properties of the comment you're modifying the default properties for all other comments created with the corresponding tool.
5. Click OK to close the dialog box.

Note   If Acrobat Password Security has been applied to the document and commenting is not allowed, you won't be able to edit comments unless the settings are changed. If Acrobat Certificate Security has been assigned to the document, you will be able to edit comments if the document author grants you permission to edit comments. For more information on Acrobat security, see Chapter 10.

Reply to Comments

When you receive a document for review, you can reply to comments other reviewers have added to the document. If you set the status for a comment, you can add a reply to let the reviewer know why you chose a particular status, or just add a general reply to add your two-cents worth to the review. To reply to a comment, follow these steps:

1. Open the Comments List, as outlined previously in the section "Navigate to a Comment."
2. Select the comment to which you want to respond.
3. Click the down arrow to the right of the author's name and choose Reply. Acrobat displays a new title nested within the original comment with a Reply icon and a text field to the right of the comment title.
4. Enter your reply and then click outside of the reply window.

Replies are nested within the original note and are also displayed in the Comments List. The number of replies is listed to the right of the comment. Click the plus sign to reveal the reply. After reading the reply, click the minus sign to hide the reply. When other reviewers see your reply, they can continue the thread by displaying your reply and then clicking the down arrow and choosing Reply from the menu.

Tip To edit a reply, double-click it to open the reply in its own window. Your cursor becomes an I-beam, enabling you to edit any or all of the reply. To delete a reply, click the down arrow to the right of the author's name and choose Delete from the menu.

Add Comments

When you receive or send a PDF document, you can add comments to the document. Comments are a handy way to communicate among team members or clients. Comments are readily accessible in the Comments panel and can easily be added with the click of a mouse. You can add sticky notes or audio comments, or create comments in text boxes.

Note If the document you're viewing is part of a review, you can display any changes made to an annotation created with a commenting tool. To do so, select the comment, right-click and choose Properties from the context menu. After the comment's Properties dialog box appears, click the Review History panel to view a list of any changes to the document.

Use the Sticky Note Tool

Use the Sticky Note tool when you want to add a quick comment that's pertinent to a certain part of the document. When you use the Sticky Note tool, a sticky note icon appears in the document. The icon can be double-clicked to see the note in another window, or viewers can pause their cursor over the icon to see a Tooltip that displays the contents of the note. When you create a comment with the Sticky Note tool, you can define the size of the note window as well as the type and color of the note icon, and you can enter your comments. To add a comment to a PDF document with the Sticky Note tool, follow these steps:

1. Navigate to the point in the document where you want to add the note.
2. Click Comment | Annotations and then select the Sticky Note tool. Alternatively, you can choose View | Comments | Annotations to display the Annotations panel shown here.
3. Click the point in the document where you want the note to appear. When you create a note in this manner, Acrobat opens a blank note window of the default size. When you use the default window size, scroll bars are provided for use when reading lengthy notes. After you create the window, a blinking cursor appears in the window, signifying Acrobat is ready for you to enter some text.
4. Enter the text you want to appear in the comment window. Click outside the note window when you finish entering text.

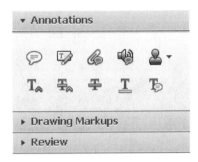

After you click outside the sticky note window, the note closes. Viewers can double-click the note to read it in its original window, or pause their cursor over the sticky note icon to view the contents of the note in a Tooltip. After you create a note, you can modify the appearance of the sticky note icon and its colors by changing its properties.

About the Sticky Note Options Menu

When you add a note to a document, an Options icon appears in the upper-right corner of the note. You can use the commands from this menu to modify note properties, set note status, and more. To display the Sticky Note Options menu, click the Options icon in the upper-right corner of the pop-up note.

Set Sticky Note Properties

The default icon for a sticky note looks like a Post-it note with a cloud inside and, in keeping with that paradigm, the Acrobat designers gave the icon a default color of bright yellow. If you don't like bright yellow for your virtual sticky notes, you can change the characteristics of the icon by following these steps:

1. To select the sticky note you want to modify, click its name in the Comments List, as discussed previously, or click the actual note in the document. You can select the sticky note with the Hand tool, Sticky Note tool, or Select tool.
2. Right-click and choose Properties from the context menu. The Sticky Note Properties dialog box appears.
3. On the Appearance panel, choose an icon from the list in the Icon window.
4. Click the Color button and choose a color from the color picker. Alternatively, click the Other Color icon and choose a color from the system color picker. When you choose colors from the system color picker, they may not look the same when viewed cross-platform.
5. Enter a value in the Opacity field or drag the slider to specify note opacity. This determines how much of the document is visible through the note icon. The note icon is totally opaque (nontransparent) at the default setting of 100 percent. Opacity isn't supported in Acrobat 5.0 and older.
6. Click the General tab, shown next, which will enable you to enter text to change the author's name or the note subject. For the Author field, Acrobat's default is to use the comment author's name (as given when the application owner registered the product with Adobe). Notice the timestamp at the bottom of this section. After you modify the note properties, the timestamp updates to reflect the time the properties were changed.

7. Click the Locked check box in the lower-left corner of the dialog box to lock the position of the note in the document and prevent any property changes until the note is unlocked by once again clicking the check box.

> **Tip** Even though you have locked a comment, another reviewer can unlock and modify it unless you add security to the document and disallow commenting.

8. Click OK to exit the Sticky Note Properties dialog box and have Acrobat apply the changes to the note.

Modify Sticky Note Text

When you annotate a document with the Sticky Note tool, you can modify the text at any time by following these steps.

1. Select the note whose text you want to modify. The easiest way to do this is to double-click the note icon in the document to open the pop-up note.
2. Click inside the note and then drag to select the text you want to modify. You can modify a single character, word, sentence, or the entire text.

To select all text in a pop-up note, place your cursor inside the note and then press CTRL-A (Windows) or CMD-A (Macintosh).

3. Choose View | Show/Hide | Toolbar Items | Properties Bar to open the Properties bar, shown next.

4. Click the drop-down arrow to the right of the Color icon and choose a color from the color picker. This determines the color displayed for the note's icon in the document, as well as the color of the title bar of the note when it's popped up.
5. To change the color of the pop-up note text, select the text in the note, click the drop-down arrow to the right of the Text Color icon in the Properties bar, and choose a color from the color picker. Alternatively, you can click Other Color and choose a color from the system color picker.
6. To decrease the size of the selected note text, click the Decrease Text Size icon. You can click the icon repeatedly, but Acrobat stops decreasing the text size when it reaches 6 points.
7. To increase the size of the selected note text, click the Increase Text Size icon. You can click the icon repeatedly, but Acrobat stops increasing the text size when it reaches 18 points.
8. Click the applicable icon to boldface, italicize, underline, superscript, or subscript the selected text.

Edit Notes

In addition to changing the properties of a note, you can change the position of a note, edit its contents, or delete it. In a previous section, you learned how to delete a note from within the Comments List. In this section, you learn how to edit a note from within the document. To edit a note within the document, select it with the Hand tool, Sticky Note tool, or Select tool and perform one of the following tasks:

- To delete a selected note, choose Edit | Delete or choose Delete from the context menu. You can also click the Options icon to open the Sticky Note Options menu, which contains commands to delete notes, reply to a note, change note properties, and more.

Note When you position your cursor over a sticky note icon, your cursor icon becomes a diagonal arrowhead, which is the indication you can double-click and drag the note icon. Double-click the note to open it in its own window and then move your cursor inside the note body. When it becomes an I-beam, you can edit text. When you move your cursor to the lower-right corner of the note, it becomes a diagonal line with an arrowhead on each end, indicating you can resize the note window.

- To delete a reply to a note, right-click the reply within the note and then choose Delete from the context menu.
- To move a selected note, click the title bar of the note and then drag it to a new location.
- To move a note icon, select it and drag it to the desired location.
- To change the contents of a selected note, double-click its icon to open the note, edit the contents, and then close the window. If the note is already open, place your cursor inside the note and perform your edits.
- To reply to a selected note, choose Reply from the context menu or the Sticky Note Options menu.
- To reply to a reply, select the reply from within the note and then choose Reply To This Reply from the context menu. You can also reply to the original comment by choosing Reply To Original from the context menu or Reply from the Sticky Note Options menu.
- To resize the window of a selected note, double-click its icon and then click and drag the lower-right handle of the pop-up note window. To resize the window proportionately, press SHIFT while dragging.

Add Audio Comments

If you prefer the spoken word to a written comment, you can record a comment and add it to a document. Audio comments can often be more effective than written comments. You can convey excitement and enthusiasm with a recorded comment.

You record the audio comments through a microphone attached to your computer, or you can choose an audio file stored on your system. Whichever method you use, the sound is embedded with the document. To record comments with your PDF documents, your computer must have a sound card and software capable of recording from a microphone. Acrobat relies on your system recording software to create the comment embedded with the PDF document. To record an audio comment for a PDF document, follow these steps:

1. Click Comments, click Annotations, and then choose the Record Audio tool.
2. Click the spot in the document where you want to add the audio comment, and the Sound Recorder dialog box appears, as shown here. This is the Windows version of the recorder. The Macintosh version looks slightly different.

3. Click the Record button (a red circle) and speak into the microphone. When you begin recording, the Play button (a black triangle) changes to the Stop button (a solid black square). Alternatively, click the Browse button to navigate to a folder on your computer that contains a prerecorded sound you want to attach to the document.

4. Click the Stop button to stop the recording. The button changes to Play again, which you can use to review the message you just recorded.

5. Click OK. Acrobat displays the Sound Attachment Properties dialog box.

6. On the Appearance panel, accept the default icon type (Sound), as shown here, or choose a different one from the list.

7. Accept the default sound attachment icon color (blue) or click the Color button to choose a different color from the color picker. Click the Other Color icon to choose a color from the system color picker.

8. Enter a value for Opacity or drag the slider. The default value of 100 percent renders the icon totally opaque. Enter a lower value to make the icon transparent and let some of the underlying objects show through. A value of 0 makes the icon totally transparent.

9. Click the General panel and either accept the default information for the Author, Subject, and Description fields or enter different information.

10. Click OK to embed the sound in the document.

After you finish the recording, Acrobat designates the audio comment with the default speaker icon or the icon specified in the Appearance panel of the Sound Attachment Properties dialog box. To play the recording or sound file, double-click the icon. Alternatively, right-click the icon and choose Play File from the context menu.

You can modify the properties of an audio comment by right-clicking the comment icon and choosing Properties from the context menu.

Create Text Annotations

You have another Acrobat tool at your disposal for adding comments to a document: the Text Box tool. When you use the Text Box tool, you can add text notes with borders and, if you desire, a solid-color background. When you annotate a document with the

Text Box tool, you create a static note that occupies space in the document, whereas a Sticky Note tool annotation is collapsed to an icon and can be popped up when needed. You can specify the font type, size, and style of text annotations.

Use the Add Text Box Tool

You can create a comment using the Add Text Box tool at any location in the document. When you create a comment with the Add Text Box tool, the comment appears on top of the actual elements in the PDF document.

To add a comment with the Add Text Box tool, follow these steps:

1. Click Comment, click Drawing Markups, and then select the Add Text Box tool.
2. Click the point in the document where you want to add the comment, and Acrobat creates a rectangular text box (with default dimensions). A blinking cursor positions itself in the upper-left corner of the text box, prompting you to enter text.

If you find the default size of the Add Text Box tool text box isn't to your liking, you can size the box while creating it by clicking in the document and then dragging diagonally. As you drag the tool, a rectangular bounding box gives you a preview of the text box size. Release the mouse button when the box is sized to your preference.

3. Enter the text for the comment. If you enter enough text, it will wrap to a new line and increase the size of the text box.
4. After you write the comment, click outside the text box to stop entering text. You can now use the Add Text Box tool to create another text box.

You can modify the properties of an annotation created with the Add Text Box tool by choosing View | Show/Hide Toolbar Items | Properties Bar. After displaying the Properties bar, click inside the text box, and then you can change the fill color, border color, border line style, border thickness, and opacity of the note. Click More to reveal the Text Box Properties dialog box. Select the text and then change the font type, text color, text size, text justification, and text style.

Edit Text Box Annotations

When you create a comment with the Add Text Box tool, you can edit the contents of the comment, move the location of the comment, and delete the comment when it has outlived its usefulness.

To modify text created with the Add Text Box tool, select the Hand tool, the Text Box tool, or the Select tool, double-click the comment you want to edit, and do one of the following, as described on the next page.

- To select text, click and drag your cursor over the text characters you want to select.
- To select all text in the box, choose Edit | Select All. Alternatively, you can choose Select All from the context menu or press CTRL-A (Windows) or CMD-A (Macintosh).
- To modify the selected text, enter new text from your keyboard.
- To delete selected text, press DELETE, choose Edit | Delete, or choose Delete from the context menu.
- To copy selected text to the clipboard, choose Edit | Copy. Alternatively, you can choose Copy from the context menu.
- To cut selected text, choose Edit | Cut. Alternatively, you can choose Cut from the context menu or press BACKSPACE (Windows) or DELETE (Macintosh).
- To paste text from the clipboard into a selected comment, place your cursor at the point you want to display the text and then choose Edit | Paste. Alternatively, you can choose Paste from the context menu. Note that some of the formatting you apply to the text in another application may be lost when it's pasted into a text box comment.
- To look up a word in an online dictionary, select the word and choose Lookup from the context menu.
- To check the spelling of a word, select it and choose Check Spelling from the context menu.

 When you use the Add Text Box tool to edit a text box annotation, make sure you click or double-click the actual annotation. Otherwise, you create a new annotation with the tool.

To resize the text box, follow these steps:

1. Select the text box with the Hand tool, the Add Text Box tool, or the Select tool. Eight handles appear, enabling you to change the width, height, or both.
2. Click and drag a corner handle to resize the box. To resize the box proportionately, press SHIFT while dragging. As you drag, Acrobat draws a rectangular bounding box, which gives you a preview of the current size of the box. Drag a handle in the middle of the right or left side to change the width, or a handle at the top or bottom to change the height. Note that this doesn't change the size of the text.
3. Release the mouse button when the box is the desired size.
4. To move a selected text box comment, position your cursor over the comment. When you see a vertical and horizontal line with two arrowheads, click and drag the comment to the desired position.

Tip You can spell-check your comments before saving the document by choosing Edit | Check Spelling | In Comments, Fields & Editable Text.

Edit Text

When you mark up a document with text, you can modify the text by inserting text or replacing text. You perform these text edits with the Insert Text at Cursor tool and the Replace tool. Your edits are noted by an insertion caret at the point where you placed the cursor when you perform the edit. Your revisions are noted in the Comments List. To insert text, follow these steps:

1. Click Comment, click Annotations, and then select the Insert Text at Cursor tool. After you choose the tool, your cursor becomes an I-beam.
2. Click at the point where you want to insert the text. A blue pop-up note appears with a blinking cursor inside.
3. Start typing. Your edits appear in the pop-up window.
4. Click outside the pop-up window to complete your edits.

Your inserted text appears in the Comments List, covered previously in this chapter. Reviewers can also read your edits by right-clicking the blue insertion caret and choosing Open Pop-up Note from the context menu. Reviewers can reply to your edits in the same manner as they reply to a Sticky Note pop-up window, discussed previously in this chapter.

You can also replace text by following these steps:

1. Click Comment, click Annotations, and then select the Replace tool. After you choose the tool, your cursor becomes an I-beam.
2. Select the text you want to replace. A blue bounding box appears around the text and a blue pop-up note appears with a blinking cursor inside.
3. Enter the desired text.
4. Click outside the pop-up note to complete your edits.

When you're performing text edits with either tool, you can edit your work by right-clicking and choosing one of the following options from the context menu: Paste Text, Check Spelling, Remove the highlighted word from the dictionary, or Look Up the word. There's also an option to use one or more of the following text styles on highlighted text: Bold, Italic, Underline, Superscript, and Subscript.

Attach Files to a Document

You can attach any file to a document for use by another reviewer or colleague. When you use the Attach File tool to attach a file to a document, it becomes embedded in the document. Reviewers will need the software associated with the file installed on their computer to be able to view the file. To attach a file to a document, follow these steps:

1. Click Comment, click Annotations, and then select the Attach File tool.

2. Click the spot in the document where you want the File Attachment icon (a paperclip) to appear. Acrobat opens the Add Attachment dialog box.

3. Navigate to the file you want to attach and then click Select. Acrobat opens the File Attachment Properties dialog box, shown here.

4. In the Icon list of the Appearance panel, select the icon you want to appear in the document. By default, the file attachment icon is a paper clip. You can choose a different icon, though, if you feel it's a better representation of the type of document you want to attach. For example, you may want to use the graph icon when attaching a spreadsheet.

5. Click the Color button and select a color from the color picker, or click the Other Color icon to choose a color from the system color picker.

6. Enter a value in the Opacity field or drag the slider to determine the opacity of the text box background. The icon is totally opaque (nontransparent) at the default setting of 100 percent.

7. Click the General tab and accept the default information, or enter new information in the Author, Subject, and Description fields. If desired, click the Locked check box at the bottom of the panel to lock the position of the file attachment icon.

8. To make the current properties the defaults for the future use of the tool, click the Make Properties Default check box.

9. Click OK to exit the dialog box and attach the file to the document.

Tip Attaching a file to a document may considerably increase the document file size. Because Acrobat stores additional information with the embedded (attached) file, the final document file size will be above and beyond the file size of the original document, combined with the file size of the attached file.

Open a File Attachment

When you receive a PDF document with a file attachment, you open the file by double-clicking the file attachment icon. After you double-click the icon, Acrobat displays a warning dialog box saying the attached file may contain programs or macros with viruses. If you received the document from a trusted source, click Open This File to view the file. If you don't know the author of the PDF document, or you have reason to believe the attachment may have a virus, click Do Not Open, close the document, exit Acrobat, and then check the PDF document with your virus-scanning software. If you decide to open the file, Acrobat launches the application on your computer associated with the file type of the attachment. When you open an attached file, your OS creates temporary files, the location of which will vary depending on the OS you use. Note that you can also open a file using the Attachments panel, as described in the upcoming section "Use the Attachments Panel."

If your antivirus software cannot scan an attachment to a PDF document, right-click the file attachment icon and choose Save Embedded File To Disk from the context menu. Close the PDF document to which the file was attached and then, prior to opening the suspect file, use your antivirus software to scan the file you saved to disk.

Edit File Attachment Properties

When you use the File Attachment tool to embed a file within a document, you cannot change the embedded file with the File Attachment Properties dialog box. Instead, you must make and save changes to the file before attaching it to a document. To delete the previous version of an attached file and embed a different one, select the file attachment icon with the Hand or Attach File tool and delete it by choosing Edit | Delete, pressing DELETE, or by choosing Delete from the context menu. After you delete the outdated file attachment, attach an up-to-date version of the file by using the steps outlined in the previous section.

As indicated, you can't change the file attached to a document by editing its properties in the File Attachment Properties dialog box. If it's unlocked, though, you can change the position of the file attachment icon by clicking it with either the Hand tool, Selection tool, or the File Attachment tool and then dragging it to a different location. You can also edit the properties of the file attachment icon by clicking the attachment icon and then choosing Properties from the context menu to open the File Attachment Properties dialog box (shown previously). Modify the properties, as outlined in the previous section, and then click OK to exit the dialog box.

You can save an embedded file to your hard drive by clicking the file attachment icon and then choosing Save Embedded File To Disk from the context menu. Alternatively, you can click the Save Attachment button in the Attachments panel. Even if you know the author of the file, a good idea is to run a virus scan on the file before you open it, especially if it's a Word or Excel file that may contain macros, which can harbor viruses that can be harmful to your system.

Use the Attachments Panel

When you open a PDF file with attachments, the icon for the attachment appears on the page to which the attachment was added. You can view the attachment by double-clicking the icon, as outlined previously. This is fine when you're perusing a PDF document page by page. However, when you want to cut to the chase and look at the document attachments, you can easily do so by using the Attachments panel, as shown in Figure 9-3.

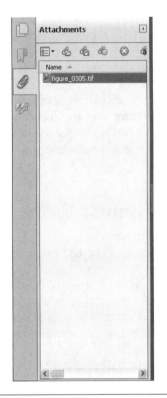

FIGURE 9-3   You use the Attachments panel to manage files that are attached to
the document.

Follow these steps to manage attachments within the Attachments panel:

1. Choose View | Show/Hide | Navigation Panes | Attachments. Alternatively,
   you can click the Attachments icon in the Navigation pane. After you open the
   Attachments panel, all file attachments are listed. Each attachment is divided
   into the following columns: Name, Description, Modified, Size, Compressed Size,
   and Location In Document. If your desktop size is not wide enough to display
   all columns, a scroll bar appears at the bottom of the panel. An icon for each
   attachment appears with the filename and extension. At the top of the panel are
   icons you use to perform tasks.
2. Click a column title to sort file attachments by that parameter. For example, if
   you click the Name column, attachments are sorted alphabetically in ascending
   order. Click the title again to sort the column in descending order.
3. Select a file attachment and do one of the following:
   • Click the Open File In Its Native Application button to open the attachment
     in the associated application. When you do this, Acrobat displays the Launch
     Attachment dialog box, which cautions you against opening the file because it
     may contain a virus. Click OK to open the document.

- Click the Options icon to reveal the Options menu. The commands on this menu match the buttons on the Attachments panel, with the additional option of editing the description of the attachment that appears in the Description column of the Attachments panel. If the attachment has no description, you can use the Edit Description command to add one. The description is only relevant in Acrobat and doesn't alter the original document in any shape or form.
- Click the Save Attachment button to display the Extract File dialog box, which enables you to save the attachment to a folder on your hard drive.
- Click the Add A New Attachment button to open the Add Files dialog box. This enables you to add a new file attachment to the document. The attachment location is listed in the Attachments panel, regardless of the page you're viewing when adding the comment.
- Click the Delete button to delete the attachment from the document.
- Click the Search icon to open the Search pane. Enter the word or phrase you're searching for and then click Search Attachments. Acrobat searches the attachments and then returns all instances of the word or phrase. Double-click a result to open it in the associated application.

Apply a Stamp

When you receive a PDF document for review, you can literally apply a stamp of approval to the document. You apply a stamp to a PDF document by using the Stamp tool, the virtual equivalent of a rubber stamp, minus the messy inkpad. You can use one of the Acrobat preset stamps on a document or create your own custom stamp. An Acrobat stamp, as it appears when applied to a document, is shown here.

open the Bookmarks panel, and then click the Options icon.

2. After you open the Bookmarks Options menu, click the menu command you want Acrobat to perform. Some of the commands in this menu were already presented; others will do the **APPROVED** counterparts. For example, to expand a bookmark, you can click the plus sign next to a collapsed bookmark or choose the Expand Current Bookmark command from the Bookmarks Options menu. Detailed information about other relevant Bookmarks Options menu commands are discussed in upcoming sections.

Tip: If you're viewing a document with long bookmarks that aren't completely visible in the Bookmarks panel, choose Wrap Long Bookmarks from the Bookmarks Options menu.

(2)Edit Bookmarks

You can edit existing bookmarks by changing the bookmark destination, renaming the bookmarks, deleting selected bookmarks, and rearranging the hierarchy of

Use the Stamp Tool

You use the Stamp tool to apply a stamp to a PDF document. You can choose from a large selection of preset stamps. After you stamp a document, you can change the color, size, and location of the stamp. You can even attach a note to a stamp. To annotate a document using the Stamp tool, follow these steps:

1. Click Comment, click Annotations, click Add Stamp, and then choose a preset from one of these categories: Dynamic, Sign Here, Standard Business, and Favorites. Move your cursor over the category title to display a fly-out menu with a preview of the category stamps. Alternatively, if you're going to use the Stamp tool repeatedly, choose Show Stamps Palette to display the Stamps Palette in the workspace.

Note When you use the Stamp tool for the first time, you are prompted to enter your name, position, and the name of your company.

2. Click the preview of the desired stamp to select it.
3. Click the location inside the document where you want the stamp to appear.
4. To move the stamp, select it with the Hand tool and drag it to another location. To resize the stamp, select it and then move your cursor toward one of the rectangular handles at each corner of the stamp. Click the handle and drag in or out to resize the stamp. Press SHIFT while dragging to constrain the stamp to its original proportions. Click the round handle at the top of the annotation to rotate the stamp.

Edit Stamp Properties

You can edit the properties of any stamp in a PDF document. You can change the appearance of the stamp, as well as the name of the author(s) and subject description. To edit stamp properties, follow these steps:

1. In the document, use the Hand tool to select the stamp whose properties you want to change. Alternatively, you can select a stamp annotation by clicking its icon in the Comments List.
2. Right-click and choose Properties from the context menu to display the Stamp Properties dialog box.
3. On the Appearance panel, you can choose a different color for the Stamp icon as it appears in the Comments List or change the opacity of the stamp in the document.
4. Click the General tab and enter new text to change the author or subject information. By default, Acrobat uses the name of the registered owner of the software for Author and the name of the stamp for Subject.
5. Click OK to exit the Stamp Properties dialog box and apply the changes.

Did You Know? **You Can Create Custom Stamps**

If your organization has a need for stamps other than the robust set of presets that comes with Acrobat, you can create your own. In your favorite image-editing program, create a graphic that's approximately 2 × 1.5 inches. In Acrobat, click Comment Annotations, select the Add Stamp tool, and choose Custom Stamps | Create Custom Stamp. Follow the prompts in the dialog box to locate the graphic you created in your image-editing program. You'll be prompted for a category name and a stamp name. When you close the dialog box, your custom stamp is available for immediate use.

Delete a Stamp

To delete a stamp, select it with the Hand tool and then choose Edit | Delete or choose Delete from the context menu.

Tip To mark a stamp as a favorite, select the desired stamp and click Comment, click Annotations, select the Add Stamp tool, and choose Add Current Stamp To Favorites. Previews of favorite stamps are conveniently located at the top of the Stamps menu for easy access.

Mark Up a Document

In addition to annotating your documents with notes, stamps, text boxes, and attached files, you can also highlight, strike through, and underline text to create annotations. You can also use graphic elements to mark up a document. You can create a circle, a rectangle, a line, or use a Draw Free Form tool to highlight areas of the document.

Use the Highlight Tools

When you want to draw attention to a block of text that needs to be changed in a paper document, you use a highlighter. Acrobat gives you similar tools that you can use to draw attention to text: the highlight tools. You have three from which to choose: the Highlight Text tool, Underline tool, and Strikethrough tool. The steps involved in using each tool are the same, as presented in the following steps:

1. Click Comment, click Annotations, and select the desired highlight tool from the Annotations panel.
2. Move the tool into the Document pane and highlight the desired text by clicking and dragging. After you select a single word with the tool, it automatically snaps to the end of the next word over which you position your cursor, and so on. If

desired, you can double-click the text you just highlighted to open the pop-up note in which you can leave comments for other people working on the document.

Double-click a word with any highlight tool to select the word.

Reviewers of the document can access a pop-up note attached to the highlighted text by double-clicking it with the Hand tool.

You can edit properties of comments created with a highlight tool by following the steps in the next section.

Edit Comment Properties

Comments created with the Highlighter, Cross-Out Text, or Underline Text tool share the same properties: color, opacity, author, and subject. To modify comment properties, follow these steps:

1. In the document, use the Hand tool to select the comment whose properties you want to modify. You can select the actual comment in the document or click its title in the Comments panel.
2. Right-click and choose Properties from the context menu to display the Highlight Properties dialog box.
3. On the Appearance tab, click the Color button to choose a color from the color picker. This changes the color of the annotation in the document and the Comments panel. Alternatively, you can click Other Color and choose a color from the system color picker.
4. Enter a value in the Opacity field. Alternatively, drag the Opacity slider to specify the level of opacity for the comment as it appears in the document.
5. Click the General tab, and you can modify the author and subject information by entering new text or editing the existing text. By default, Acrobat lists the registered owner of the application as the author and the tool name as the subject.
6. Click OK to exit the dialog box and apply the property changes.

When you change a comment's properties, this doesn't automatically change the default properties for the tool, as it did in Acrobat 6.0 and earlier. When you next use a tool, it reverts to its default settings. You can, however, make the current properties of any modified comment the tool's default by right-clicking the comment icon in the document and choosing Make Current Properties Default from the context menu.

Use Graphic Elements

Some reviewers prefer to use graphic elements to mark up a document. You can create graphic elements to mark up a document with one of the tools from the Drawing Markups panel.

Some PDF reviewers prefer to mark up a document with a combination of graphic elements and text created with the Add Text Box tool. For example, you can use the Circle tool to highlight a graphic element that needs to be modified, and then you can use the Arrow tool or the Line tool to point to text created with the Text Box tool. In Figure 9-4, the Add Text Callout tool is used to draw attention to an image in a PDF document. This tool combines a text box with a line and callout arrow. The default Add Text Callout annotation can be modified to suit the document.

Use the Draw Free Form Tool

If you're a card-carrying member of Pocket Pals Anonymous, the Draw Free Form tool is right up your alley. You can use the Draw Free Form tool to create expressive

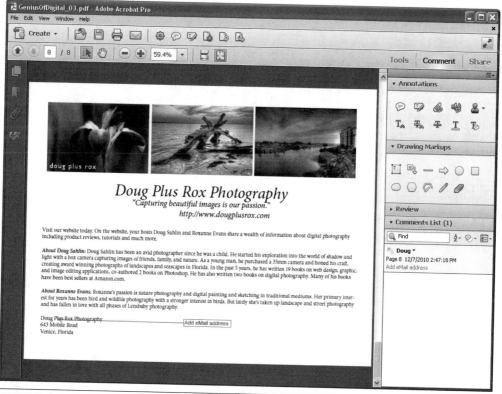

FIGURE 9-4   You can use the Add Text Callout tool to mark up a document with a text callout.

squiggles to direct another reviewer's attention to an element you feel needs correcting. When you mark up a document with the Draw Free Form tool, Acrobat smoothes out the rough spots, but it isn't possible to constrain the tool to a perfectly straight line—for that you use the Line tool. To mark up a document with the Draw Free Form tool, follow these steps:

1. Click Comment, click Drawing Markups, and then select the Draw Free Form tool.
2. Click anywhere inside the Document pane and drag to create a line.
3. Release the mouse button to finish drawing with the Draw Free Form tool.

Edit a Draw Free Form Tool Markup

After you create a markup with the Draw Free Form tool, you can move or resize it. You edit a Draw Free Form tool markup with the Hand tool. You can also edit it with the Draw Free Form tool, but if you inadvertently click outside of the markup you want to edit, you create another line. You can edit a Draw Free Form tool markup by doing one of the following:

1. To move the markup, select it with the Hand tool and drag it to another location.
2. To resize the markup proportionately, click it with the Hand tool and then click and drag one of the rectangular handles at the corners of the markup bounding box.
3. To erase part of the markup, click Comment, click Drawing Markups, and then choose Erase Free Form Tool and drag the tool across the markup to erase the unwanted portion.

Modify Draw Free Form Properties

You can change the color, opacity, and thickness of a line created with the Draw Free Form tool, as well as change the author and the subject of the comment. To modify the properties of a line drawn with the Draw Free Form tool, follow these steps:

1. Select the Hand tool.
2. Select the Draw Free Form mark whose properties you want to change.
3. Right-click and choose Properties from the context menu to open the Pencil Mark Properties dialog box.
4. Click the Appearance tab to display the appearance parameters for the comment, as shown here.
5. Click the spinner buttons to the right of the Thickness field to

increase or decrease the thickness of the line. Alternatively, you can enter a value between 0 and 12 points.

6. To change the color of the line, click the Color button and choose a color from the color picker, or click the Other Color icon to choose a color from the system color picker.

7. To change the opacity of the line, enter a new value in the Opacity field. Alternatively, you can drag the Opacity slider to set the value.

8. Click the General tab. You can modify the default listing for the Author and Subject fields by entering new text.

9. Click OK to exit the dialog box and apply the changes.

> **Tip** After changing the properties of a comment made with any tool, you can apply the new properties (except author and subject) to all future comments created with the associated tool. Before deselecting the comment, open the context menu again and then choose Make Current Properties Default.

Use the Add Text Callout Tool

If you're an author who submits illustrations to accompany your document text, you'll appreciate the Add Text Callout tool. The Add Text Callout tool enables you to create a text box with a connecting line and arrow that point to an object in the PDF document, as follows:

1. Click Comment, click Drawing Markups, and then select the Add Text Callout tool. Alternatively, you can select the Add Text Callout tool from the Comment & Markup toolbar if you've previously displayed it.

2. Click the object in the PDF to which you want the Add Text Callout to point and then drag to position the Add Text Callout text box.

3. Enter the desired text in the text box. If the text exceeds the default width of the Add Text Callout, it wraps to a new line.

4. Click anywhere in the document to finish entering text. Your completed callout is the default size and position.

When you have multiple callouts in a document, you may need to size the text box or reposition the text box relative to the callout to accommodate other callouts. To change the default size and position of a callout, follow these steps:

1. Select the callout with the Hand tool or Select tool. Acrobat displays handles around the text box and on the callout line and arrow.

2. Drag a text box handle to resize the text box.

3. Drag the handle at the end of the callout line to resize the line.

4. Drag the handle at the end of the arrowhead to reposition it.

5. Position your cursor over the text box until the cursor becomes a diagonal arrowhead with the letter T in a rectangle. Click the text box and drag it to the

desired position. As you move the text box, the connecting lines are also resized and repositioned.

6. Double-click inside the text box, and your cursor becomes an I-beam, signifying you can edit the text.

You can edit the properties of a callout by right-clicking and then choosing Properties from the context menu. On the Appearance tab, you can modify the shape of the line-ending arrowhead, line thickness, line style, color of the text box, and color of the text box border. On the General tab, you can modify the author and subject information. To apply edited callout properties to other annotations created with the Add Text Callout tool, access the context menu again and choose Make Current Properties Default.

Use the Drawing Tools

You can use shapes to draw attention to certain parts of a document. When you annotate a PDF document with drawing tools, you can select the tools from the Drawing Markups panel, shown here. The Add Text, Add Text Callout, Draw Free Form, and Erase Free Form tools have been covered previously. In this section, you learn how to use the remaining tools.

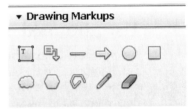

All the tools function in a similar manner. The following steps describe the process of commenting with one of the drawing tools:

1. Select a drawing tool from the Drawing Markups panel by clicking Comment, clicking Drawing Markups, and then selecting the desired tool from the Drawing Markups panel.

2. Click the spot in the document where you want the comment to appear and do one of the following:
   - **Draw Line tool**   Click the spot where you want the line to begin and then drag. Press SHIFT while dragging vertically or horizontally to create a vertical or horizontal line. Press SHIFT while dragging diagonally to constrain the line to 45 degrees.
   - **Draw Arrow tool**   Click and drag to create a line with arrowheads. Press SHIFT while dragging vertically or horizontally to constrain the line to 90-degree increments, or to 45-degree increments while dragging diagonally.
   - **Draw Oval tool**   Click and drag diagonally to create the oval. Press SHIFT while dragging to create a circle.
   - **Draw Rectangle tool**   Click and drag diagonally to create the shape. Press SHIFT while using the tool to create a square.
   - **Draw Cloud tool**   Click to create the first point and then click to create the additional points that define the cloud's shape. Double-click to close the shape.

- **Draw Polygon tool**   Click to create the first point and then click to add additional points to the shape. Double-click to close the shape.
- **Draw Polygon Line tool**   Click to create the first point and then click to add additional points to the line.

Editing a Drawing Tool Comment's Properties

As you know from reading previous sections of this chapter, comments have properties you can modify. Comments created with the drawing tools are no exception. The following steps show how to modify the properties of a comment created with the Rectangle tool. These steps also follow suit for comments created with the other closed-shaped commenting tools (Draw Cloud, Draw Oval, and Draw Polygon).

1. Select the comment whose properties you want to modify, right-click, and choose Properties from the context menu. The Properties dialog box for the tool appears. The Rectangle Properties dialog box is shown here.
2. Click the Style drop-down arrow and choose an option from the drop-down menu. This option determines the appearance of the shape's border (or line).
3. Click the spinner buttons to the right of the Thickness field to specify line thickness. Alternatively, you can enter a value between 0 and 12 points.
4. Click the Color button and then choose a color from the color picker. The selected color determines the color of the shape's border. Alternatively, click Other Color to select a color from the system color picker.
5. Click the Fill Color button and then choose a color from the color picker. This determines the color of the inside of the shape. Accept the default no-color option to create an outline of a shape.
6. Enter a value in the Opacity field to determine the comment's opacity. Alternatively, you can click and drag the Opacity slider to set this value.
7. Click the General tab to modify the author and subject information by entering new information in each field.
8. Click OK to exit the dialog box and apply the changes.

Customize the Toolbars

If you've used earlier versions of Acrobat, you know each toolbar was jam-packed with tools. In fact, nearly every available tool had a spot on some toolbar. To simplify matters, the Acrobat design team put the toolbars on a diet, displaying only the most popular tools. You can, however, modify the toolbars by adding and/or removing tools. To customize a toolbar, follow these steps:

1. Choose | Show/Hide | Toolbar items to display all the toolbar groups.
2. Select the toolbar group you want to modify. The Page Navigation tools are shown here. Tools with a checkmark are displayed on the toolbar.

Rotate View	▶		
Page Navigation	▶	⊼	First Page
Page Display	▶	✔ ⬆	Previous Page
Select & Zoom	▶	✔ ⬇	Next Page
File	▶	⊻	Last Page
Edit	▶	✔	Page Number
⚙ Quick Tools…		◀	Previous View
Properties Bar	Ctrl+E	▶	Next View
⊟ Hide Toolbars	F8		Show All Page Navigation Tools
Reset Toolbars	Alt+F8		Reset Page Navigation Tools

3. Click a tool without a checkmark to add it to the tool group, or click a tool with a checkmark to remove it from the tool group. You can also choose to show all tools for a tool group, or to reset a tool group to its default.

Edit a Pop-Up Note

You can edit a pop-up note attached to an annotation by moving it to a new position or by changing the text of the pop-up note. You can also reset a pop-up note to its default position. To edit a pop-up note, double-click the comment or markup the note is attached to and do one of the following:

1. Click the note title bar and drag it to a new location.
2. Select text to edit and enter new text.
3. Select text to delete and then choose Edit | Delete.

Note To display a pop-up note when a user pauses his cursor over it, choose Edit (Windows) or Acrobat (Macintosh) and then choose Preferences. In the Commenting section, click the Automatically Open Pop-Ups On Mouse Rollover option.

Export Comments

You can export comments from one document and use them in another version of the same document. Exported comments are saved as an FDF file. The comment file contains all the comments exported from the document in their original positions, but not the actual document elements. You can export all comments from a document or export selected comments.

Follow these steps to export all comments from a document:

1. Click Comment, click Comments List, and then choose Export All To Data File to open the Export Comments dialog box.
2. Choose the desired file type from the Save As Type drop-down menu. You can save comments as an Acrobat FDF (Forms Data Format) or Acrobat XFDF (XML Forms Data Format) file.
3. Accept the default name for the comments (the document filename with the .fdf or .xfdf extension) or enter a different name.
4. Navigate to the folder where you want the comment file saved and then click Save.

You can also export selected comments from a document—for example, all comments created by a particular reviewer. Here's how to export selected comments:

1. Open the Comments List, as shown previously.
2. Select the comments you want to export.
3. Click the Options icon and choose Export Selected To Data File.
4. In the Export Comments dialog box, enter a name for the comment file, navigate to the folder you want to save the file in, and then click Save.

Note You can also export comments as a Word document by choosing Export To Word from the Comments List Options menu. Note that you must have Word 2002 or newer installed on your system to use this feature. You can also export comments to AutoCAD by choosing Export To AutoCAD from the Comments List Options menu.

Import Comments

You can import a comment file into a different version of a document. When you import comments, they appear in their original positions. If you receive several versions of the same document marked up by different reviewers, you can collate each reviewer's comments in a single document. First, export the comments from each document, as outlined in the previous section. Second, open the master copy of the document into which you want to collate the comments. Third, follow these steps:

1. Choose Import Data File from the Comments List Options menu to open the Import Comments dialog box. You can now import comments by having Acrobat strip comments from a PDF file or by importing an FDF or XFDF file.
2. Click the Files Of Type drop-down arrow and choose Acrobat FDF Files, Adobe PDF Files, or Acrobat XFDF Files to view only files from the selected format. Alternatively, you can select the desired file from the folder, as only supported file types appear in the dialog box.
3. Choose the file and then click Select.

After you invoke the command, Acrobat imports the comments and places them in the exact location they appeared in the document from which they were extracted. If you choose to import comments from a PDF file, this may take a while if the document is large and contains many comments.

You can compare two versions of the same document by choosing View | Compare Documents. After you choose the documents to compare, you can choose to compare visual differences and textual differences and have Acrobat generate a report that annotates the differences with a side-by-side comparison.

Summary

In this chapter, you learned how to generate an e-mail review. You discovered how to keep tabs on the review with the Tracker. Other chapter topics showed you how to annotate a PDF document with notes, shapes, and text, as well as display comments from other reviewers by using the Comments panel. You learned how to reply to a comment, and you also discovered how to manage file attachments with the new Attachments panel. In the next chapter, you learn how to add security to the PDF documents you create.

10

Add Digital Signatures and Document Security

HOW TO...

- Remove sensitive content
- Use digital signatures
- Modify signature appearance
- Use the Signatures panel
- Use Acrobat Password Security
- Use Acrobat Certificate Security

When you create a document for use with several team members in a corporate environment, you can keep track of who did what to the document with digital signatures. When a reviewer or team member digitally signs a document, Acrobat acknowledges the reviewer and creates a timestamp. All changes to the document are noted as being performed by the digital signer. When more than one person digitally signs a document, you can compare different versions of the document.

Documents created in a corporate environment are often confidential. When this is the case, you can assign security to a document. Before applying security to a document, however, you might want to remove sensitive information from the document, such as passwords, credit card information, addresses, and similar details. You can easily do so using the enhanced redaction feature available only in Acrobat X Pro. After removing sensitive content, you can apply security to the document. When you add security to a document, you limit a viewer's access to the document. When you use Acrobat Password Security, you can assign a password to the document. Before a document can be viewed, the user must enter the proper password. You can also assign a permissions password to the document, which limits the viewer's ability to edit a document, print it, and so on. If a permissions password is assigned to a document, the user must enter it to modify any of the security settings. When you use Acrobat Certificate Security, you limit access to the document to certain team members, and you can create different user permissions for each team member. For example, you can disallow editing and printing for certain team members, while giving other team members carte blanche access to the document. Another option is to create a custom policy using the Adobe LiveCycle Policy Server, a service to which you can subscribe. After your company subscribes to this service, policies can be created that are stored on your company's server, which means you change security settings dynamically.

Remove Sensitive Content

When you have a PDF document that contains sensitive information, you can permanently remove sensitive content, such as personal information. You remove sensitive content with the features in the Protection panel located in the Tools pane. The process of removing sensitive information is known as *redaction.* When you redact a document, you can replace the removed content with colored boxes or leave the area blank. You can also specify that custom text or redaction codes appear over the redaction marks.

Mark Objects for Redaction

If you've ever seen television documentaries that show FBI documents with sensitive information removed, you know the document is a photocopy and the sensitive content is obliterated with black ink. The document is then photocopied, which is what the public sees. This is known as redaction. The tools in the Protection panel perform the same function with equal efficiency on a PDF document. Redaction of sensitive content is a two-step process. First, you mark text or pages for redaction.

After you mark text and graphics for redaction, you can still make changes. When you apply redaction, the marked text and graphics are permanently removed from the document. Here's how to redact content in a document:

1. Click Tools, click Protect to open the Protection panel (shown here), and then choose Mark For Redaction.

 When you choose the Mark For Redaction command, Acrobat displays a dialog box explaining the redaction process. You can prevent this dialog box from appearing again by clicking the Don't Show Again check box.

2. Mark objects for redaction by doing one of the following:
    - To mark text for redaction, move the tool toward text you want to mark. When your cursor becomes an I-beam inside a square, click and drag across the text you want to mark for redaction. You can also double-click a word to mark it for redaction.
    - To mark a graphic object for redaction, move the tool toward the object you want to mark. When your cursor becomes a crosshair, click and drag diagonally to select the object. As you drag the tool, a bounding box shows the area you selected. Release the mouse button when the bounding box surrounds the graphic you want to mark for redaction.

An object marked for redaction is surrounded by a red rectangle. A pop-up note also appears after you mark text or a graphic for redaction. This is handy when you're working with colleagues to redact a document. Any comment you add to a redaction appears in the Comments List.

To preview what the redacted content will look like when you apply redaction, pause your cursor over the content marked for redaction. If you're satisfied with the appearance of the redacted content, you can apply redaction. If not, you can modify redaction properties.

 You can redact a page or range of pages by clicking Tools, clicking Protection, and then choosing Mark Pages To Redact to open the Mark Page Range dialog box. The default option Mark Current Page For Redaction is selected. To redact more than one page, click Mark Specific Page Range For Redaction and then enter the page numbers in the Page Range text field.

Search for Text to Redact

If you're working with a multipage object that needs to be marked for redaction, you can speed the process by searching for the text you want to redact. This is similar to searching a document with the exception that you can mark results from the search from within the Search dialog box. The Search And Remove feature only works for searchable text, not for graphic objects that have text. Follow these steps to search for text you want to mark for redaction:

1. Click Tools, click Protection, and then choose Search And Remove Text to display the Search dialog box. When you select this tool for the first time, a dialog box appears telling you that documents with images and line art that contain text cannot be found with the Search & Remove Text tool. The dialog box also warns you to perform a final review to remove any images or graphics that may contain text of a confidential nature. You can prevent this dialog box from appearing again by clicking the Do Not Show This Message Again check box.
2. Choose an option in the Where Would You Like To Search? section of the dialog box. You can search in the current document, which is the default option, or choose to search for the word or phrase in PDF documents in a specific folder.

The latter option is useful when you need to redact several documents that contain the same sensitive information.

3. Enter the text in the What Word Or Phrase Would You Like To Search For? text field. Alternatively, you can choose the Multiple Words Or Phrase option, which opens the Words And Phrases To Search And Redact dialog box. Enter the desired words or phrase in the dialog box and then click OK to search the document for the words and phrases. You can further refine your search by choosing either or both of the following options: Whole Words Only or Case-Sensitive.

4. Click Search And Redact. Acrobat displays all instances of the search word or phrase. You can locate individual search results in the document by clicking the text in the Search panel.

5. To select search results you want to mark for redaction, do one of the following:
   - Click a search result instance's check box to select this instance of the search word or phrase for redaction.
   - Click Check All to select all instances of the search word or phrase for redaction.

6. In the Redaction Marks Options section, choose one of the following options: Mark Whole Word(s) For Redaction, or Mark Partial Word(s) For Redaction. The second option will redact part of a word that contains the word or phrase entered in your query.

7. Click Mark Checked Results For Redaction.

Modify Redaction Properties

Redaction is an ongoing process. After you make an initial pass over the document, you may find that you need to mark other objects for redaction, or change the properties of objects you've marked for redaction. By default, a black rectangle replaces redacted content. You can modify the appearance of the redacted objects in the document by changing redaction properties.

Follow these steps to modify redaction properties:

1. Click Tools, click Protection, and then choose Redaction Properties to display the Redaction Tool Properties dialog box, shown here.

2. Accept the default black fill color for redacted areas, or click the color swatch and choose the desired color from the Color Picker.

3. Click the Use Overlay Text check box if you want to display text over areas where content has been redacted. If you choose this option, specify the text attributes, such as font type, color, size, and so on, in the Overlay Text area.
4. Enter text in the Custom Text field. Alternatively, click the Redaction Code radio button, choose the desired code set and code entries from the Code Sets and Code Entries areas, and then click Add Selected Entry. After you choose a redaction code, Add Selected Entry becomes Remove Selected Entry, which you use to remove the current redaction code.

Tip   If you're familiar with redaction codes, click the Edit Codes button to display the Redaction Code Editor dialog box, which enables you to add or remove code sets, import or export code sets, and add, remove, or rename individual code entries.

5. In the General section you can modify the subject by selecting the default subject text (Redact) and entering different text.
6. Click OK to apply the properties to the Redaction tool.

Apply Redaction to Marked Objects

After marking instances of sensitive text and graphic objects you want to remove, the next step is to permanently remove the marked objects from the document and replace them with filled rectangles, and/or overlay text as specified in the Redaction Tool Properties dialog box. To remove sensitive information marked for redaction, follow these steps:

1. To permanently remove objects marked for redaction, click Tools, click Protection, and then click Apply Redactions. After you use the tool, Acrobat displays a dialog box warning you that you're about to permanently remove all items from the document that are marked for redaction. By default, Acrobat saves the redacted document, appending the current title with _Redacted, which leaves your original document unaltered.
2. Click OK to exit the Adobe Acrobat warning dialog box and apply redaction. After Acrobat redacts the selected objects, it displays a dialog box that enables you to examine the document for additional objects to redact, such as hidden text, metadata, and so on. This dialog box has an option that tells Acrobat to always perform the option you choose.
3. Click Yes to mark additional objects or text for redaction, or click No to apply redaction to marked objects. Figure 10-1 shows a Word document with objects that were permanently removed and replaced with filled black rectangles.

Remove Hidden Information

If you have a document that doesn't contain information you need to hide, but does contain hidden information in the form of metadata, file attachments, or bookmarks

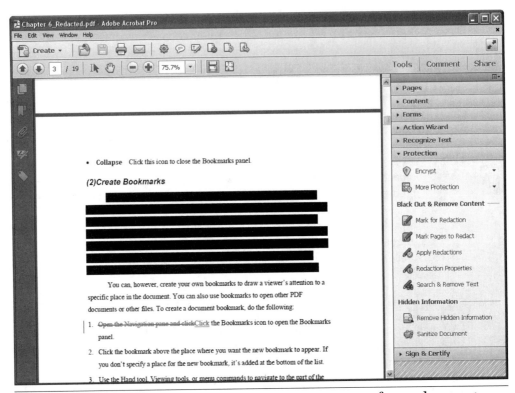

FIGURE 10-1 You can permanently remove sensitive content from a document.

that may contain sensitive information, you can easily remove hidden information with Acrobat X Pro. This information, although not visible to casual Acrobat users, can be viewed by people who have the full version of Acrobat. You can easily remove hidden information by performing the following steps:

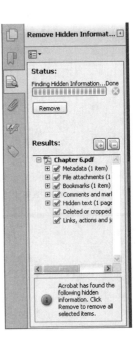

1. Click Tools, click Protection, and then choose Remove Hidden Information. After choosing this option, Acrobat scans the document and displays the results in the Remove Hidden Information panel, shown here.
2. Click the plus sign next to a hidden information category such as Metadata to reveal all instances of the category.
3. Click a hidden information listing to show a preview of the currently selected instance of hidden information.
4. To keep information in the document discovered by Acrobat, click the check box next to the listing in the Remove Hidden Information panel to remove the green checkmark.

5. Click Remove to remove the hidden information from the document. A dialog box appears telling you that you also remove digital signatures, Adobe Reader Extensions, review and form workflows, plus any information added by third-party applications.

6. Click OK to exit the Remove Hidden Information dialog box and complete the operation.

7. Save the document. Save the document with a different filename or in a different folder if you want the original document to remain intact.

Tip   You can also remove hidden information with the Sanitize Document command, which you find in the Protection panel. This removes all instances of hidden information. This command is quicker than removing hidden information, but doesn't give you the option to review what's being removed before saving the document.

Did You Know?

Add Bates Numbering Header or Footer

Bates numbering is a method of indexing legal documents that makes it easy to identify and retrieve them. Bates numbering is used by legal firms. When Bates numbering is applied to a document, each page of the document receives a unique number that also indicates its relationship to other Bates-numbered documents. Bates numbers appear in headers or footers on the pages of each PDF to which Bates numbering has been applied.

You apply Bates numbering by clicking Tools, clicking Pages, and then choosing Bates Numbering | Add Bates Numbering. The Bates Numbering dialog box prompts you for the documents to which you'll apply Bates numbering. After selecting documents, you can also modify the order in which documents are arranged. The next step is to click Output Options and specify the folder in which the documents are saved, filenaming options, and then choose the Bates numbering options and decide whether the numbering will be added to the header or footer. At this stage, you can add additional text to the header and/or footer.

About Digital Signatures

With Acrobat, documents can be digitally signed. A digital signature is like an electronic thumbprint; it identifies the signer of the document. A digital signature also records any changes made by the signer and stores information about the signer with the document.

When you add Acrobat Certificate Security to a document, only a team member with an authorized digital signature can view the document. Acrobat users with digital signatures can select their digital ID and log in prior to working on secure documents. Secure documents open without requesting the user for a password if an authorized user has selected their digital ID and logged in prior to opening the document.

If you use Acrobat to send contracts to clients, digital signatures can be used to approve contracts. If both parties accept a digital signature as an electronic facsimile of a handwritten signature, a digitally signed contract may be legally binding. Before you accept a digital signature as legally binding authorization to proceed with a contract, it's best to seek the advice of legal counsel.

Use Digital Signatures

When you decide to use digital signatures to verify the identities of users modifying your documents, you can use the default Acrobat Certificate Security or the Adobe LiveCycle Policy Server, or you can specify a third-party service to handle digital signatures. After you decide on a signature handler, you need to create a digital ID. Your digital ID stores information about you. You can use the default Acrobat graphic for a digital signature or customize the digital signature with a photo or other graphics, such as a logo. When you work with colleagues with whom you'll exchange secure documents, you can create a list of trusted identities. Trusted identities are digital signature certificates you have imported, which are files in FDF, P7C, P7B, CER, or CRT format used to verify digital signatures. You can request digital IDs of colleagues via e-mail, and share your certificate with other colleagues so your digital signature can be verified.

Documents can be signed multiple times by multiple authors. Whenever a document is digitally signed, Acrobat records the changes made since the document was last digitally signed. When you open a document with multiple signatures, you view the most current version of the document.

You can view earlier versions of a digitally signed document and compare different versions. When you compare different versions of a document, you can also view the changes made by each signer.

Note You can create a digital ID from within Acrobat and send your certificate to other parties to verify your signature. If you intend to distribute the document widely, this can be tedious. You can, however, secure a digital ID from a trusted Adobe party, which enables any user of Adobe Reader 7.0 or later, Acrobat X Standard, or Acrobat X Pro to verify your digital signature.

Create a User Profile

You create a user profile to create identification and a password that links to your digital signature. You can create more than one user profile if you sign documents in different capacities. To create your first user profile, follow these steps:

1. Click Tools, click Protection, and then choose More Protection | Security Settings to open the Security Settings dialog box.
2. Click Digital IDs to display the options for Digital IDs.

3. Click the Add ID button to open the Add Digital ID Wizard. On the first page (shown next), choose My Existing Digital ID From and then select one of these options: A File, A Roaming Digital ID Stored On A Server, or A Device Connected To This Computer. Alternatively, to create a new digital ID, choose A New Digital ID I Want To Create Now.

4. Click Next. The following steps assume you selected A New Digital ID I Want To Create Now.

Note   If you already have an existing digital ID, such as a Windows certificate, on your computer, click the A File radio button and then click Next. The next wizard page prompts you to locate the ID file and enter your password. After following these steps, you can use the digital ID from within Acrobat to certify documents and apply security settings.

The second Add Digital ID Wizard page, shown on the next page, enables you to choose one of the following options to specify where you want to store your self-signed digital ID:

- **New PKCS#12 Digital ID File**   Creates a digital ID file using the PKCS#12 standard. Digital IDs created with this standard have a .pfx or .p12 file extension, and they can be used with most applications that require secure digital IDs, including certain browsers.
- **Windows Certificate Store**   Creates a digital ID file that can be used with most applications supported by Windows.

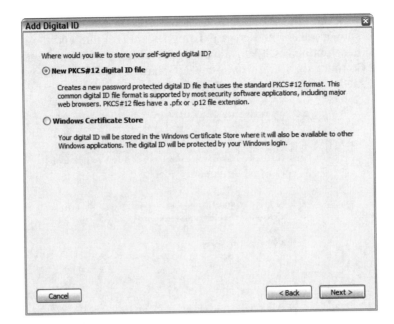

5. Click Next to open the next page of the Add Digital ID Wizard, shown here.

6. Enter your name in the Name field. If desired, supply additional contact information in the Organizational Unit and Organizational Name fields.

7. Enter your e-mail address in the Email Address field.

8. Click the Country/Region drop-down arrow and choose an option from the drop-down menu.

9. Click the Enable Unicode Support check box if you want to include Unicode information with the certificate. The Unicode standard provides a unique number for every character. Each number is cross-platform. The Unicode standard for most English documents is UTF-8. If you choose this option, Unicode fields appear to the right of your contact information. Enter the appropriate Unicode information in the desired fields.

10. Click the Key Algorithm drop-down arrow and choose 1024-bit RSA or 2048-bit RSA. The latter choice offers better security, but it may not be available to all users.

11. Click the Use Digital ID For drop-down arrow and choose an option from the drop-down menu. The default option, Digital Signatures And Data Encryption, enables you to use the digital ID for signing documents and encrypting. Alternatively, you can choose Digital Signatures Or Data Encryption to limit your use of the digital ID.

12. Click Next to open the password page of the Add Digital ID Wizard.

13. Accept the default location and filename for your digital ID, or enter a different path and filename. Alternatively, you can click Browse to open the Save Digital ID dialog box, which enables you to navigate to the desired folder and enter the desired filename.

14. Enter and confirm your password. Your password must be at least six characters and cannot contain any of the following symbols:

    ! @ # $ % ^ & * , | \ < > _ or "

This version of Acrobat has a password rater, which is a very useful feature. When you enter characters for your password, the rating changes from Weak to Medium, to Strong, to Best. Create a password with a rating of Strong or Best. These are the types of passwords that are hard to hack.

15. Click Finish to complete the process and exit the wizard. Your new digital signature appears in the Digital IDs section of the Security Settings dialog box.

16. Close the Security Settings dialog box.

Create Signature Appearance

When you digitally sign a document, Acrobat uses a default text-only signature with the Acrobat logo in the background. You can create an alternate of your digital signature by creating a file in a graphics program and converting it to PDF format. For that matter, you can choose File | Create | PDF From Scanner, or click the Create button and choose PDF From Scanner, after which you scan a copy of your actual signature and save it as a PDF file. You can also import a graphic file saved with any file format supported by Acrobat. To create a digital signature with a graphic, follow these steps:

1. Choose Edit | Preferences to open the Preferences dialog box.
2. Click Security, and then in the Appearance section, click New to open the Configure Signature Appearance dialog box, shown here.
3. In the Title field, enter a name for the signature configuration.
4. In the Configure Graphic section, choose No Graphic, Imported Graphic, or Name. If you choose Imported Graphic, click the File button to open the Select Picture dialog box. Click the Browse button, navigate to the PDF file that contains the image for your digital signature, and then click Select. Acrobat displays a sample of the image in the Preview window. If the desired image is not a PDF file, click the Files Of Type drop-down arrow and select an option from the drop-down menu, which contains all the image file formats supported by Acrobat. Next, navigate to and select the desired graphic format to display all files of that type. Select the desired image and then click OK.
5. If the image is acceptable, click OK to close the Select Picture dialog box.
6. In the Configure Text section, choose the options you want displayed with your digital signature. Every option is selected by default. For example, if you deselect Logo, the Acrobat logo won't be displayed with your new digital signature.
7. In the Text Properties section, choose the desired option to determine how the text and graphic are displayed. As you change the options, Acrobat updates the preview in real time, as shown next.

8. Click OK to close the dialog box, and Acrobat adds your custom signature to the list, as shown in the illustration below. Notice when you select the signature, you have options to edit, duplicate, and delete the custom signature.

9. Click Advanced Preferences and then click the Creation tab. Choose the desired preferences from the following:

   • **Include Signature's Revocation Status When Signing**   Choose this option to embed information about your certificate's validity. Choosing this option expedites the validation process because your recipient won't have to go online to determine whether the certificate has been revoked.

- **Show Reasons When Signing** Choose this option, and a field with a drop-down menu arrow appears when you sign a document, enabling you to specify a reason for signing the document.
- **Show Location And Contact Information When Signing** Choose this option to have your location information added to the digital signature. Your contact information appears in the Signer tab of the Signature Properties dialog box. When you add a digital signature to a PDF, text boxes appear in the Sign Document dialog box where you enter the desired location and contact information.
- **Enable Reviewing Of Document Warnings** Choose an option from the drop-down menu, which, when you apply your digital signature, analyzes a document for content that might change the document appearance. Your options are Always, Never, and When Certifying A Document. Then, provide the option in the Sign Document dialog box to review this content.
- **Prevent Signing Until Document Warnings Are Reviewed** Choose an option to require the signer to review document warnings before signing the document. Your options vary depending on which option you choose to enable reviewing of document warnings.

10. Click OK to exit the Preferences dialog box.

How to... **Create a Secure Password**

When creating a password, many people create one that's easy to remember, such as their birthday, a relative's birthday, or a combination of initials from their name and their spouse's name. Passwords such as these are easy to decipher. When you need to create a secure password, create one with at least eight characters. Create a combination of alphabetic characters interspersed with numeric characters, such as j87ty91w!~98. Refer to the Acrobat Password strength rater when creating a password for a digital ID until you get a password that rates Strong or Best. After creating the password, make sure you archive a hard copy of the password in a safe and remote location. You may also want to consider saving a digital copy of your password to your PDA (personal digital assistant) if it is secure.

Sign a Document

After you create a user profile, you can digitally sign documents. When you digitally sign a document, you're required to save it. When you save the document for the first time, Acrobat saves it in an append-only format. From this point forward, you won't be able to do a full save, because the Save option is unavailable for a digitally signed document. After you sign a document, your signature appears in the Signatures panel, discussed in the section "Use the Signatures Panel." To digitally sign a document, follow these steps shown next.

1. Finalize all your required changes prior to signing the document. If necessary, remove sensitive information using commands in the Protection section of the Tools pane. If you digitally sign the document and then make additional changes, the document will be marked as modified since your digital signature was applied.

2. Click Tools, click Sign & Certify, and then choose Sign Document. After you choose to sign the document, a dialog box appears with instructions on how to place the signature within the document. Click OK to exit the dialog box. You can prevent this dialog box from appearing again by clicking the Do Not Show This Message Again check box.

3. Click and drag diagonally to define the area in which your digital signature will appear.

4. After you release the mouse button, the Sign Document dialog box appears, as shown here.

5. Choose the desired digital ID from the Sign As drop-down list.

6. Enter the password associated with the digital ID you selected.

7. In the Appearance field, accept the default Standard Text signature, or click the drop-down arrow and choose a signature you created.

8. If the Lock Document After Signing check box is available, click it to prevent further changes to the document after you sign it. This option is not available if there are unsigned signature fields in the document, or if the document is being managed with the Adobe LiveCycle Workflow Server.

9. Click the Sign button. The Save As dialog box appears.

10. Enter a filename for the document and click Save. After you save the document, your digital signature appears on the document as noted in the Signatures panel.

 To display a document in Preview Document mode prior to signing a document, choose Edit | Preferences, choose the Security category, and then click the View Documents In Preview Mode When Signing check box.

 If you prefer to create a reasonable facsimile of your signature when signing a document, click Tools, click Sign & Certify, and then choose Apply Ink Signature. You can then create a signature with your system pointing device. This option works better if you have a digital tablet and stylus connected to your computer.

Choose a Digital ID

If you launch Acrobat for the purpose of reviewing documents with digital signatures, you need to choose the digital ID with which you'll be reviewing and signing the documents. When you choose a digital ID, you can validate digital signatures from your list of trusted identities as soon as you open a document. To choose a digital ID, follow these steps:

1. Click Tools, click Sign & Certify, and then choose More Sign & Certify | Security Settings. The Security Settings dialog box appears with a list of all digital IDs you created or that already exist on your system. If it's not already expanded, click the plus sign (+) to the left of Digital IDs to view all available options.
2. In the left pane, expand Digital ID Files to display all digital IDs you've created.
3. Click Digital ID Files in the expanded tree, and then from the right pane, select the digital ID file with which you want to work.
4. Click Login at the top of the Security Settings dialog box (shown next) to open the dialog box for the digital ID.

5. Enter the correct password.
6. Click OK to exit the digital ID dialog box.
7. Close the Security Settings dialog box.

After selecting a digital ID, you can sign documents with the digital ID and validate signatures, as shown in upcoming sections.

Tip From within the Security Settings dialog box, you can add additional IDs and remove selected IDs, as well as view the settings for selected digital IDs. You can also export a copy of your digital ID to a folder on your hard drive. The exported digital ID serves as a backup if you ever have to reinstall Acrobat.

Change Digital ID Password

If you feel security has been breached, you can change the password for your digital ID. To change your digital ID password, follow these steps:

1. Click Tools, click Sign & Certify, and then choose More Sign & Certify | Security Settings to access the Security Settings dialog box, shown previously.
2. Click the plus sign (+) to the left of Digital ID Files; then in the right pane, select the file you want to modify.
3. Click Change Password to open the Change Digital ID File Password dialog box.
4. Enter your current password in the Old Password field.
5. Enter your new password in the New Password field and then confirm your new password.
6. Click OK to close the Change Digital ID File Password dialog box.
7. Click Close to exit the Security Settings dialog box.

Change Password Timeout Settings

By default, you're required to enter your password every time you sign a document. This feature prevents other people from using your digital signature on a document when you temporarily vacate your workstation while using Acrobat. You can, however, change password settings to avoid having to enter your password every time you digitally sign a document. The following steps explain how to change password settings:

1. Click Tools, click Sign & Certify, and then choose More Sign & Certify | Security Settings to access the Security Settings dialog box, shown previously.
2. Expand the Digital IDs listing in the left pane of the dialog box and then click Digital ID Files.
3. In the right pane of the dialog box, select the file you want to modify. The Security Settings dialog box reconfigures, as shown previously.
4. Click Password Timeout. If you're not already logged in, Acrobat prompts you to enter the password for the digital signature. If you are logged in, the Password Timeout Policy dialog box appears.
5. Enter the correct password and then click OK to open the Password Timeout Policy dialog box, shown next.

Here are your options:

- **Always**   This option is selected by default and requires a password every time you digitally sign a document. You can deselect this option if you're a sole entrepreneur or you secure your computer when you're not at your workstation.
- **After**   Click this button and then click the drop-down arrow to choose a time interval after which you will be required to enter your password when digitally signing a document.
- **Once Per Session**   Choose this option and you'll be prompted to enter your password the first time you digitally sign a document. You won't have to enter your password again until you close and launch Acrobat again.
- **Never**   Choose this option and you never have to enter your password while working in Acrobat.

6. Click OK to apply the new settings.

Use the Signatures Panel

After you or another author digitally signs a document, information concerning the signature appears in the Signatures panel. You can select a signature in the panel and find out when the document was signed, who the author was, and the validity of the signature. You use the Signatures panel to manage the signatures in the document, as well as perform other functions. To open the Signatures panel, shown here, open the Navigation pane and click the Signatures icon.

The Signatures panel has an extensive Options menu with

commands pertaining to digital signatures. To open the Signatures panel Options menu, shown here, click the Options icon in the Signatures panel.

In the following sections, you learn how to use commands from this menu to sign signature fields, clear and delete signature fields, verify signatures, view different versions of the document, and more.

View Digital Signatures

After you open the Signatures panel, you see a single listing for each signature in the document. The listing notes the author's name, e-mail address, the verification status of the signature, and the date the signature was added to the document. Verifying signatures is discussed in the upcoming section "Validate Signatures."

To the left of the signature is a minus sign (–), as shown previously. Click the minus sign to collapse the signature. A collapsed signature is designated by a plus sign. Click the plus sign to expand the signature.

Clear Signature Fields

When you or another author digitally signs a document, you create a field that contains a digital signature. You can also clear a digital signature field for use by another reviewer by following these steps:

1. In the Navigation pane, click the Signatures icon to open the Signatures panel.
2. Click the name of the digital signature whose field you want to clear.
3. Choose Clear Signature from the Options menu. If you want to clear all signature fields, choose Clear All Signature Fields from the Options menu.

After you clear a signature field, it's represented in the Signatures panel with a signature icon followed by a title that designates the signature field by a number and the document page on which the signature appears. In the document, the cleared signature is represented by the signature field icon. You can sign a blank signature field by selecting it in the Signatures panel and then choosing Sign Document from the Options menu, or by clicking the field in the document with the Hand tool. Either method opens the Sign Document dialog box, discussed previously in the section "Sign a Document."

Sign Signature Fields

When you have a blank signature field in a document, you can sign the field in one of two ways: Click the field with the Hand tool within the document, or select the signature field in the Signatures panel and then choose Sign Document from the Options menu. After you choose to sign the field using one of these methods, follow the previously discussed steps to sign the signature field.

Validate Signatures

When you open a document with digital signatures, they are verified by default, unless you deselect the Verify Signatures When The Document Is Opened check box in the Security category of the Preferences dialog box. Acrobat checks the authenticity of the signature to see if the document or signature has been changed since the signing. If you select a digital ID prior to opening a document, Acrobat checks all signers' digital IDs against the list of trusted identities in your user profile. If the signature matches one of the certificates, Acrobat verifies the signature. If the document has been modified after the signature was placed, Acrobat displays a warning icon. You can verify selected signatures or all signatures.

To verify signatures, do one of the following:

- Click a signature in the document with the Hand tool.
- Open the Signatures panel, select the signature you want to verify, and then choose Validate Signature from the Options menu.
- Open the Signatures panel and then choose Validate All Signatures from the Options menu. This option may take a while if you're validating multiple signatures on a large document.
- Click Tools, click Sign & Certify, and then choose Validate All Signatures.

When you validate one signature in the Signatures panel or within the document, Acrobat displays the Signature Validation Status dialog box. If the document has been modified after being digitally signed, Acrobat displays text to that effect in the Signature Validation Status dialog box, shown here.

To accept the verification and continue working, click the Close button.

View Document Version

When a document is digitally signed, Acrobat remembers the exact contents of the document at that stage of the revision process. You can use the Signatures panel or menu commands to view any version of the document. Here's how to view a signed version of the document:

1. In the Navigation pane, click the Signatures icon.
2. Click the digital signature that corresponds to the version of the document you want to view.
3. Choose View Signed Version from the Options menu. Alternatively, click Tools, click Sign & Certify, and then choose More Sign & Certify | View Signed Version.

After you invoke this command, Acrobat re-creates a version of the document as it appeared at that stage of the revision process and displays it in another window. You can view as many signed versions of the document as needed. You can compare signed versions with the original by following the previous steps to re-create previous versions of the document, choosing Window | Tile, and then choosing Horizontally or Vertical.

> **Tip**
>
> To navigate to a signature field location within the document, open the Signatures panel, select the signature to which you want to navigate, and then choose Go To Signature Field from the Options menu.

> **Did You Know?**
>
> ## You Can Compare Documents
>
> If you own Acrobat X Pro or Acrobat X Pro Extended, choose View | Compare Documents. This opens a dialog box that enables you to choose which versions of the document you want to compare. After selecting two versions, click OK. Acrobat X Pro creates a side-by-side comparison (or a detailed report if you choose that option) of each page of the document. You can see differences between versions by scrolling through the pages.
>
> You can also compare a signed version to the current version by selecting a digital signature in the Signatures panel and then choosing | Compare Signed Version To Current Version from the Options menu. Acrobat displays the signed version beside the current version of the document and displays a pink rectangle for each difference.

View Digital Signature Properties

You can learn everything you want to know about a digital signature by viewing its properties. When you view a digital signature's properties, you can verify the signature and get information about the author of the digital signature. To view the properties of a digital signature, follow these steps shown next.

1. In the Navigation pane, click the Signatures icon to open the Signatures panel.

2. Click a digital signature to select it.

3. Choose Show Signature Properties from the Options menu to open the Signature Properties dialog box, shown here.

4. On the Summary tab of the dialog box, you can perform the following operations:

   - Click the Validate Signature button at the bottom of the tab to verify the digital signature.

   - Click the Show Certificate button to display the Certificate Viewer dialog box, which is divided into the following tabs: Summary, Details, Revocation, Trust, Policies, and Legal Notice. If the creator of the certificate isn't on your trusted identities list, you can add the certificate owner to the list by clicking the Add To Trusted Identities button on the Trust tab of the dialog box. After viewing information about the certificate, click Close to exit the Certificate Viewer dialog box.

5. Click the Document tab, shown on the next page, to reveal information about the version of the document associated with the digital signature. From within this tab, you can verify whether the document was altered or modified after the digital signature was applied and view the associated version of the document by clicking the View Signed Version button.

6. Click the Compute Modifications List button to reveal a detailed list of the changes made to the version of the document associated with the selected digital signature.

7. Click the Signer tab to reveal information about the signer associated with the selected signature. From within this tab, you can click the Show Certificate button to view the signer's certificate.

8. Click the Date/Time tab to view the date and time the selected digital signature was applied to the document. If the date and time stamp are from the signer's computer, Acrobat displays a yellow exclamation point and warning text.
9. Click the Legal tab to view the Legal Notice, which contains additional information about the digital ID and a disclaimer. From within this tab, you can click the Signer Legal Notice button to view the Legal Notice tab of the Certificate Viewer dialog box.

Note You have another option on the Legal tab of the Signature Properties dialog box. This option is to click the View Document Integrity Properties button to display the PDF Signature Report dialog box, which contains warnings about potential problems with the document, such as links that open URLs in web browsers. If the document doesn't contain any problems, Acrobat displays a dialog box to that effect.

10. Click Close to exit the Signature Properties dialog box.

About Acrobat Security

When you assign security to a document, you can limit user access to the document. For example, you can prohibit printing of the document and copying elements from the document. You have three versions of Acrobat Security: Acrobat Password Security, Acrobat Certificate Security, and Adobe LiveCycle Policy Server.

With Acrobat Password Security, you can password-protect a document and require a permissions password to change the document password or security settings. When you use Acrobat Password Security, the same permissions level is granted to all recipients of the document. Acrobat Password Security is available with 40-bit encryption for Acrobat 3.x or Acrobat 4.x, and is available with 128-bit encryption for Acrobat 5.x and 6.0. Acrobat 7.0 and later have a different version of 128-bit encryption, which is compatible with Acrobat 7.0 and later, as well as Adobe Reader 7.0 and later.

If you need to assign different levels of permission for different recipients of your document, use Acrobat Certificate Security. When you secure a document with Acrobat Certificate Security, a user can open the document only if you selected that user from your list of trusted certificates and they are logged in with the corresponding digital signature. You can assign differing levels of permission for each user on your trusted identities list, as discussed in the upcoming section "Use Acrobat Certificate Security."

If your organization has decided to subscribe to the Adobe LiveCycle Policy Server service, you can tailor security policies for the documents you create. For example, you can create a policy that disables opening a document after a certain date. When you choose Adobe LiveCycle Policy Server, you're prompted to log in with the credentials assigned by your system administrator. You can then create security policies online, which, after completed, are stored online on the Adobe LiveCycle Policy Server. General information on the Adobe LiveCycle Policy Server can be found at www.adobe.com/products/livecycle/rightsmanagement/.

Certify a Document

When you certify a document, you digitally sign it to verify its contents. Other reviewers will be able to fill in form fields and digitally sign the document, but if they attempt to change any of the other document attributes—such as links, text, and so on—the document is no longer listed as certified. To certify a document, follow these steps:

1. Choose the digital ID with which you want to certify the document, as discussed earlier in the section "Choose a Digital ID."
2. Choose File | Save As | Certified PDF. Acrobat displays a dialog box with information about certifying documents. You also have the option of clicking the Get Digital ID From Adobe Partner button, which transports you to a web page on the Adobe website where you can procure a third-party digital ID. Third-party digital IDs may be easier for recipients to validate if you widely distribute the

document. Alternatively, you can click Tools, click Sign & Certify, and from the Certify section choose With Visible Signature.

3. Click OK. Acrobat displays a dialog box with instructions on how to create a signature field. After you certify a few documents, you may find this dialog box is intrusive. You can prevent the dialog box from appearing again by clicking the Do Not Show This Message Again check box.

4. Click OK and then create a digital signature, as outlined previously. After you create the digital signature, the Certify Document dialog box appears.

5. Choose a digital signature from the Sign As drop-down menu and then enter your password.

6. Choose a signature appearance.

7. Click the Permitted Changes After Certifying drop-down arrow and choose one of the following options:

   - **No Changes Allowed**   Prevents any document changes by future viewers.
   - **Form Fill-in And Digital Signatures**   Enables future viewers of the document to fill in form fields and apply a digital signature.
   - **Annotations, Form Fill-in And Digital Signatures**   Allows future viewers of the document to create annotations with any of the commenting tools, fill in form fields, and digitally sign the document.

8. Click Sign. Acrobat displays the Save As dialog box.

9. Enter a name for the document and click Save.

When the document is opened again, a blue ribbon appears in a light blue field at the top of the document. The name of the certifier is listed along with the validity of the digital signature. The reader of the document can click the Signature Properties icon to display the Signature Properties dialog box.

Use Acrobat Password Security

In today's economy, corporations often have branches in different counties, states, and countries. Before the advent of e-mail, corporations had to send documents via courier, an expensive way to communicate. With e-mail, corporate documents can be sent as e-mail attachments. However, anyone with a bit of computer savvy can access an e-mail message and, with the proper software, view sensitive communications. When you use Acrobat Password Security, you can assign to a document a password that must be entered to open the document. When a user tries to open a password-protected document, Acrobat prompts the user for a password. The document can only be opened with the proper password. When you password-protect a document, you can assign permissions to the document to restrict what changes the user can perform to the document after accessing it with the correct password. For example, you can specify whether a viewer with Acrobat can edit the document. To limit access to a document by using Acrobat Password Security, follow these steps:

1. Click Tools, click Protection, and then choose | Encrypt | Encrypt With Password. After you choose the command, Acrobat displays the Applying New

Security Settings dialog box, which asks you if you're sure you want to change the security of the document.

Tip Click the Do Not Show This Message Again check box to prevent the Applying New Security Settings dialog box from appearing in the future.

2. Click Yes to display the Password Security – Settings dialog box.

Password Security - Settings

Compatibility: [Acrobat 7.0 and later ▾]

Encryption Level: 128-bit AES

Select Document Components to Encrypt
- ⦿ Encrypt all document contents
- ○ Encrypt all document contents except metadata (Acrobat 6 and later compatible)
- ○ Encrypt only file attachments (Acrobat 7 and later compatible)
- ⓘ All contents of the document will be encrypted and search engines will not be able to access the document's metadata.

☐ Require a password to open the document

Document Open Password: [   ] [▮▮▮▮▮] Not Rated

ⓘ No password will be required to open this document.

Permissions

☐ Restrict editing and printing of the document. A password will be required in order to change these permission settings.

Change Permissions Password: [   ] [▮▮▮▮▮] Not Rated

Printing Allowed: [High Resolution ▾]

Changes Allowed: [Any except extracting pages ▾]

☑ Enable copying of text, images, and other content

☑ Enable text access for screen reader devices for the visually impaired

[Help] [OK] [Cancel]

3. Click the Compatibility drop-down arrow and choose one of the following: Acrobat 3.0 And Later, Acrobat 5.0 And Later, Acrobat 6.0 And Later, Acrobat 7.0 And Later, or Acrobat X.0 And Later. Choosing 6.0, 7.0, or X.0 gives you the best security, but the document will be available only to users with Adobe Reader 6.0 and later, Adobe Reader 7.0 and later, or Adobe Reader X.0 and later.

4. Select the desired option in the Select Document Components To Encrypt section.

Note If you choose compatibility for Acrobat 5.0 and later, or an earlier version, your only option is to encrypt all document components, which means the document metadata will be unavailable to search engines. If you choose compatibility for Acrobat 6.0 and later, you can encrypt all document components except metadata. If you choose compatibility for Acrobat 7.0 and later, you have the additional option to encrypt only file attachments to the document.

5. To assign a password to the document, check the Require A Password To Open The Document box. The Document Open Password field then becomes available.

If you encrypt document attachments, Require A Password To Open File Attachments is selected by default.

6. In the Document Open Password field, enter the password that will be required to open the document. If you choose to encrypt only file attachments, this field is listed as File Attachment Open Password. As you type each letter of the password, an asterisk appears to prevent prying eyes from seeing the password you enter. Make sure you take advantage of the new password rating feature and create a password that rates Strong or Best to ensure maximum security.

7. To restrict document printing and editing, click the Restrict Editing And Printing Of The Document check box. The Change Permissions Password field then becomes active. When you assign a permissions password to a document, a user who enters the proper document-open password can view the document, but cannot change the document-open password and can only perform the tasks allowed by the permissions settings. If the viewer enters the proper password in the Change Permissions Password field, they can change the document password as well as the permissions allowed to future viewers of the document.

8. In the Change Permissions Password field, enter the password that must be entered to change document passwords or permissions. As you enter text in the Permissions Password field, each letter appears as an asterisk. The document-open password and permissions password must be unique. For security reasons, a good idea is to use dissimilar passwords.

Tip To prevent being locked out of a document you created, consider copying your document passwords in a safe place—for example, your PDA, if you use one. If you frequently secure documents, consider creating a spreadsheet that lists documents with fields for date, title, and password. Refer to the spreadsheet to quickly locate the password of a document based on its title or the date it was created.

9. Click the Printing Allowed drop-down arrow and choose an option. Your choices vary depending on the compatibility option you choose in step 4. If you choose Acrobat 5.0 And Later, your options are None, Low Resolution (150 DPI), and High Resolution. If you choose Low Resolution and a document viewer chooses Acrobat Distiller as the printing device, the resulting PDF file is also printed at low resolution, which prevents the user from pirating a high-resolution copy of the document.

10. Click the Changes Allowed drop-down arrow and choose an option. If you chose Acrobat 5.0 And Later, choose one of the following options:
    - **None**   Viewers cannot make any changes to the document.
    - **Inserting, Deleting, And Rotating Pages**   Viewers can only insert, delete, and rotate pages.
    - **Filling In Form Fields And Signing Existing Signature Fields**   Viewers can fill in form fields and sign signature fields, but they cannot create them.

- **Commenting, Filling In Form Fields, And Signing Existing Signature Fields**   Viewers can add comments to the document and fill in and sign the document, but they cannot create or otherwise alter form fields.
- **Any Except Extracting Of Pages**   Viewers have full access to the document with the exception of extracting pages, within the limits of the version of Acrobat or Adobe Reader being used to view the document.

11. Click the Enable Copying Of Text, Images, And Other Content check box to allow Acrobat users to use the applicable tools to copy content to the clipboard for use in other PDF documents or applications.

12. Check the Enable Text Access For Screen Reader Devices For The Visually Impaired box to allow the visually impaired to read the document with their screen readers. They will be unable to copy or extract objects from the document.

13. Click OK to set document security. If you password-protected the opening of the document, the Confirm Document Open Password dialog box appears.

14. Confirm the document password and click OK. Acrobat displays a warning dialog box, telling you the viewers using third-party products to view the document may be able to circumvent the security you apply.

To prevent this warning about third-party security products from appearing in the future, click the Do Not Show This Message Again check box.

15. Click OK to exit the warning dialog box. If you assigned a permissions password to the document as well, the Confirm Permissions Password dialog box appears again, prompting you to confirm the permissions password.

16. Confirm the permissions password and click OK.

17. Choose File | Save. When the document opens again, the security measures you selected are assigned to the document.

If changes in your organization prompt a change in document security permissions settings, you can easily change them by opening the document whose security permissions settings you need to change and then clicking Tools, clicking Protection, choosing More Protection, and then choosing Security Properties. Click the Change Settings button. After correctly entering the document permissions password, you can change the security settings, as outlined in this section.

Use Acrobat Certificate Security

When you use Acrobat Certificate Security, you have complete control over who is permitted to open the document and who is permitted to edit the document. You can assign varying degrees of permission as well, which is useful if you create a document to be distributed in a corporate environment.

You can allow some team members to have complete access to the document and allow other team members to have varying degrees of access. For example, if the document needs to be available to a recent hire, you can disable that person's access to edit, print, and extract elements from the document. When you assign Acrobat Certificate Security, you choose the users who can have access to the document from your list of trusted identities.

Build a List of Trusted Identities

Before you can assign Acrobat Certificate Security to a document, you need to build a list of trusted identities. Trusted identities are Acrobat users who have sent you their certificates. When users create a digital ID, they have the option to export to a file the certificate associated with their digital ID. You can exchange certificates with other members of your team via e-mail, as discussed in the following section.

Exchange Certificates

The first step in building a list of trusted identities is to exchange certificates. You can import certificates received from other team members, or you can request a certificate from a recipient via e-mail. To exchange certificates via e-mail, follow these steps:

1. Click Tools, click Sign & Certify, and then choose More Sign & Certify | Manage Trusted Identities to access the Manage Trusted Identities dialog box.
2. Click the Display drop-down arrow and choose Certificates to display a list of your trusted identities, as shown here.

3. Click Request Contact to display the Email A Request dialog box.
4. Enter your name in the My Name field and your e-mail address in My Email Address field, similar to what is shown on the next page.
5. If desired, enter information in the My Contact Information field. For example, you may want to enter a phone number that recipients can use to verify your certificate.

6. Click Next to display the Selecting Digital IDs To Export dialog box, which contains a list of your digital IDs.

7. Accept the default option to include your certificate with the request. This option sends your certificate as an e-mail attachment. Your recipient can add your certificate to his or her list of trusted identities by double-clicking the attachment and following the prompts.

8. Accept the default option (Email Request) or click the Save Request As A File radio button to save the digital ID to a folder on your hard drive.

9. Click Next to open the Selecting Digital IDs To Export dialog box.

10. Select the digital ID you want to export and then click Select to display the Compose Email dialog box. Note that you can select only one digital ID to export.

11. After Acrobat opens the Compose Email dialog box, do the following:
    - Enter the recipient's e-mail address in the To field.
    - Accept the default Subject message or delete the message and enter your own. Note that you can modify the subject title as well as the body of the message.

12. Log on to the Internet, click the Email button, and Acrobat launches your default e-mail application with the recipient's e-mail address filled in along with the subject and message. Use your e-mail application's Send command to send the message and certificate. When the recipient opens your e-mail, the certificate appears as an attachment.

After you click the Email button, your certificate is sent to the recipient as an e-mail attachment. Your e-mail recipient can add your certificate by double-clicking the file attachment, which launches Acrobat and displays the Data Exchange File – Import Contact dialog box, shown next. Note that a certificate comprises two components: a public key and a private key. The public key can be viewed by someone who intercepts a certificate you send via e-mail, but the private key is invisible and cannot be reverse-engineered (RE).

Recipients can add your certificate to their trusted identities list by clicking the Set Contact Trust button, which opens the Import Contact Settings dialog box. Recipients can select the options for which the certificate will be trusted and then click OK to add the certificate to your trusted identities list. If you requested a return certificate, the user can send it by clicking the Email Your Certificate button.

Data Exchange File - Import Contact

You have opened an Acrobat FDF Data Exchange File containing the following data:

Contact Information

Sender

Name: Doug Sahlin

Email Address:

Add Certificate to List of Trusted Identities

This file contains Contact information for Doug Sahlin. Click Set Contact Trust to set options on how to include this Contact in your list of trusted identities. Contact information includes certificates that, once trusted, can be used to validate signatures from and encrypt documents for the associated Contact.

Set Contact Trust...

Close

Import a Certificate

After exchanging certificates, your next step in building your list of trusted identities is importing the certificate. E-mail is an efficient way to exchange certificates. The files are small and can be sent quickly with even the slowest Internet connection. However, you may receive certificates on floppy disk or other media. When you receive a certificate in this manner, you can import it. To import a certificate into your list of trusted identities, follow these steps:

1. Click Tools, click Sign & Certify, and then choose More Sign & Certify | Manage Trusted Identities to open the Manage Trusted Identities dialog box.
2. Click the Display drop-down arrow and choose Certificates.
3. Click Add Contacts to open the Choose Contacts To Import dialog box.
4. Click Browse to open the Locate Certificate File dialog box, navigate to the folder where the certificate you want to add to the list is stored, select it, and then click Open.
5. Click Import to add the issuer of the digital ID to your list of contacts. Note that you can only import one certificate at a time. Repeat steps 3 through 5 to import additional contacts.
6. Click OK to exit the Select Contacts To Add dialog box.
7. Click Close to exit the Manage Trusted Identities dialog box. Acrobat adds the certificate to your list of trusted identities and to your contacts list, if you performed step 6.

Tip After importing a contact into your trusted certificates list, select the contact and then click Edit Trust to select the options for which the certificate will be trusted.

Add Certificate Security to a Document

After the members of your team are added to your list of trusted identities, you can begin to secure your documents with Acrobat Certificate Security. When you set up Certificate

Security, you don't have to enter passwords. Each team member's password information is stored with their own certificate. Document recipients will have access to the document after they log in with the digital ID whose certificate you chose from your list of trusted identities. All you need to do is determine which members of your list of trusted identities have access to the document and which level of permissions each team member will have. You then create a list of recipients who will have the same privileges and then add security. To add Acrobat Certificate Security to a document, follow these steps:

1. Click Tools, click Protection, and then choose Encrypt | Encrypt With Certificate. Acrobat displays a warning dialog box asking if you want to change security on the document.

Tip   Click the Do Not Show This Message Again check box to prevent this dialog box from being displayed in the future.

2. Click Yes to exit the warning dialog box. Acrobat displays the Certificate Security Settings dialog box, shown next.
3. In the Select Document Components to Encrypt section, choose one of the following options:
   - Encrypt All Document Contents

- Encrypt All Document Contents Except Metadata (Acrobat 6 And Later Compatible)
- Encrypt Only File Attachments (Acrobat 7 And Later Compatible)

4. Choose an option from the Encryption Algorithm drop-down menu. Your choices are 128-bit RC4 (Compatible With Acrobat 6.0 And Later), 128-bit AES (Compatible With Acrobat 7.0 And Later), and 256-bit AES (Compatible With Acrobat 9.0 And Later). The last option offers the greatest security. Make sure you choose an option that is compatible with the version of Acrobat or the Adobe Reader your intended recipients use.

5. Click Next.

Note If you have more than one digital ID, the Document Security-Digital ID Selection dialog box appears, which enables you to select the digital ID with which you want to certify the document. If this is the case, choose the desired Digital ID and click OK to access the Search For Recipients dialog box.

6. Click Search to open the Search For Recipients dialog box. From within this dialog box, you can search for recipients by entering contact information in the Search area and then clicking the Search button. This method returns recipients from your e-mail address book and other locations that have valid digital IDs. You can choose recipients from the Search Results field. However, if you've already gone to the trouble of importing certificates as trusted identities, go to step 7.

7. Deselect the Search All Directories check box, click the Directories drop-down arrow, and then choose Trusted Identities from the drop-down list to display the recipients on your Trusted Identities list, as shown here.

8. Choose the desired recipients from the Search Results field and then click OK. The recipients are added to the Certificate Security Settings dialog box.

9. Select one or more recipients and then click Permissions. Acrobat displays the Acrobat Security dialog box, informing you that viewers using third-party products to view the document may be able to bypass the security.

Tip Click the Do Not Show This Message Again check box to prevent the dialog box from appearing in the future.

10. Click OK to reveal the Permissions Settings dialog box. By default, no restrictions are applied.
11. Choose an option from the Printing Allowed and Changes Allowed drop-down menus. These are the same options discussed earlier in the section "Use Acrobat Security."
12. Click the Enable Copying Of Text, Images, And Other Content check box to allow this permission to the selected recipient(s). By default, the option to enable text access for screen readers is enabled. Click the check box to disallow this permission for the selected recipient(s).
13. Click OK to apply the permissions to the selected recipient(s). The Permissions section of the dialog box updates to show the permissions you granted to the selected recipient(s).
14. Repeat steps 6 through 9 for the other recipients on your list. Remember, you can assign different permissions for each user, which is what makes Acrobat Certificate Security such a powerful tool.
15. Click Next. Acrobat displays a summary telling you the details of the encryption you've applied to the document.
16. Click Finish. Acrobat displays a dialog box telling you the settings will not be applied until you save the document.

Create a Security Envelope

If you have confidential files such as Word documents or Excel spreadsheets that you want to send as editable documents to colleagues, you can send them via e-mail. But if a third party intercepts the e-mail, they'll be able to open the documents using the associated application. To prevent this, you can employ the Secure Envelope feature in Acrobat. When you create a security envelope, you use a secure PDF document as the envelope for the editable documents, which you also encrypt. Follow these steps to create a security envelope:

1. Click Tools, click Protection, and then choose More Protection | Create Security Envelope to display the Create Security Envelope dialog box. Any documents currently open appear in the dialog box, as shown next. To add additional files to the security envelope, click the Add File To Send button, which reveals the Files To Enclose section of the Create Security Envelope dialog box.
2. Select the files you want to enclose in the security envelope and then click Open.
3. Click Next to reveal the Envelope Template section of the Create Security Envelope dialog box. This section lists the default Acrobat security envelope templates. You can substitute an envelope of your own design, which has been saved as a PDF document, by clicking the Browse button and then selecting the desired PDF document.
4. After choosing a template, click Next to reveal the Delivery Method section of the Create Security Envelope dialog box.

5. Choose the method of delivery. Your options are to send the envelope later, in which case the completed envelope is saved to your hard drive, or to send the envelope now, in which case you're prompted for a list of recipients to whom you'll e-mail the envelope.

6. Click Next to display the Security Policy section of the dialog box. At this stage of the process, you can click the New Policy button to create a new policy, or click the Show All Policies check box to show all security policies associated with Acrobat, as shown next. The default Certificate Encrypt and Password Encrypt methods of security aren't recommended for PDF documents with attached files, however. If you don't have a security policy that encrypts document attachments, your best bet is to create a new policy. If you already have a security policy that encrypts file attachments, go to step 15.

7. Click the New Policy button to reveal the first page of the New Security Policy dialog box, shown next.

8. Choose the Use Passwords option. The reason for choosing this option for the new policy is because file attachments can be encrypted when Acrobat 7.0 and later compatibility has been specified.
9. Click Next to reveal the General Settings section of the dialog box.
10. Enter the desired information in the Policy Name and Description fields. You can also choose to save passwords with the policy, which is the default option.
11. Click Next to reveal the Document Restrictions section of the dialog box. The options in this dialog box are identical to those found in the Password Security – Settings dialog box, previously discussed in the section "Use Acrobat Password Security." When you're choosing settings, make sure you choose Acrobat 7.0 And Later Compatibility, which encrypts the document as well as the attachments. Use the Acrobat password rater to create a password with a rating of Strong or Best.
12. After completing the Document Restrictions section of the dialog box, click Next. At this stage, you're prompted to confirm your passwords.

13. Confirm the password(s) and then click OK to reveal the Summary section of the New Security Policy dialog box, which lists the details of the new policy. At this stage, you can click the Back button to navigate to a previous section and change settings.

14. If the details on the Summary page are acceptable, click Finish to return to the Create Security Envelope dialog box. Your new policy is shown on the list.

15. Select the desired policy and then click Next to reveal the Identity section of the Create Security Envelope dialog box. By default, Acrobat lists your name, title, and the name of your organization as entered when you installed Acrobat on your computer. If desired, you can also enter your organization unit and e-mail address. If you use the same identity information for each security envelope you create, click Do Not Show Again. Acrobat stores your identity information and uses it on all security envelopes you create in the future.

16. Click Next to reveal the summary, which shows the files included with the security envelope and the template that will be used.

17. Click Finish. What happens next depends on the method of delivery you choose. If you choose to send the envelope now, your default e-mail application opens and you're prompted for recipients to whom you want to send the envelope. Otherwise, you're prompted to save the envelope.

Summary

In this chapter, you learned how to remove sensitive content from a document, add your digital signature to a document, add signature fields to a document, and verify other colleagues' digital signatures. Certifying a document was another topic of discussion. You also discovered how to restrict a document by adding password security or certificate security to it. The final topic of discussion showed you how to create a security envelope in which you could enclose files for distribution to colleagues. In the next chapter, you will learn how to optimize PDF documents for specific destinations.

11

Optimize PDF Documents

HOW TO...

- Optimize documents for the visually impaired
- Optimize documents for print
- Optimize documents for CD/DVD applications
- Optimize documents for the Web
- Customize Distiller conversion settings

When you create a PDF document using Acrobat Distiller or PDFMaker, you can optimize it for a specific destination or for several destinations by choosing the proper conversion settings. If you create a document in an authoring application and (if available) use the PDF export feature of the application, or use Adobe PDF to print the file as a PDF document, you can modify the output settings for an intended destination by changing Adobe PDF Settings in the Adobe PDF Document Properties dialog box. When you change Adobe PDF Settings, you can specify how Adobe PDF compresses the images in your document and how it adjusts color settings for the intended destination of the document. You can also specify whether fonts are embedded.

Previous chapters covered how to use preset Adobe PDF Settings when converting documents into PDF format. In this chapter, you find out how to fine-tune Adobe PDF Settings to suit the intended destination of the document. Fonts are an important consideration when you create a PDF document, so this chapter discusses font issues as well as when it's necessary to embed fonts. You learn specific strategies for optimizing your documents for an intended destination. You also see how to create a document that can be reflowed for easier reading in devices with different monitor sizes, and how to modify a document for the visually impaired. Finally, you find out how to fine-tune document graphics for the intended destination of the PDF.

About Tagged Documents

When you create a document that will be distributed to users who view the document on screen readers or other devices with a limited viewing area, you can create a tagged document that can be reflowed to any window or screen size. When a user reflows a tagged document, the font size remains unchanged, so it's legible even on a smaller viewing device. Images, however, are reduced in size to accommodate the reduced viewing area. If your tagged PDF document will be viewed on devices such as a handheld PDA (personal digital assistant) or some of the smaller e-book readers, viewers with Adobe Reader or Acrobat can reflow the document to fit the smaller viewing area.

You can create a tagged PDF in several key ways:

- Create using Acrobat PDFMaker
- Create manually
- Create by converting already structured content, such as HTML or XML

Create a Tagged Document

You can create a tagged document by converting web pages to PDF format or by creating a document within a Microsoft Office application and then using Acrobat PDFMaker to convert the document to PDF. To create a tagged document from a Microsoft Office application, you modify the Application Settings option in the Settings section of the Acrobat PDFMaker dialog box, as detailed in the upcoming section "Customize Acrobat Distiller Conversion Settings."

To create a tagged document from web pages and HTML documents, follow these steps:

1. Choose File | Create | PDF From Web Page. Alternatively, you can click Create and then choose PDF From Web Page.
2. In the URL field, enter the URL of the page you want to convert to a tagged document. Remember, you can also capture an HTML document located on your computer by entering the relative path to the file.
3. Click the Settings button to open the Web Page Conversion Settings dialog box.
4. In the PDF Settings section, click the Create PDF Tags check box and then click OK to close the dialog box.
5. Click Create. Acrobat captures the web page with PDF tags. For more information on converting web pages to PDF documents, refer to Chapter 5.

Reflow a Tagged Document

The recipients of a tagged document can reflow the document to fit the viewing area of the device they use to view the document. Tagged PDF files are optimized for accessibility, making them available to viewers using screen-reader devices. To reflow a document with Acrobat or Adobe Reader, choose View | Zoom | Reflow.

Optimize Documents for the Visually Impaired

When you create a document that will be viewed by visually impaired people using onscreen readers, a different challenge presents itself to you—the document will be viewed at varying degrees of magnification. Creating a tagged document eliminates the problem of reflowing the document, but the issue of images in the document still exists. When a document is greatly magnified, only a portion of the image will be rendered. To offset this difficulty, you must provide a way for visually impaired readers to identify what the image is. To accomplish this, provide alternate text for tagged, nontext elements in the document by using the Tags panel.

Use the Tags Panel

You use the Tags panel to view the logical order of a tagged document. To open the Tags panel, choose View | Show/Hide | Navigation Panes | Tags. When you open the Tags panel, you see the logical structure of the document, which is a visual representation of the organization of the document elements. Elements are objects, such as a block of text, an image, a document page, and so on. You can use the Tags panel to modify tags in a document. For example, many onscreen readers can take advantage of alternate text for a tagged element. The alternate text gives the visually impaired person a description of the element. You can also use tag information to specify the text language of the document. Some tags in the Tags panel shown in the illustration here have been expanded. When you initially open the Tags panel, tags have a plus sign (+) to their left, indicating other tags are nested within. Click each plus sign to expand the tag. If the document isn't tagged, No Tags Available displays at the top of the panel.

Tip If you open the Tags panel and see No Tags Available, you can add tags by choosing New Tag from the Tags panel Options menu.

If you create a tagged document with images to be viewed with onscreen reading devices that have limited graphics capabilities, you can add an alternate tag that describes what the image shows. To add an alternate text tag to a nontext element, follow these steps:

1. Open the Tags panel (View | Show/Hide | Navigation Panes | Tags).
2. Select the tag that denotes the image in the PDF document. If you have a hard time determining which tag is associated with which element in the text, click the Options icon in the upper-left corner of the panel and choose Highlight Content. When you enable this option, Acrobat highlights the element in the document when you select the corresponding tag. Also note that graphic elements have different icons in the Tags panel.
3. Click the Options icon and choose Properties to open the TouchUp Properties dialog box. Alternatively, you can right-click the desired tag in the Tags panel and then choose Properties from the context menu.
4. To add alternate text to an image tag, in the Alternate Text field, enter a description of the image. For example, if the image depicts El Capitan in Yosemite National Park, you might enter the following: **This image is a photograph of El Capitan in Yosemite National Park.**
5. Click Close to assign the alternate text to the tag. Alternate text is displayed in a screen reader.

Optimize Documents for Your Local Printer

When you create a PDF document for print, you modify the Press Quality or High Quality Print Adobe PDF conversion settings (in either Acrobat Distiller or when using the PDFMaker in a Microsoft Office application) to match the intended output device. If the document is to be printed by a service center, check with the service center technicians to get the necessary information about the printing device with which your documents will be printed. This is the information you need to modify conversion settings—in particular, when you're modifying the Color and Advanced settings of either the Press Quality conversion settings or, if the document contains high-resolution images, the High Quality Print conversion settings. You should also pay careful attention to image resolution. If the document is for print only and file size isn't a concern, you can choose Maximum for the Image Quality settings in the Images section of the Adobe PDF Settings dialog box to maintain maximum image quality. If you create documents that will be printed by a service center or on a printer attached to a different computer, embed all fonts to ensure the document prints properly.

The default resolution of 2400 dpi (dots per inch) is fine for most commercial printing devices; however, it's higher than needed for most laser and inkjet printers. You can change the resolution setting to match your laser or inkjet printer in the General section of the Press Quality – Adobe PDF Settings dialog box or the High Quality Print – Adobe PDF Settings dialog box. Modifying conversion settings is discussed in detail in the section "Customize Acrobat Distiller Conversion Settings." Alternatively, you can also choose the Press Quality conversion settings as the basis for documents you print in-house on laser or inkjet printers. If you're optimizing documents for a commercial printer, you use one of the PDF-X conversion settings. Optimizing PDF documents for commercial printers is covered in detail in Chapter 14.

Optimize Documents for CD/DVD Applications

When you optimize a document for a CD/DVD application, use the Standard conversion settings as a starting point. This option has compression settings with higher resolutions than those generally needed for screen viewing, but when you create a CD/DVD, file size is generally not an issue. If you choose the High option in the Image Quality drop-down lists in the Images section of the Adobe PDF Settings dialog box, the document images will have low compression and your viewers will be able to zoom in on document images with little or no loss in quality. In fact, you may want to use the Maximum Image Quality setting and disable downsampling if your CD/DVD presentation has many intricate images, such as maps that will be examined at higher magnification settings, and the required files will fit on the CD/DVD with high-image resolution settings.

Optimize Documents for the Web

When you optimize documents for viewing on the Web, begin with the Smallest File Size conversion settings. The default settings resample document images to 100 pixels per inch (PPI). The resulting file is a compromise between file size and image quality. Experiment with the Low and Minimum settings in the Image Quality drop-down list box. These settings will result in images of lower quality because of the higher compression applied. If the images in the original document were high quality, you may be able to produce an acceptable document using the Low or Minimum image-quality settings.

You can create a document using the default Smallest File Size conversion settings (Low image quality) and then create another document using the Smallest File Size conversion settings with Minimum image quality settings. Compare the two documents in Acrobat, arranged in tile format. Increase the magnification level of each document to 100 percent or greater, and you will be able to see the difference in image quality between the different compression settings.

By default, documents created with the Smallest File Size conversion settings are optimized for byteserving (sending a document to a web browser a page at a time) over the Web if the web-hosting service supports byteserving.

Customize Acrobat Distiller Conversion Settings

When you create a document for a specific destination using Acrobat Distiller or Adobe PDFMaker, you can use one of the preset Adobe PDF conversion settings to convert the file. You can also customize any of the preset conversion settings by modifying the parameters to suit your needs. To modify an Adobe PDF conversion setting, you begin with a preset that closely suits your needs, apply the needed changes, and then save the Adobe PDF conversion setting with a different filename. After you save a modified Adobe PDF Setting, the new setting appears on the Default Settings drop-down menu in Acrobat Distiller, and on the Conversion Settings menu of the Acrobat PDFMaker dialog box, which you access from the Adobe PDF menu in Microsoft Office applications (except on Macintosh computers).

Each Adobe PDF Settings dialog box is composed of six sections in Acrobat X Pro. You can modify as many or as few sections as needed to create the optimal conversion for your document(s). To create a custom-conversion setting in Acrobat Distiller, follow these steps:

1. In the Adobe PDF Settings area, click the Default Settings drop-down arrow and choose a conversion setting from the drop-down menu. Choose a conversion setting that closely matches the intended destination of the document. For example, if you're customizing settings for documents that will be viewed on a website, choose Smallest File Size.
2. Choose Settings | Edit Adobe PDF Settings to open the Adobe PDF Settings dialog box, shown in Figure 11-1. Note that the dialog box shown in Figure 11-1 is for the Standard – Adobe PDF Settings as viewed in Acrobat Distiller. The title of the dialog box changes, depending on the conversion setting you're modifying. For example, if you modify Press Quality Adobe PDF Settings, the dialog box title reads Press Quality – Adobe PDF Settings.

You can also modify Adobe PDF Settings from within a Microsoft Office application. When you modify a conversion setting from within a Microsoft Office application, you're modifying an Adobe PDF Settings job option. Adobe PDF Settings

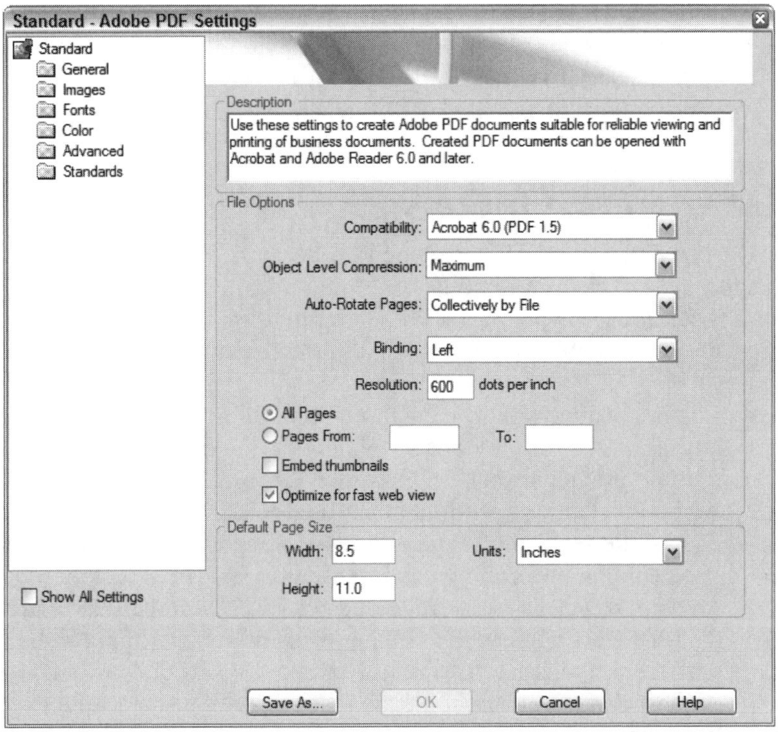

FIGURE 11-1   You can customize Adobe PDF Settings to suit the documents you convert to PDF.

created in Acrobat Distiller can be used to convert a document to PDF in a Microsoft Office application. You have access to the same settings in Acrobat Distiller. To modify an Adobe PDF Settings option from within a Windows Microsoft Office application, follow these steps:

1. Click the Acrobat tab on the Ribbon and choose Preferences.
2. Click the Conversion Settings drop-down arrow and choose a conversion setting to modify.
3. Click the Advanced Settings button to open the Adobe PDF Settings dialog box, previously shown in Figure 11-1.

After you open the Adobe PDF Settings dialog box, modify the conversion settings by making changes in each section. To access the settings in each section, click the section folder. The following sections of this chapter discuss the conversion settings you can modify in each section of the Adobe PDF Settings dialog box.

Note   Acrobat Distiller defaults to the last conversion setting used. Before converting a document to PDF with Acrobat Distiller, using Adobe PDF as a printing device, or using PDFMaker in a Microsoft Office application, choose the desired PDF Setting from the Change Conversion Settings menu (PDFMaker), the Default Settings drop-down list (Acrobat Distiller), or the Default Settings drop-down list in the Adobe PDF Document Properties dialog box when using Adobe PDF as a printer. Your document will be created with the new conversion settings.

Set General Options

In the General section of the Adobe PDF Settings dialog box, you determine which version of Acrobat is compatible with the published document. Also, you can optimize the file for fast Web viewing, set the document resolution for printing, and set the page size of the published document. To set General job options, follow these steps:

1. Choose a conversion setting to modify and open the Adobe PDF Settings dialog box, as discussed previously. By default, the dialog box opens to the General section, previously shown in Figure 11-1.
2. In the File Options section, click the Compatibility drop-down arrow and choose the version of Acrobat with which you want the published document to be compatible. You can choose Acrobat 3.0 (PDF 1.2), Acrobat 4.0 (PDF 1.3), Acrobat 5.0 (PDF 1.4), Acrobat 6.0 (PDF 1.5), Acrobat 7.0 (PDF 1.6), or Acrobat 8.0 (PDF 1.7). Choose the version of Acrobat that supports the features in the document you created. Remember, take into account which version of Acrobat, Acrobat Reader, or Adobe Reader the majority of your target audience is likely to have installed on their computers. If a PDF is created with a version of Acrobat that is newer than a viewer's Acrobat Reader or Adobe Reader, a dialog box to that effect appears. When a PDF version higher than the viewer's reader is opened, some of the features authored into the document might not work.
3. After you choose the version of Acrobat with which documents created with this conversion setting will be compatible, you can modify the following settings:
   - **Object Level Compression** Choose Off, Tags Only, or Maximum. The latter option applies maximum compression to all objects in the document.
   - **Auto-Rotate Pages** Choose this option to have Acrobat automatically rotate document pages when the page should be rotated for viewing without scrolling. You can choose Off, in which case Acrobat won't rotate pages, Collectively By File, or Individually, to rotate all pages based on the orientation of the majority of pages within the document.
   - **Binding** Choose either Left or Right binding to determine how Acrobat displays the document in Continuous-Facing viewing mode, and how thumbnails are displayed when the thumbnails are resized so they can be viewed side by side. Thumbnails are arranged from left to right when you choose Left binding, and right to left when you choose Right binding.
   - **Resolution** Enter a value that matches the resolution of the device on which the document will be printed. When you create a PDF file with Acrobat Distiller or Acrobat Distiller in the guise of Adobe PDF, the device is printing a PostScript file for display in PDF format. The value you enter for Resolution emulates the resolution setting of a printing device. If you specify a higher

resolution, recipients of your document can print the file on a high-resolution device, but the file size will be larger.

- **All Pages**   This default option converts all pages in the document to PDF.
- **Pages From [ ] To [ ]**   Choose this option to specify a range of pages to convert to PDF by entering the first page to convert in the Pages From field and the last page to convert in the To field.
- **Embed Thumbnails**   Choose this option to have Acrobat Distiller embed a thumbnail for each page of documents converted to PDF with this conversion setting. Remember, this increases the file size of the published document. If you choose not to select this option, Acrobat automatically generates thumbnails on the fly when the document viewer opens the Thumbnails panel. If, however, you're creating large PDF documents with hundreds of pages, you may want to consider embedding thumbnails because generating hundreds of thumbnails every time the Pages panel is open can severely tax the system resources of the computer used to view the document.
- **Optimize For Fast Web View**   Choose this option if you create a document to view on the Web. When you choose this option, Acrobat converts documents created with this job option for page-at-a-time downloading (byteserving) from the host web server.

4. In the Default Page Size section, enter values in the Width and Height fields and then choose a unit of measure from the Units drop-down menu. The settings you enter here determine the dimensions of the files Acrobat creates with this conversion setting. Enter dimensions that match those of documents you create in the authoring application, which you use as the basis for PDF files created with this conversion setting. Remember, if you use Adobe PDF as a printing device to convert a Microsoft Office file to PDF format, you must configure Adobe PDF to match the page dimensions specified in the Conversion Settings setting. Otherwise, Adobe PDF (which is using Acrobat Distiller to print the PDF file) reverts to the default dimensions for Acrobat Distiller. For more information on configuring Acrobat Distiller page size, refer to Chapter 4.

After you modify the General settings of an Adobe PDF conversion setting, you can click a folder to modify other settings or save the modified conversion setting, as described in the later section "Save Conversion Settings."

Set Conversion Settings Images Options

When you choose a specific conversion settings option to create a PDF document, Acrobat compresses the document text, line art, and images using settings deemed optimal for the conversion setting. You can, however, modify the compression settings to suit documents you create for specific applications. You can modify the settings to reduce file size by applying more compression to images, or enhance the quality of the published document by specifying a higher quality for document images. With a bit of experimentation, you can modify compression settings for optimal file size while still maintaining a high level of detail in the published document.

Acrobat Distiller Compression Methods

The compression method you choose greatly affects the overall quality of the images in your published document. When you modify compression settings, you can have Acrobat Distiller automatically choose the compression method deemed right for the images in the document, or you can choose one of the following Acrobat Distiller compression methods:

- **ZIP**   Use the ZIP (Adobe's variation of the ZIP filter, as derived from the zlib package of Jean-loup Gailly and Mark Adler) method of compression for images with large areas of solid color, such as GIF images. This method of compression works well with simple images created in painting applications, such as Windows Paintbrush and Corel Painter, and artwork created in vector-based drawing programs, such as Adobe Illustrator and CorelDRAW. You can use ZIP compression with 4-bit and 8-bit color depth. If you choose 4-bit color depth on an 8-bit image, you end up with a smaller file size but degraded image quality because you lose data when the image is compressed.

- **JPEG**   Use the Joint Photographic Experts Group (JPEG) method of compression on full-color or grayscale images, such as photographs. When you use JPEG compression, you can control the size of the file by telling Acrobat how much compression to apply to the images. You can modify the settings to create a PDF document with high-quality images at the expense of a larger file size, or you can apply a higher level of compression and your published PDF file will be smaller, but the images won't be as detailed due to the data lost during compression. JPEG compression is also known as *lossy* compression, because data is lost when the document images are compressed. JPEG has compression options from Minimum to Maximum. JPEG compression is best suited for photographs. If you have images with large areas of solid color, such as GIF images, in your document, use ZIP compression.

- **Automatic (JPEG)**   When you choose this option, Acrobat determines the best settings to achieve the highest image quality using the JPEG compression method.

- **JPEG 2000**   This option is available if you choose Acrobat 6.0 (PDF 1.5) or later for compatibility. JPEG 2000 is the new international standard for attaining high-quality images through superior compression and packaging. JPEG 2000 has six compression settings, from Minimum to Lossless.

- **Automatic JPEG 2000**   This option is available if you choose Acrobat 6.0 (PDF 1.5) or later for compatibility. When you choose this option, Acrobat determines the optimum compression settings using the JPEG 2000 compression method.

- **CCITT**   Use the International Consultative Committee for International Telephone & Telegraph (CCITT) method of compression for 1-bit black-and-white images, such as faxes. When you use the CCITT method of compression, no data is lost. Use the CCITT Group 4 method for general-purpose compression of monochrome images. Use the CCITT Group 3 method for faxed documents.

- **Run Length**   Use this option when your document contains images with large areas of solid black or white. Run Length is a lossless compression method.

Acrobat Distiller Resampling

When Acrobat Distiller compresses images, it also resamples them. When you use software to resample an image, pixels are either added or removed from the image to change the resolution in pixels per inch (PPI) at which the image is displayed. When pixels are added to an image to increase resolution, image degradation generally occurs because you're asking the software to interpolate between neighboring pixels to create new pixels. Starting with a high-resolution image is always best, and then downsample it to the desired resolution when converting it to PDF. You can specify one of the following interpolation methods to resample images. These settings are found in the Downsample drop-down lists in the Color Images, Grayscale Images, and Monochrome Images sections of the Images section of the conversion setting you're modifying:

- **Off** Acrobat Distiller doesn't interpolate when the image is downsampled. This option is applicable only when the document contains high-resolution images and you've selected High or Maximum for the Image Quality setting.
- **Average Downsampling** Acrobat Distiller creates new pixels at the specified resolution using the average color of neighboring pixels within a given area.
- **Bicubic Downsampling** Acrobat Distiller creates new pixels at the specified resolution using a weighted average to determine pixel color. In other words, the resulting color is weighted toward the dominant color in each area Acrobat Distiller samples. This is the slowest method, but it gives you the highest quality images.
- **Subsampling** Acrobat Distiller creates new pixels at the specified resolution using the color of a pixel in the center of the sampled area. Because this method of interpolation uses a single pixel to create new pixels, this is the quickest interpolation method, but it can lead to images with harsh transitions between adjacent pixels.

Set Image Compression Settings

Each Adobe PDF Settings option has a specific set of compression options that you can modify for documents you create. You modify compression settings to determine the quality of the text, line art, and images in the published PDF document. To modify image compression settings for an Adobe PDF conversion setting, follow these steps:

1. Choose a Conversion Settings option to modify and open the Adobe PDF Settings dialog box, as discussed previously.
2. Click the Images folder to open the Images section of the Adobe PDF Settings dialog box, shown on the next page.
3. In the Color Images and Grayscale Images sections, click the Downsample drop-down arrow and choose an option.
4. In the Color Images and Grayscale Images sections, click the Compression drop-down arrow and choose a compression method. By default, Acrobat

Distiller compresses images and, based on the selected Adobe PDF job option, automatically chooses the compression option it deems best for the color and grayscale images in the document. You can choose Off to have Acrobat Distiller convert the file to PDF without compressing it.

5. In the Color Images and Grayscale Images sections, to the right of the Downsample field, enter the PPI value to which you want Acrobat Distiller to downsample color and grayscale images. Alternatively, click the spinner buttons to specify the desired resolution.

6. In the Color Images and Grayscale Images sections, enter a value (in PPI) in the For Images Above fields. Alternatively, click the spinner buttons to specify the desired resolution. When you convert a document to PDF using the conversion setting you're editing, Acrobat Distiller downsamples all images above the resolution you enter in this field to the lower output resolution you entered in step 5.

7. In the Color Images and Grayscale Images sections, click the Image Quality drop-down arrow and choose an option. This setting varies, depending on the Adobe PDF Settings job option you're modifying. Choose High or Maximum to create a better-looking document with a larger file size, or choose Minimum or Low to create a PDF document with a smaller file size and less-detailed images.

8. In the Monochrome Images section, click the Downsample drop-down arrow and choose an option.

9. In the field to the right of the Downsample field, enter the pixels per inch value to which you want Acrobat Distiller to downsample monochrome images. Alternatively, click the spinner buttons to specify the desired resolution.
10. In the For Images Above field, enter the value above which you want Acrobat Distiller to downsample images to the value entered in step 9. Alternatively, click the spinner buttons to specify the desired resolution.

 If a PDF document converted with applied downsampling doesn't properly display black-and-white images, modify the Adobe PDF Settings option and choose Off for the Monochrome Images Downsample option.

11. In the Monochrome Images section, click the Compression drop-down arrow and choose an option.
12. Click the Anti-Alias To Gray drop-down arrow (anti-aliasing blends neighboring pixels of different colors to avoid jagged edges) and choose Off (the default option), 2-bit, 4-bit, or 8-bit. This option determines how many levels of gray are used to smooth edges in the image. Choose 8-bit (256 levels of gray) for the best results.
13. Click the Policy button to reveal the Image Policy dialog box. In this box, you specify processing options for images that are less than the specified resolutions. For each color setting, you have the following choices: Ignore, Warn And Continue, and Cancel Job.

After you modify the Images settings of an Adobe PDF conversion setting, you can click a panel to modify other settings or save the modified conversion setting, as described in the section "Save Conversion Settings."

Set Fonts Options

When you want to ensure that a document appears exactly as you created it, you embed the font set with the document. When you embed fonts with a document, the document displays and prints correctly, even if the user's computer doesn't have the document fonts installed. Acrobat Distiller can embed most modern fonts, but certain fonts cannot be embedded due to licensing issues.

Specify which fonts to embed when you convert documents to PDFs by modifying the settings in the Fonts section of the Adobe PDF Settings dialog box, as follows:

1. Choose a conversion settings option to modify and open the Adobe PDF Settings dialog box, as discussed previously in the section "Customize Acrobat Distiller Conversion Settings."
2. Click the Fonts folder to reveal the Fonts section of the Adobe PDF Settings dialog box, shown next.
3. Enable the Embed All Fonts option (selected by default) to embed all fonts used in the document.

4. Enable the Embed All OpenType fonts to embed OpenType fonts that were used in the document. This option is grayed out if the document contains no OpenType fonts.

5. Enable the Subset Embedded Fonts When Percent Of Characters Used Is Less Than [ ] % option and enter a percentage value. When you choose this option, Acrobat Distiller embeds only the characters used to create the document when the percentage of characters used from the font set falls below the value you specify. For example, if you enter a value of 60, Acrobat Distiller embeds only characters used to create the document when less than 60 percent of the font set is used.

6. Click the When Embedding Fails drop-down arrow and choose one of the following: Ignore, Warn And Continue, or Cancel Job.

7. To select a different font list, click the Font Source drop-down arrow and select the desired font folder from the drop-down menu.

8. If you always want to embed a certain font set with documents created using this Conversion Settings option, select the font family or families from the left pane and click the Add button to the left of the Always Embed pane to add the fonts to the Always Embed list.

9. To add a font to the Never Embed list, select the font family from the left pane and click the Add button to the left of the Never Embed pane. To remove a font from the Never Embed list, select the font from the Never Embed list and click the Remove button.

10. Click Add Name if the font you want to embed or never embed is not in a folder. This opens the Add Font Name dialog box. Enter the name of the font, choose the Always Embed list or Never Embed list, and then click Add. After you finish adding font names, click Done.

> **Note** Licensing issues prohibit you from embedding certain fonts in a document. If you select a font with licensing issues, Acrobat Distiller displays a key icon before the font name and a warning at the bottom of the dialog box saying the font cannot be embedded because of licensing issues.

After you change the Fonts folder conversion settings parameters, click another folder to modify different settings, or save the job option by following the steps in the section "Save Conversion Settings."

> **Note** When you install Acrobat, the install utility locates every folder in your system that contains fonts. If you add a new font folder to your system after installing Acrobat, launch Acrobat Distiller and choose Settings | Font Locations to open the Acrobat Distiller – Font Locations dialog box. Click the Add button, navigate to the folder that contains the fonts you want to use with Acrobat Distiller, select the folder, click OK, and then close the Font Locations dialog box. The next time you launch Acrobat Distiller, the font folder will be available.

Set Color Options

When you convert a document to PDF format using Acrobat Distiller or PDFMaker, you can modify the color options. You can choose a color-management settings file and let Acrobat Distiller manage the color of the images during conversion, or you can modify the color settings to suit a specific output device. To set color options, follow these steps:

1. Choose a Conversion Settings option to modify and open the Adobe PDF Settings dialog box, as discussed previously.
2. Click the Color folder to open the Color section of the Adobe PDF Settings dialog box, shown on the next page.
3. To use a preset color settings file, click the Settings File drop-down arrow and choose an option. When you choose one of the color-management setting files, all the color options are dimmed out. You can choose None (the default) for no color management, Monitor Color for documents that will be displayed on a monitor, or one of the Prepress defaults.
4. Accept the default settings option, which varies depending on the setting you're modifying, or click the Color Management Policies drop-down arrow and choose one of the following:
   - **Leave Color Unchanged**   Choose this option, and Acrobat Distiller doesn't modify device-dependent colors. Instead, Distiller processes device-independent colors to the nearest match in the resulting PDF. Use this option

if the file will be printed by a color-calibrated device that specifies all color management.

- **Tag Everything For Color Management**   When you choose this option and specify Acrobat 4.0, 5.0, 6.0, 7.0, or 8.0 compatibility in the General section of the Adobe PDF Settings dialog box, Acrobat Distiller embeds an International Color Consortium (ICC) color profile with the document. The ICC color profile calibrates image color and makes the colors in the converted PDF document device-independent. Device-dependent colors in the original files (RGB, Grayscale, and CMYK) are converted to device-independent color spaces (CalRGB, CalGrayscale, and LAB) in the resulting PDF file. (Cal, in these names, stands for calibrated.)

- **Tag Only Images For Color Management**   Choose this option so that when Acrobat Distiller converts a document to PDF format, it embeds ICC color profiles with document images, but not with text or line art.

- **Convert All Colors To sRGB**   When you choose this option, all images with RGB and CMYK colors are converted to standard RGB (sRGB).

- **Convert All Colors To CMYK**   When you choose this option, all images with RGB and CMYK colors are converted to DeviceGray or DeviceCMYK.

5. Click the Document Rendering Intent drop-down arrow and specify how Acrobat Distiller maps color between the color spaces. Choose from the following options:

- **Preserve**   Preserves color spaces in the original document.
- **Perceptual**   The original color values of the document images are mapped to the gamut of the output device. This method preserves the visual relationship between different colors, but color values may change.
- **Saturation**   The file that Acrobat Distiller produces maintains the same relative color saturation as the original image pixels. Choose this method when document color saturation is more important than maintaining the visual relationship between colors of the original document.
- **Absolute Colormetric**   Acrobat Distiller disables the black-and-white point matching when converting colors in the document. This option isn't recommended unless your intent is to preserve specific colors used in a trademark or logo.
- **Relative Colormetric**   Acrobat Distiller preserves all colors within the output device gamut range. Colors in the original document that are out of the printing-device gamut range convert to brightness values within the printer gamut.

6. If you choose any Color Management Policies option other than Leave Color Unchanged, in the Working Spaces section you will be able to choose an ICC profile for managing grayscale, RGB, and CMYK color conversion, as described here:

   - **Gray (Grayscale)**   Choose None from the drop-down menu, and Acrobat Distiller doesn't convert grayscale colors. The default option is determined by your operating system (OS): Gray Gamma 2.2 for Windows or Gray Gamma 1.8 for Macintosh. Alternatively, you can choose one of the Dot Gain options (10 percent to 30 percent in 5 percent increments). Choose a lower Dot Gain value to lighten document images or a higher value to darken document images. Your other options are Black And White and sGray.
   - **RGB**   Choose a color-management profile from the drop-down menu. The available options are the color profiles installed on your computer. If you're uncertain about which profile to choose, the default option (sRGB IEC61966-2.1) yields good results with most printers. Choose None, and Acrobat Distiller doesn't convert colors in RGB images when distilling them to PDF.
   - **CMYK**   Choose one of the options from the drop-down menu to specify how Acrobat Distiller handles colors in CMYK images when converting them to PDF format. If in doubt, choose U.S. Web Coated (SWOP) v2 or the default CMYK color profile for the country in which you live. If you choose None, Acrobat Distiller doesn't convert colors in CMYK images when distilling them to PDF.

7. If you click the Preserve CMYK Values For Calibrated CMYK Color Spaces check box, device-independent color values will be treated as device-dependent (DeviceCMYK) color values, and device-independent color spaces will be ignored and discarded. This option is grayed out unless you choose the Convert All Colors To CMYK color management policy.

8. In the Device-Dependent Data section, choose from the options on the following page that pertain to the device with which the converted documents will be printed (these options have no effect on screen viewing).

- **Preserve Under Color Removal And Black Generation**   Choose this option if the documents you want to convert with this job option are PostScript files that contain Color Removal and Black Generation settings.
- **When Transfer Functions Are Found**   Click the drop-down arrow and choose one of the following options:
  - **Remove**   Acrobat Distiller removes all applied transfer functions when converting the file to PDF. You should choose this option unless the resulting PDF file will be printed on the same device for which the PostScript file was created.
  - **Preserve**   Acrobat Distiller preserves transfer functions if they're present in the original file. Transfer functions are traditionally used to compensate for dot gain or dot loss when an image transfers to film.
  - **Apply**   Acrobat Distiller applies the transfer functions to the file. This option changes the colors in the file.
- **Preserve Halftone Information**   The resulting file that Acrobat Distiller produces preserves halftone information embedded in the original PostScript document. Halftone screens control the amount of ink deposited in specific locations when the file prints. By varying the dot size, halftone screens simulate the illusion of flowing color and varying shades of gray. CMYK images have four halftone screens, one for each color (cyan, magenta, yellow, and black).

After you modify the Conversion Settings Color folder settings, click another tab to modify another setting or save the job option, as outlined in the section "Save Conversion Settings."

Tip   If you're modifying multiple settings, click the Show All Settings check box to display all conversion settings in the Adobe PDF Settings dialog box. Click a setting title to display the parameters in each settings folder.

Set Advanced Options

The Advanced section in the Adobe PDF Settings dialog box enables you to modify Document Structuring Convention (DSC) comments that appear in the original PostScript file, as well as other options that affect the conversion from PostScript to PDF. To modify Advanced Options for a conversion setting, follow these steps:

1. Choose a Conversion Settings option to modify and open the Adobe PDF Settings dialog box, following the steps presented earlier in this chapter.
2. Click the Advanced folder to reveal the Advanced section of the Adobe PDF Settings dialog box, shown next. In the Options section, choose from the following:
   - **Allow PostScript File To Override Adobe PDF Settings**   Choose this option if you're reasonably certain the PostScript files you convert with this job option contain the necessary information for the intended output device. Deselect this option if you want conversion settings to take precedence over

any settings embedded in the PostScript files that you intend to convert with this job option.

- **Allow PostScript XObjects**   Choose this option to have Acrobat Distiller create XObjects (eXternal Objects) that store information that appears on multiple pages of the same file. This can result in faster printing, but it requires more printer memory because the XObjects are stored in printer memory and called when needed.

- **Convert Gradients To Smooth Shades**   When you choose this option, Acrobat Distiller smoothes gradients from the original files, creating a seamless blend. This option has no effect on how the document appears onscreen. If you print the converted file to a PostScript 3 device, however, you will notice a marked improvement in quality. Note that if you choose this option, it may take longer for Acrobat to render the gradient onscreen.

- **Convert Smooth Lines To Curves**   Choose this option if the files you're converting are CAD drawings. When you choose this option, Acrobat Distiller reduces the number of points used to define gentle curves, which results in a smaller PDF file.

- **Preserve Level 2 Copypage Semantics**   Choose this option to have Acrobat Distiller use the copypage editor defined in LanguageLevel 2 PostScript, instead of the one defined in LanguageLevel 3 PostScript. Don't choose this option if you're printing to LanguageLevel 3 PostScript devices. If the converted file will be sent to a service center, check with the technicians to see which PostScript level its devices support.

- **Preserve Overprint Settings** Choose this option if the PDFs you intend to create with this job option originally had overprint information. An overprint is when two or more colors are printed on top of each other to produce another color.
- **Overprinting Default Is Nonzero Overprinting** If you choose this option, files with overprints that contain zero CMYK information won't prevent underlying colors from printing.
- **Save Adobe PDF Settings Inside PDF File** Choose this option, and Acrobat Distiller includes the settings used to create the file as a file attachment within the PDF document. This document can be accessed by other applications to duplicate the settings.
- **Save Original JPEG Images In PDF If Possible** Choose this option to have Acrobat Distiller save JPEG images from the original file in the resulting PDF file with the compression settings from the original file.
- **Save Portable Job Ticket Inside PDF File** Choose this option to have Acrobat Distiller create a job ticket that contains information about the PostScript file used to create the PDF document. The job ticket includes information such as page size and orientation, resolution, halftone information, and so on. Disable this option if the PDF documents you create with this job option are strictly for screen viewing.
- **Use Prologue.ps And Epilogue.ps** Choose this option to send a prologue and epilogue file with each document Acrobat Distiller converts with this job option. Epilogue files can be edited to append information to the PDF file. Prologue files can be edited to resolve procedure problems with PostScript files. Sample Prologue.ps and Epilogue.ps files are located in the Distiller folder. Neither file contains data, but you can use them as templates. Unless you're familiar with creating PostScript code, you should disable this option.

3. In the Document Structuring Conventions (DSC) section, enable the Process DSC Comments option to have Acrobat Distiller preserve DSC information from the original PostScript file. With this default option, you can include any of the following:
   - **Process DSC Comments** Preserves DSC comments from a PostScript file with the resulting PDF file.
   - **Log DSC Warnings** Choose this option, and Acrobat Distiller displays warning messages about troublesome DSC comments in the original PostScript file and creates a text file log of these errors. Choose this option if the files you process with this job option contain DSC comments.
   - **Preserve EPS Information From DSC** Choose this option when processing EPS files with DSC comments, and the DSC comments will be preserved when the file converts to PDF.
   - **Preserve OPI Comments** Choose this option, and when Acrobat Distiller processes files with For Placement Only (FPO) images or comments, they are replaced with the high-resolution image located on servers supporting Open Press Interface (OPI) versions 1.3 and 2.0.

- **Preserve Document Information From DSC**   Choose this option, and Acrobat Distiller includes the title, creation date, and time information when you use this job option to convert files to PDF. When the PDF file opens, this information appears in the Document Summary and can be accessed by choosing File | Document Summary.
- **Resize Page And Center Artwork For EPS Files**   Choose this option when processing EPS files, and Acrobat Distiller resizes the page to the document artwork and centers the artwork.

After modifying the settings for a conversion settings' Advanced folder, you can click another tab to modify different settings or save the job option file, as covered in the upcoming section "Save Conversion Settings."

Set Standards Options

Acrobat X Pro gives you the option to modify PDF/A and PDF/X settings. PDF/A (Portable Document Format/Archive) is an ISO standard used for longtime archiving of electronic files. PDF/X (Portable Document Format Exchange) is an ISO standard used for print production. The PDF/X format combines all print and workflow settings for the PDF document in a single file. To set PDF/X options for a conversion setting, follow these steps:

1. Choose a Conversion Settings option to modify and open the Adobe PDF Settings dialog box, following the steps presented earlier in this chapter.
2. Click the Standards folder to open the Standards section of the Adobe PDF Settings dialog box, shown here.

3. Click the Compliance Standard drop-down arrow and choose a compliance option from the drop-down menu, shown here. Note that the options vary depending on the setting you are modifying.

| None |
| PDF/X-1a (Acrobat 4.0 Compatible) |
| PDF/X-3 (Acrobat 4.0 Compatible) |
| PDF/X-1a (Acrobat 5.0 Compatible) |
| PDF/X-3 (Acrobat 5.0 Compatible) |
| PDF/A-1b (Acrobat 5.0 Compatible) |

   - PDF/X-compliant PDF documents are used for high-resolution print jobs. Accept the default PDF/X settings, unless the document is being used for print production.

Note PDF/X-1a (Acrobat 4.0 Compatible) is available only when you choose Acrobat 4.0 (PDF 1.5) compatibility in the General tab of the Adobe PDF Settings dialog box. If you choose Acrobat 5.0 (PDF 1.6) or higher, these options are grayed out.

   - PDF/A-compliant PDF documents are generally used for archiving of electronic files. PDF/A files can contain only text, raster images (bitmaps), and vector graphics. PDF/A doesn't support including scripts with the archived document.

4. Click the When Not Compliant drop-down arrow and choose one of the following options:
   - **Continue**   Creates the PDF file anyway and lists the compliancy issues in the report.
   - **Cancel Job**   Aborts creation of the PDF file when compliancy issues occur.

5. In the If Neither TrimBox Nor ArtBox Are Specified section, choose from the following options:
   - **Report As Error**   If neither option is specified in the PostScript document, this is reported as an error.
   - **Set TrimBox To MediaBox With Offset (Inches)**   Choose this option and enter values in four fields: Left, Right, Top, and Bottom. The TrimBox is always the same size or smaller than the MediaBox.

6. In the If BleedBox Is Not Specified section, choose one of the following options:
   - **Set BleedBox To MediaBox**   Sets the BleedBox dimension equal to the MediaBox dimensions.
   - **Set BleedBox To TrimBox With Offsets (Inches)**   Choose this option and enter values in four fields that let you set the offset from BleedBox size to TrimBox size. The BleedBox is always the same size or larger than the TrimBox.

7. Click the Output Intent Profile Name drop-down arrow and choose an option. This option indicates the printing profile with which the document will be printed if this option isn't included with the PostScript file from which the PDF document is being created.

8. An entry is automatically made in the Output Condition Identifier field if you choose an Output Intent Profile Name with a known output condition identifier. The option also becomes available if you choose Use Output Condition Identifier from the Output Intent Profile drop-down list, whereupon you enter the output condition identifier manually.

9. Enter text in the Output Condition field (optional) to describe the intended printing condition. This parameter isn't required, but when used, it provides useful information to recipients of the PDF document.

10. An entry is automatically made in the RegistryName (URL) field when you choose an Output Intent Profile with a known URL. If no entry is provided, enter a URL for the website associated with the ICC profile associated with the document. A URL is provided by default for the ICC registry names associated with the document. More information about the ICC registry can be found at the URL provided.

11. Click the Trapped drop-down arrow and choose an option for color trapped state, which determines whether colors in the document are trapped. This is required for PDF/X compliance. Choose from Leave Undefined (when the PostScript document specifies this option), Insert True, and Insert False.

Save Conversion Settings

After you modify an Adobe PDF Settings option, you can save it for future use. To save a conversion setting and close the Adobe PDF Settings dialog box, follow these steps:

1. Click the Save As button to open the Save Adobe PDF Settings As dialog box. By default, the Adobe PDF Settings option you use to create the new setting is appended by the next available number—for example, Standard(1).

2. Accept the default filename or enter a different name. Choose a name that reflects the intended source of documents you create with this conversion setting. For example, if the documents you create with this job option will be included on a CD/DVD-ROM, enter **CD/DVD-ROM**.

3. Click Save.

After you save the new job option, it appears on the Acrobat Distiller Default Settings drop-down menu. If you use Microsoft Office applications, the job option appears on the Adobe PDF Conversion Settings menu.

PDF Font Considerations

When you create a document in an authoring application, a little time spent choosing fonts can produce a better-looking document. Try to avoid highly stylized fonts with long swooping curves. They may look great printed, but they often don't display properly on monitors. If you choose a large bold font, the center of characters such as *a, o,* and *p* fill in and are hard to read, unless the user greatly magnifies the PDF document. When you're in doubt about whether a particular font style will display well in Acrobat, create a test document in the authoring application using every character from the font set in both uppercase and lowercase. Convert the document to PDF format and view the document in Acrobat at 100-percent magnification. One look and you'll know whether to use the font.

You should also be cautious about mixing fonts. If you create a document with multiple fonts, make sure the finished document is aesthetically pleasing. A document with multiple fonts can be hard to read. The actual number of fonts you can safely include in a document is a matter of personal taste and document size. For example, creating a single-page document with more than two fonts wouldn't be a good idea. Also, when you create a document with multiple fonts and embed those fonts, the file size of the document increases dramatically.

When you create a PDF document and view the output on your computer, everything may look as you planned, with crystal-clear images and sharp and stylish text. If your intended audience doesn't have the fonts used in the document installed on their computer, though, the document will look quite different, especially if you selected highly stylized fonts. If you don't embed fonts and a viewer doesn't have the document fonts installed on their system, Acrobat substitutes either the AdobeSansMM font or the AdobeSerifMM font. (MM is the acronym for Multiple Master.) Through the use of these fonts, Acrobat tries to create a reasonable facsimile of the original font, while maintaining the width of the original font to preserve line breaks from the original document.

Embed Fonts

When you embed fonts, you can rest assured that viewers of your document will see the document as you intended. Embedding several fonts, however, can dramatically increase the file size of the document. You can embed fonts when you modify Adobe PDF Settings for Acrobat Distiller, but make sure you don't violate any font-licensing agreement when you decide to embed a specific font. For more information on embedding fonts when setting Adobe PDF Settings, refer to the earlier section "Set Fonts Options."

You should embed fonts whenever you need the published document to look identical to the original. If, for example, your clients use a font as part of their corporation identity package, embed the font. If you use a stylized font that's difficult for Acrobat to re-create with an MM font, then embed the font.

Subset a Font

When you embed a font, you can reduce the file size of the resulting PDF document by subsetting the font. When you subset a font, you embed only the characters used in the document being converted to PDF format. You can have Acrobat subset a font when the percentage of characters used drops below a certain value. By default, Acrobat subsets a font when the percentage of characters used drops below 100 percent. To subset a font, click the Fonts tab in the Adobe PDF Setting you're modifying, choose the option to subset fonts, and then specify the value Acrobat uses as its signal to embed the entire font set or subset the font set.

The only disadvantage to subsetting a font is when you (or a third party) edit a document with subset fonts. If you don't have the font set installed on your computer, you can only edit the document with the subset characters and you cannot add other characters from the font set.

Preview an Unembedded Font in Acrobat

If you have any question as to whether you should embed a font, create a test document in an authoring application and view it in Acrobat without using local fonts. When you view a PDF document in Acrobat without using local fonts, fonts installed on your system are disregarded and Acrobat goes into font-substitution mode. To preview an unembedded font in Acrobat, follow these steps:

1. Create a document in a word processing application using every character of the font set in both uppercase and lowercase.
2. Choose Adobe PDF from the application's Print command or, if you're in a Windows Microsoft Office application, choose Create PDF from the Acrobat ribbon.
3. Edit the Adobe PDF Settings you're using to convert the document and, in the Fonts section, deselect the Embed All Fonts option, as outlined previously in the section "Set Fonts Options."
4. Convert the document to PDF format.
5. Launch Acrobat.
6. Choose Edit | Preferences (Windows) or Acrobat | Preferences (Macintosh) and select the Page Display category.
7. Deselect the Use Local Fonts check box and then click OK.
8. Open the document with unembedded fonts. If a font cannot be substituted, Acrobat displays the text as bullets and an error message appears.

When this preferences option is deselected (unchecked), Acrobat substitutes document fonts with MM fonts. You see what the document looks like on a viewer's system without the document fonts installed. When you deselect Use Local Fonts, you can also print a copy of the document using the Adobe substituted fonts. If the test document isn't satisfactory, embed the fonts when you create the final document.

Summary

In this chapter, you learned about tagged PDF documents and how to optimize documents for intended destinations. You also learned how to modify default Adobe PDF Settings to suit the documents you create and to save the new settings. The topic of fonts and whether to embed them was also presented. In the next chapter, you will learn how to create PDF documents for the Web.

12

Acrobat Online

HOW TO...

- View PDF documents in a web browser
- Use the Acrobat plug-in
- Prepare PDF documents for the Internet
- Create links to websites
- Initiate a shared review
- Use PDF forms on the Internet

In this chapter, you learn how to view PDF documents within a web browser and prepare PDF documents for use on the Internet. Also covered are web browser considerations and information about the Acrobat plug-in. In addition, you learn how to initiate a shared review, create links from PDF documents to websites, and utilize PDF forms on the Internet.

View PDF Documents in a Web Browser

When you view non-HTML documents from a website, your web browser detects the document type and loads the necessary helper application so you can view the document in the web browser. Depending on the type of document you view, the helper application (or plug-in, as it's known to web developers) may load within the browser or externally. Some applications give web designers the freedom to embed a document and call up the plug-in interface within the HTML document or open the application in an external window. When you view PDF documents from websites, your version of Adobe Acrobat appears in your web browser.

For viewers who don't own the full version of Acrobat, but who have Adobe Reader installed on their systems, Adobe Reader launches in the web browser when a PDF document is encountered. Alternatively, in Acrobat or Adobe Reader, you can display a PDF document from a website by choosing Edit | Preferences (Windows) or Acrobat | Preferences (Macintosh) and then disabling the Display PDF In Browser option in the Internet section. If you own a Macintosh computer, Previewer may launch when you open a PDF document.

When you view documents online, Acrobat provides you with a slightly different set of tools. You can select objects from the document, review and comment on the document, and digitally sign the document. However, there are no menu commands—only the Acrobat tools and the web browser menu commands and tools. With the stripped-down web browser version of Acrobat, you only have tools to view the document, save a copy of the document, and annotate the document. The tools and menus in your web browser don't change, though. When you finish viewing a document, use the web browser controls to navigate to a different website or back to the page called the PDF document.

After you open a PDF document within your web browser, you can save a copy of the document for future use. After you save a copy of the document, you can open the document in Acrobat and use the menu commands and tools to modify the document, provided security hasn't been applied to it.

You can also download PDF documents directly from the Internet to your hard drive by means of the hyperlink to the document. To download a PDF document using Mozilla Firefox, right-click the document link and then choose Save Link As from the context menu. If you use Internet Explorer (IE), right-click the link and then choose Save Target As from the context menu to download a PDF document. Follow the prompts to download the document to the desired folder on your hard drive. If you use Safari for your default web browser, right-click and choose Save Link To Downloads. After downloading the file, you can access the file from your Downloads folder for future use.

About PDF Web Browser Plug-ins

When you install Acrobat, the install utility automatically detects the Internet Explorer, Mozilla, or Safari web browser installed on your system, and Acrobat is configured as the default application for the following Multipurpose Internet Mail Extensions (MIME) types:

Note If you have web browsers other than IE or Mozilla Firefox installed on your system, you might have to manually configure the browser to use Acrobat as the application to read the listed MIME types.

- **PDF** When you click a website link to a PDF file, it's displayed in your web browser using the Acrobat plug-in.
- **FDF** When you create a PDF form with the Submit action applied to a button, you have the option to send form results via e-mail in the FDF (Forms Data Format) format. When the recipient double-clicks the e-mail attachment, Acrobat launches, opens the original form, and adds the data contained in the FDF file to the form.
- **XFDF** When you receive form data via e-mail in XFDF format, double-click the attachment to launch Acrobat, open the associated form, and add the data from the XFDF file.

- **RMF**   When you purchase locked PDF documents, the seller sends RMF files that contain the licensing information Web Buy (a plug-in used to authorize a computer to view a locked PDF) used to unlock the document.

Note   If you install Acrobat on a new system, be sure to install your web browser first. If you install Acrobat first, to view PDF documents in a web browser, you must manually configure each web browser on your system or reinstall Acrobat and perform a custom installation, choosing only the web browser plug-in.

Download Adobe Reader

A large majority of Internet users already have a version of Adobe Acrobat or Adobe Reader installed on their systems. If, however, you post a PDF document on your website or on a client's website and some visitors to that website don't have Adobe Reader, they will be unable to view your document. To accommodate website visitors who don't have a copy of Adobe Reader, you can include a link to the Adobe web page from which visitors can download a free copy of Adobe Reader. The following URL takes the viewer to the Adobe Reader download page: http://get.adobe.com/reader/.

Distribute Adobe Reader

You can post the Adobe Reader installer on a company intranet or a local network. You can also distribute the Adobe Reader installation software on a CD-ROM, provided you accept the conditions of the Acrobat electronic End User License Agreement (EULA) and complete and submit the Adobe Reader Distribution Agreement. When users install the Adobe Reader, they are also prompted to accept the conditions of the EULA.

You cannot distribute Adobe Reader from a website. Adobe requires any third-party website that wants to make the Adobe Reader available for visitors to include a link to the Adobe Reader. You'll find the information on how to distribute Adobe Reader from your website and apply for a license at http://www.adobe.com/products/reader/distribution.html. If you post a link to the web page from which Adobe Reader can be downloaded, include a Get Adobe Reader logo or an Adobe PDF logo as a link to the site. You can download both logos in the web logos section of the following web page: http://www.adobe.com/misc/linking.html.

Conduct a Shared Review

A shared review is the ideal option if all users are on the same network behind a firewall, and if they all have read and write access to the folder where the comments are stored. After a shared review is initiated, reviewers receive notification they have been requested to review a document. Review participants are notified after new comments have been posted by other reviewers.

Initiate a Shared Review

You can initiate a shared review from within Acrobat. You select the document to review, specify where comments will be stored, and then invite reviewers. To initiate a shared review, follow these steps:

1. Click Comment, click Review, and then choose Send For Shared Review to open the Send PDF For Share Review dialog box, shown next.

2. Choose an option from the How Do You Want To Collect Comments From Your Reviewers? drop-down menu. Your choices are Automatically Download & Track Comments With Acrobat.com and Automatically Collect Comments On My Internal Server. If you choose the former, you send a secure link that directs reviewers to your file. Reviewers can comment using Acrobat X or Adobe Reader X. You are notified when new comments are made. Comments can be viewed by all reviewers. You track the review using the Tracker. Acrobat.com is a subscription service. You can sign up for a free trial and find out more information at https://acrobat.com/pricing.html. The following steps cover a shared review on an internal server.
3. Click Next to display the second step of the Send For Shared Review dialog box, shown next.
4. Choose the desired folder type from the following options:
   - **Network Folder** Choose this option if all review participants have access to a local area network (LAN), such as a corporate intranet. All participants must have read and write access for the folder in which the comments are stored.

- **SharePoint Workspace**   Choose this option if all review participants are within a LAN and have read and write privileges for the folder in which the comments will be stored. This option requires a Windows server running SharePoint Services.
- **Web Server Folder**   Choose this option if the comments will be stored in a folder on a web server that supports the web server protocol. Choose this option if some of the review participants are outside the network firewall.

5. Enter the path to the shared network folder. Alternatively, you can click the Browse button and browse to the folder on your local server.
6. Click Next to open the third step of the Send PDF For Shared Review initialization process.
7. Choose the manner in which you're going to send the invitation. You can use Acrobat to send the document to reviewers as an attachment to the message, or include a link to the network review folder in which the document is stored within the body of the e-mail message. Alternatively, you can choose to save a copy locally and send it later.
8. Click Next to reveal the fourth step of the Send PDF For Shared Review initialization process.
9. Enter a name for the server profile and then click Next to reveal the next step of the Send PDF For Shared Review initialization process.
10. Specify the required reviewers in the To field and, if desired, add optional reviewers in the Cc field. You can select reviewers from your address book or manually enter each reviewer's e-mail address. Separate each e-mail address with a semicolon, or press ENTER or RETURN after entering an e-mail address.

11. Accept the default deadline or click the Review Deadline link to open the Change Review Deadline dialog box. Your options are New Review Deadline, which enables you to select a new deadline date and time using a calendar or spinner buttons, and No Deadline.

12. Accept the default Subject and Message of the e-mail that will be sent to reviewers. You can modify the subject or message, as desired, by adding and deleting text.

13. Click Send. The Create Shared Review Progress dialog box appears. The message is sent to your default e-mail application. If your e-mail application is not set up to automatically send messages from the outbox, you'll have to manually send the message to your reviewers. After the shared review is sent to your e-mail application, a dialog box appears telling you the document has been distributed to reviewers and has been saved to the network folder and local hard drive.

Participate in a Shared Review

When you initiate a review, a review-enabled copy of the document appears immediately after you complete the last step in the Send PDF For Shared Review dialog box. Reviewers are notified by e-mail with either a review-enabled version of the document attached or the path to the network folder where the review document is stored.

Reviewers can participate in the review by double-clicking the e-mail attachment, which launches Acrobat and displays a welcome message, or by navigating to the network folder and then opening the document. After reading the welcome message, reviewers can annotate the document using the tools in the Comment pane. After adding comments to the document, a reviewer can check for new comments, publish comments, or check server status. The reviewer can click the Server Status drop-down arrow to reveal a drop-down menu, which enables the reviewer to open the Review Tracker, save an archive copy of the document, or work offline.

A shared review is similar to an e-mail review, with the exception that the reviewer's comments are stored in an XML file in the network folder specified by the review initiator or at Acrobat.com if the review is hosted there. The review initiator and reviewers can keep track of comments using the Comments panel, and they can keep track of all their reviews using the Tracker. For more information on the Comments List and the Tracker, refer to Chapter 9.

When a reviewer opens the document again, a dialog box welcomes back the reviewer and displays a list of changes since the document was last viewed. The reviewer can add new comments to their copy of the document by clicking Check For New Comments. After reviewing other reviewers' comments and adding new comments, they can post their comments to the shared review by clicking Publish Comments.

Prepare PDF Documents for the Internet

When you prepare a document for the Internet, the first step is to optimize the document in the authoring application, as discussed in Chapter 11. The most important consideration in optimizing a document for the Internet is to get the file size as small as possible. Remember to resample all images to a resolution of 72 dots per inch (dpi) and enable Fast Web View (the default option with all conversion settings except PDF/A and PDF/X) when converting the document to PDF format. You can modify conversion settings in the Images section to resample the images to 72 dpi. If you modify the converted document in Acrobat, you need to use the Save As command to enable Fast Web View, as outlined in the section "Save the Document for the Internet."

You should also consider document security issues, document description information, and the manner in which the first page of the document is displayed when a viewer downloads it. If you include document description information, the website visitor can get an idea of the information included in the document. Add document security if you want to prevent website visitors from extracting content from the document or printing the document. If you assign security to the document, be sure to include a permissions password. Also, be sure to use Acrobat 6.0 or greater compatibility, so the document metadata is available for search engines. For more information about Acrobat security, refer to Chapter 10. For more information on modifying the document description and document-open options, refer to Chapter 3. Note that if you choose the Open In Full Screen Mode option in the Initial View section of the Document Properties dialog box, the document won't be displayed in full-screen mode when viewed in a web browser.

But that's only the beginning of your task. After you convert the original document to PDF format, you apply the finishing touches in Acrobat.

Add a Base URL to the Document

If all the web links in a document are within the same website, you can enter the relative path (directory and document name, such as documents/pdfdocs.htm) for the web link. If all the links point to another site, though, you need to enter the absolute path to the URL (website domain, directory, and document name, such as http://www.othersite.com/documents/pdfdocs.htm). If all the web links are to the same external site, you can simplify matters by adding a base URL to the document. When you add a base URL, you only need to enter the relative path to the document you want to open. Acrobat automatically links the relative path to the base URL.

To specify a base URL for the document, follow these steps:

1. Choose File | Properties and then click the Advanced tab of the Document Properties dialog box.

2. Enter the absolute path to base URL of the document in the Base URL field, as shown here.

3. Click OK to close the dialog box.

Create Links to Websites

When you create PDF documents for viewing from a website, you may need to create one or more links to other web pages. If you have several interlinked PDF documents, you also need to create some sort of link back to the HTML pages of the website. You can ask visitors to rely on the Back button of the web browser. If a viewer has navigated through several documents, however, clicking the Back button several times to exit Acrobat and return to the HTML portion of the website can be annoying. You can create a link to a website by defining the area of the document that will link to an external website with the Link tool, and for the link action, choose Open A Web Page. Enter the URL for the web page you want the link to launch, and viewers can then get back to the HTML page with a single click.

Create Named Destinations and Links

When you create links from an HTML document to a PDF document, the link destination can be the document itself or a named destination (a named link to a specific location within a PDF document). When you create a destination, you can change the view to zoom in on a specific image or paragraph within a document.

You can link to a named destination from within an HTML document. In Acrobat, create a named destination for each part of the document you want to link to from within an HTML document. For example, if you post a PDF product manual on the Web, you can create a named destination for each product. Remember to use proper naming conventions for web browsers, because you will be using each destination name as part of a web link. With this in mind, the destination name should be eight characters or less with no spaces. For more information on creating named destinations, refer to Chapter 7. For more information on creating a link to a named destination, refer to the section "Create HTML Hyperlinks to Named Destinations."

How to... **Create an E-Mail Link**

When you create a PDF document for a website, you can create an e-mail link within the PDF document. When viewers of your PDF document click the e-mail link, their default e-mail application opens with a blank message window addressed to the e-mail address of your choice. To create an e-mail link in a PDF document, choose the Link command in the Content section of the Tools pane and then define the target for your e-mail link. In the Create Link dialog box, click the Open A Web Page radio button and, in the Address field, enter **mailto:** followed by the desired recipient's e-mail address (for example, **mailto: JoeSmith64@webserver.com**).

You should also create a link within the document that takes viewers back to the HTML page after they have viewed the information. You may also need to create links from within the document to other web pages, and you can use text or images within the document as the basis for your links. You can also create a button in the PDF document that acts as a link. If you create several buttons within a document, however, you increase the file size, which isn't a desirable outcome when creating documents for the Web. For more information on creating links, refer to Chapter 6.

Create a Welcome Page

If you have a large collection of PDF documents at a website, you can link the documents together using PDF navigation. When you do this, create a welcome page in PDF format that explains what the document collection is about. On the welcome page, you can create a text menu and then use the Link tool to create links from menu titles to the other PDF documents. When you create a welcome page in this manner, as long as the other PDF documents are in the same folder, you can use the Open A File action to open a specific document when the user clicks the link.

You can also create a welcome page by using HTML. Create hyperlinks on the welcome page for each document, as outlined in the section "Create HTML Hyperlinks to PDF Documents."

Use PDF Forms on the Internet

You can use PDF forms to get feedback from visitors of a website, to conduct an online opinion poll, to build a customer database, and much more. When you create a PDF form for the Internet, add a button and use the Submit A Form action to forward the information to the site webmaster or site owner.

After filling in the form, the user clicks the Submit button to submit the information to the specified recipient. Some web-hosting services have preformatted CGI scripts that you can modify to forward form results. CGI scripts can be used to password-protect websites, create guest books, and much more. In this case, you need a CGI script that collects the information from the PDF form and forwards it to a specified person. Add a Submit button to the form that links to the web server script.

With most web servers, CGI scripts are stored within a folder named cgi-bin. Check with the web-hosting service's technical support staff for the relative path to the mail-forwarding CGI script. For more information on creating PDF forms with Acrobat, refer to Chapter 13.

Tip In lieu of using a CGI script, you can forward the form results to an e-mail address. After you create the Submit button, choose the Submit A Form action. Click the Add button and, instead of entering the URL to a web page, enter **mailto:** followed by the e-mail address of the recipient. When a visitor to the website fills in the form and clicks the Submit button, the viewer's default e-mail application opens. The viewer can add a message or send the e-mail as is. When the recipient receives the e-mail, the form results are attached as an HTML, FDF, or XFDF file, or as the complete PDF document, depending on which option you selected with the Submit A Form action.

Save the Document for the Internet

Before you upload the document to a website, double-check your work. Make sure all links function properly. If any of the document links are to a website, make sure you have the correct URL. Nothing is more frustrating for a web visitor than trying to open a link and getting a Not Found error. Remember to test your links in a browser; otherwise, Acrobat will append the current document with the web page specified in the link.

If all the links are formatted properly, choose File | Save As | Optimized PDF. This opens the PDF Optimizer. With the PDF Optimizer, you can remove any bookmarks or links with invalid destinations, and reduce the file size by specifying compression settings for images in the document and removing unused objects. If you created any named destinations that you intend to use as link destinations from an HTML document or other PDF document, deselect the Discard Unreferenced Named Destinations check box in the Clean Up section of the PDF Optimizer, shown here.

Tip   If you frequently use the same settings to optimize PDF documents, click the Preset drop-down arrow and choose Custom. After you select the desired optimize options and specify optimize parameters, click the Save button to open a dialog box that prompts you for a name for the custom settings. After you save the custom settings, the name you specify appears in the Preset drop-down list.

About Byteserving

When you view a PDF document optimized for fast web viewing from a website that supports byteserving, you see a page load almost immediately. If you've ever waited for a 350-page PDF document to download before viewing a single page, you realize the value of fast web viewing. When you optimize a document for fast web viewing, you create a document that can be downloaded a page at a time, provided the hosting service of the website supports byteserving. Unless the user has disabled the Allow Fast Web View option in the Internet section of Acrobat Preferences, Acrobat or Adobe

Reader communicates directly with the web server. If, for example, a website visitor opens a lengthy PDF document, it opens to the link specified in the HTML document in the Navigation window, and the viewer doesn't have to wait for the preceding pages to load. If the viewer enters 50, Acrobat requests page 50 and the page is downloaded from the web server or the linking PDF document.

Note After the first page of a PDF file is optimized for fast web viewing downloads, Acrobat continues downloading the rest of the document by default. To disable this option, choose Edit | Preferences | Internet (Windows) or Acrobat | Preferences | Internet (Macintosh) and deselect Allow Speculative Downloading In The Background.

Create Byteserving PDF Files

Even though you specify fast web viewing when optimizing the conversion of the document to PDF from within an authoring application, after you add navigation links and other interactive features in Acrobat, you must once again save the document in a manner that produces a file optimized for the Web. If you use the Save command to save the document to file, Acrobat doesn't create a file optimized for fast web viewing. To create a PDF document optimized for fast web viewing, choose File | Save As and then choose one of the PDF options. By default, the Save As command optimizes a document for fast web viewing unless you disable this option by editing Acrobat Document Preferences.

Name the Document

When you name a document for distribution on the Internet, remember different web browsers react differently. Refrain from using spaces within a filename and always include the .pdf extension. Web browsers are configured to use Acrobat or Adobe Reader as the default application to view PDF files. Another good idea is to refrain from using long filenames. When in doubt, stick with DOS naming conventions by using filenames with eight characters or less and no spaces.

Tip When you create a document for the Internet and you want the smallest possible file size, choose File | Save As | Reduced Size PDF. This opens a dialog box in which you choose the version of Acrobat for which you want the file optimized. Choosing an earlier version of Acrobat results in a smaller file size. Don't choose an earlier version of Acrobat if you have added features such as page transitions that are supported only in Acrobat 6.0 or later.

Combine HTML and PDF Files

When you create PDF documents that will be viewed from a website, use HTML pages as the basis for the website and create links from within the HTML pages to PDF documents. After you create the HTML pages for your website, you need to create the links that will open the PDF documents in the website visitor's browser. You can link directly to a PDF document, or you can link to a named destination within a PDF document. You can also create links from within PDF documents to websites.

Create HTML Hyperlinks to PDF Documents

After you create your web pages, you need to create hyperlinks to open the PDF documents within the website visitor's browser. As long as the PDF documents are stored at the same website as the HTML documents, you need to enter only the relative path to the document when creating the hyperlink. If the PDF documents are in the same folder as the HTML pages, your hyperlink is equal to the filename of the PDF document, with the .pdf extension. The following example shows a text link to a PDF document:

```
<a href="empMan.pdf"> Employee Manual </a>
```

Refer to your HTML editing software documentation for more information on creating hyperlinks.

Create HTML Hyperlinks to Named Destinations

If the PDF documents you create for web viewing have named destinations, you can create links that open directly to the named destinations. When the viewer clicks a link to a named destination, Acrobat or Adobe Reader launches in the viewer's web browser, and the document opens to the named destination rather than to the first page of the document. To create a link to a named destination, follow these steps:

1. Create the HTML page in your HTML editor.
2. Create a hyperlink to the named destination. You format a hyperlink to a named destination the same way you format a link to a bookmark within an HTML page. The hyperlink (href) is equal to the filename of the document, with the .pdf extension, which is then followed by the pound sign (#) and the name of the destination exactly as it appears in the PDF document. Refer to your HTML editing software user manual for more information on creating hyperlinks. The following example shows a text hyperlink to a named destination (Cat1) within a PDF document (myDoc.pdf). When you create the hyperlink, make sure you use the proper case for the named destination; otherwise, the document will open at the first page, rather than the named destination. Also refrain from using any spaces when entering a name for a named destination that will be used on the Web. For more information on named destinations, see Chapter 7.

   ```
   <a href="myDoc.pdf#Cat1"> Catalog Number 1 </a>
   ```

 Linking to a named destination isn't supported by some browsers. If your viewing audience is likely to have older web browsers or web browsers tailored for an Internet service provider (ISP) such as AOL, add a note telling viewers which web browsers the document is optimized for, and provide a link where viewers can download the web browser. Also, tell your viewers they need Acrobat 4.0 and later, or Adobe Reader 7.0 and later to view the document properly, and then provide a link to download the proper version.

Create and Distribute PDF Documents via E-Mail

As you learned throughout the course of this book, Acrobat PDF documents can be shared with anyone who has Acrobat or Adobe Reader installed. PDF documents are often referred to as e-paper, or electronic paper. What better way to share an electronic document than to send it via e-mail? In Chapter 4, you learned to convert a document from a Microsoft Office application to PDF format and e-mail it to an associate. You can also e-mail any document you create or append within Acrobat. After you digitally sign a PDF file and add your comments or otherwise mark up the document, you can send it via e-mail without leaving Acrobat by following these steps:

1. Log on to your ISP.
2. From within Acrobat, choose File | Attach To Email. Acrobat launches your default system e-mail application.
3. Within the e-mail composition window, enter any message to accompany the file and then send it. Acrobat automatically sends the PDF document as an e-mail attachment.

Summary

In this chapter, you learned how to work with PDF documents that will be posted to the Internet. You discovered how to initiate and participate in a shared review. You also learned how to prepare documents for the Internet, create links to named destinations, save documents for fast web viewing, and reduce the file size of PDF documents. In the next chapter, you will learn how to create interactive PDF forms.

13

Create Forms

Acrobat X makes it possible for you to add form fields to your PDF documents. You use form fields to retrieve information from readers of your PDF documents. You can also create forms for orders, questionnaires, and for getting viewer feedback from a website. You can create forms that tally the results of an online purchase and then submit the order to the online seller.

In this chapter, you learn to use the basic Acrobat form elements to create your own forms. A PDF form is a compilation of form fields you use to accumulate data from people to whom you distribute the form. The fields can be used to collect text and numeric data. You can specify field formatting to determine the type and look of the data entered. Your form can be a combination of text boxes, check boxes, combo boxes, list boxes, radio buttons, and signature fields. You can create buttons for the users to submit the data or reset the form. If you create a form for web use and the web host server supports Common Gateway Interface (CGI) scripting, you can have the form results forwarded to a website or entered into a database.

Create a PDF Form

When you create a PDF form, you can scan an existing paper form into Acrobat, use the tools from the Forms section of the Tools pane to create a form, and then add interactive form fields in the same position as the fields in the scanned document. You can also create a form in Acrobat by opening a document that contains elements that look like form fields and then invoking the Create command in the Forms section

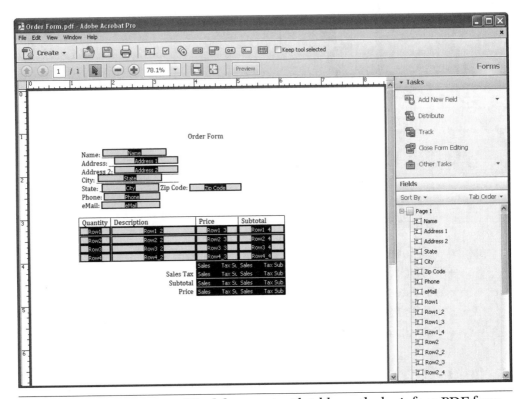

FIGURE 13-1 You can use a Word document with tables as the basis for a PDF form.

of the Tools pane. The form fields are automatically detected when you create the form. Figure 13-1 shows a Word document that was opened in Acrobat. The Form Wizard was used to detect objects that looked like form fields. For example, if you create a Word document with a table, Acrobat will detect the cells as text fields.

Fill Out a PDF Form

When users decide to fill out a form in the full version of Acrobat or Adobe Reader, such as the form previously shown in Figure 13-1, they click inside a field with the Hand tool. In Adobe Reader 7.0 and later, and in Acrobat, users have the option to highlight fields. When users click inside the form field, the cursor becomes an I-beam, indicating that data can be entered from the users' keyboard. To navigate to another field, users can either click inside another field after selecting the Hand tool or press TAB to advance to the next field. Users can correct an entry error by clicking inside the field with the Hand tool, selecting a word or letter that needs to be changed, and then entering the new data. If the form is equipped with a properly programmed Reset button, users can start over by clicking the button.

About Acrobat Form Fields

To create fields in your PDF forms, you click Tools, click Forms, and then choose Create. This starts the process to recognize form fields in an existing document created in another application such as Microsoft Word. You can also add forms to a currently open document by clicking Tools, clicking Forms, and then choosing Edit. After invoking this command, Acrobat attempts to find fields in the existing document. If nothing resembles a field, you can then add new fields to the document. In Acrobat, you can create these types of form fields:

- **Button**   You can create a text-only button, an icon-only button, or a button with both an icon and text. You can create an invisible button and place it over an existing graphic on a form you scanned and converted to PDF format, which gives the appearance that the graphic is executing the action instead of the form field.
- **Check Box**   You can create a group of check boxes when you want the user to choose from a set of options. For example, if you create a PDF questionnaire, you can create a series of check boxes for the user to select one or more items, such as frequently read publications.
- **Combo Box**   When you create a combo box, you give the user a choice of options. A combo box is identified by the presence of a drop-down arrow. When the arrow is clicked, a menu drops down with a list of available choices.
- **List Box**   You create a list box to display a list of available choices for the user. You can specify parameters that enable the user to make multiple selections from a list box (something that isn't possible with a combo box). If the number of items in the list box exceeds the dimensions of the box, Acrobat provides scroll bars.
- **Radio Button**   You can create a group of radio buttons to limit the user's choice to one item per group of radio buttons. For example, if you design an online order form, you can create a group of radio buttons with credit card options. The user chooses the one option that applies.
- **Text Field**   You create a text field to accept user input or to display data, such as the current date.
- **Digital Signature Field**   You can create digital signature fields for authorized users to digitally sign the form.
- **Barcode Field**   You can create a barcode field when you want to translate data from a form that was printed or faxed to you. Barcode fields eliminate the need to manually read and record data from a form that hasn't been submitted electronically. You must purchase Adobe's Barcoded Paper Forms software to process printed forms with a barcode field.

Design a Form

You can use any existing PDF document as the basis for your form. You create the labels for all your fields by creating read-only text boxes, and then you create the fields for user input data. The easiest method of creating a form, though, is to lay out the basic design of the form in an authoring application such as Microsoft Word and convert the file to PDF format. Then open the PDF file in Acrobat to add and format the form fields, or use the Create command in the Forms section of the Tools pane to recognize form fields. Another alternative is to scan an existing form into Acrobat and create the necessary form fields or have the Form command recognize existing form fields.

Use the Layout Grid

Whether you decide to create your form from an existing document or lay out one from scratch, you can use the Layout Grid to provide a visual reference while creating and aligning form fields. To enable the Layout Grid, shown in Figure 13-2, choose View | Show/Hide | Rulers and Grids | Grid. Rulers are also enabled when you add or edit form fields.

Use the Snap To Grid Command

When you enable the Layout Grid, you can visually align and size items to intersecting grid points. Use any of the Viewing tools to zoom in on your work. For exact alignment and sizing, choose View | Show/Hide | Rulers and Grids | Snap To

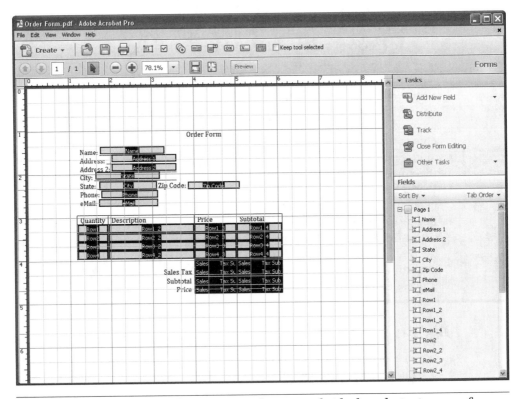

FIGURE 13-2 You can use the Layout Grid as a visual aid when designing your form.

Grid. When you use this command, the Layout Grid develops a magnetic personality, and any object you create snaps to the grid points.

> **Tip** The default color and grid spacing work well in most instances, but you can modify the color and spacing if they're unsuited to your preferences or the document you're modifying. Choose Edit | Preferences (Windows), or Acrobat | Preferences (Mac), and then click Units And Guides. Within this section of the Preferences dialog box, you can modify grid spacing, color, width between lines, and so on. You can also change the guide color, which, by default, is the same light blue as the grid line color.

Use Rulers and Guides

When you use the Create command in the Forms section of the Tools pane to add or edit form fields, rulers are displayed by default. From the rulers you can create guides wherever you need them. To create a guide, click a ruler and drag a guide into the Document pane. Release the mouse button when the guide is in the desired position. You can use the visual reference of the opposite ruler to precisely position the guide. To reposition a guide, move your cursor toward the guide. When your cursor becomes an angled arrow, click and drag the guide to the desired position. To remove a guide, select it and then drag it out of the Document pane.

Use the Form Create Command

The Create command in the Forms section of the Tools pane has the capability to recognize objects that look like form fields. This is a tremendous timesaver. For example, you can scan a paper form into Acrobat and then invoke the Create command in the Forms section of the Tools pane. After you invoke the command, Acrobat recognizes elements in the document that resemble form fields. To have Acrobat recognize objects that resemble form fields, follow these steps:

1. Choose File | Create | PDF From File and then open the file that is the basis for your form.
2. Click Tools, click Forms, and then choose Create to open the Create Or Edit Form dialog box (shown here) to start the process of recognizing form fields. You have two options: Use the current document as the basis for your form if you have one open in Acrobat, browse for a file, or scan a paper form.
3. Choose the desired option and then click Next to open the next section of the Create Or Edit

Create or Edit Form

Choose source:

◉ Use the current document or browse to a file

   (PDF, Word, Excel or other file type)

○ Scan a paper form

[Next >]   [Cancel]

Form dialog box, shown here. This section gives you the option to use the existing document or to browse for another document. After you choose an option, Acrobat scans for objects that look like form fields. If none are found, a dialog box to that effect appears. Click OK to exit this dialog box and begin creating the form. After you exit the dialog box, another dialog box appears prompting you to save the document.

After the document has been saved, Acrobat attempts to find objects that look like form fields. If Acrobat detects objects that look like form fields, they are displayed in the Fields panel, as shown in Figure 13-3.

4. Modify the fields or add new fields using the Form tools. After you've modified the document, save it. Creating form fields is covered in the following sections.

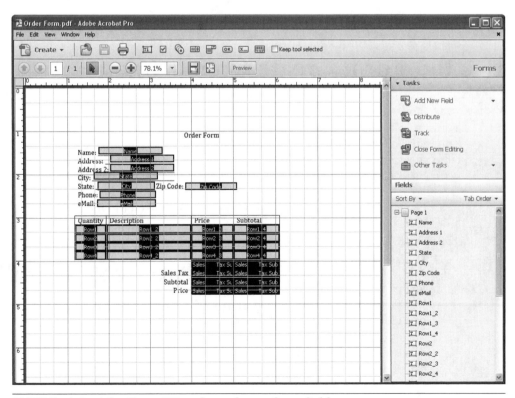

FIGURE 13-3 The Form Wizard can detect form fields.

Create Form Fields

After you create the PDF document that's the basis for your form, you're ready to start creating interactive form fields. You create form fields by selecting the desired command from the Add New Fields section of the Tasks panel and defining the field area with that tool. After you define the field area, a dialog box appears with the default name and value associated with the field. After naming the field, you can choose to display all of the field's properties, which opens another dialog box. Each field type has its own unique parameters, which you use to modify the field to suit the needs of the form you're creating. If the form fields contain text, you can also spell-check the field. To create a form field, follow these steps:

1. Open the PDF document you want to add form fields to and then click Tools, click Forms, and choose Edit. If there are no form fields in the document, a dialog box is displayed asking if you want Acrobat to detect form fields. Click Yes, and Acrobat detects anything that resembles a form field. This command enables rulers and displays the Fields panel in the Navigation pane. If you know there are no form fields in the document, click No. Either choice reconfigures Acrobat to create forms. The Forms pane appears on the right side of the interface, which is composed of Tasks and Fields panels, as previously shown.

2. Click Add New Field and then choose the desired command to add the desired form object to the document. The following illustration shows a form with several fields added. Notice the Forms tools above the Preview button.

3. Choose the desired command or select a tool from the Forms toolbar, click the point where you want the form field to begin, and then drag diagonally. As you drag the tool to define a field, a bounding box gives you a preview of the form field area. You can also click without dragging to create a form field of the default size and then edit it later. When the form field is the desired size, release the mouse button to open the Field Name dialog box. The following illustration shows the field and dialog box that appear after a form field has been created with the Text Field tool.

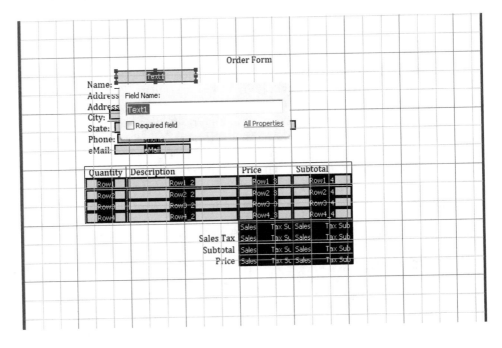

4. In the Field Name field, enter a name for the field. Acrobat gives the field a default name based on the tool that created the field, followed by a number. However, when you're creating a complex form with multiple fields, it's important to give each field a unique name. For example, if you're creating a form that retrieves contact information, the first field would have a name such as firstName.

When you name a field, it's considered good practice to have no spaces in the name, especially if you're using JavaScript code that addresses the form field.

5. Click the Required Field check box if the information is required. When you enable this option and the user attempts to complete or submit the form without entering information in the field, a warning dialog box to that effect appears.

6. Click Show All Properties to display the properties dialog box for the field. The illustration here shows the properties for a text field. Notice that the name is carried over from the previous dialog box.

7. In the Tooltip field, enter any text you want displayed as a Tooltip when a user hovers his mouse over the form field. This step is optional.

8. In the Common Properties section, click the Form Field drop-down arrow and choose one of the following options: Visible, Hidden, Visible But Doesn't Print, or Hidden But Printable.

9. Click the Orientation drop-down arrow and choose one of the following options: 0, 90, 180, or 270 degrees. This determines how the field data is oriented to the document.

 If text is in the field, it's rotated the same number of degrees. The quality of rotated text may be unacceptable with certain fonts.

10. Click the Read Only check box to make the field read-only. When you choose this option, users will be able to see the content of the form field, but they won't be able to interact with the form field.

11. Click the Required check box if users are required to interact with the form field. For example, if you choose this option on a text field, users are required to enter information in the field. If the document in which the text field is included has a Submit button and the user attempts to submit the form without filling in a required field, a warning dialog box appears, telling the user the required field was found empty during export. If you've already selected this option from the previous dialog box, the check box is filled.

12. Click the Appearance tab and select appearance options for the field. For specific instructions on setting appearance parameters, refer to the upcoming section "Specify Field Appearance."

13. Click the Options tab and specify the options for the field. The choices in this tab differ for each field type and are discussed in detail in upcoming sections.

14. Click the Actions tab and, from the Select Trigger drop-down menu, choose one of the following options to trigger the action:
    - **Mouse Up**   The action executes when the user releases the mouse button.
    - **Mouse Down**   The action occurs when the user presses the mouse button.

- **Mouse Enter**   The action occurs when the user passes the mouse over the field boundaries.
- **Mouse Exit**   The action executes when the user moves the mouse beyond the field target area.
- **On Focus**   The action occurs when the field is selected, either through a mouse action or tabbing.
- **On Blur**   The action occurs when the field is deselected as a result of a mouse action or tabbing.

15. Choose an action from the Select Action drop-down menu and then click the Add button. Actions were discussed in detail in Chapter 6 and are presented in this chapter as they apply to individual field types.
16. Click OK to complete the creation of the form field.

Specify Field Appearance

When you create a PDF form, you can change the appearance of a field to suit the document. You can choose whether to have a border and/or a background, and, if applicable, specify border and background colors. You can also control text attributes. To specify the appearance of a form field, do the following:

1. Create a form field, as outlined in the previous section, and then click Show All Properties to display the properties for the field type.
2. Click the Appearance tab to reconfigure the dialog box, as shown here.

```
Text Field Properties                                                ☒

  General | Appearance | Options | Actions | Format | Validate | Calculate

   ┌─Borders and Colors────────────────────────────────────┐
   │                                                        │
   │   Border Color:  ▣    Line Thickness:  [ Thin    ▼]    │
   │                                                        │
   │   Fill Color:    ◪    Line Style:      [ Solid   ▼]    │
   │                                                        │
   └────────────────────────────────────────────────────────┘

   ┌─Text───────────────────────────────────────────────────┐
   │                                                        │
   │   Font Size:  [ Auto      ▼]      Text Color:  ■        │
   │                                                        │
   │   Font:       [ Helvetica              ▼]              │
   │                                                        │
   │                                                        │
   └────────────────────────────────────────────────────────┘

  ☐ Locked                                         [  Close  ]
```

3. In the Borders And Colors section, click the Border Color swatch and choose a color for the field border. Then click the Fill Color swatch and choose a color for

the field background. Some field objects have a diagonal red slash through both swatches, which means the default option for the element is no border color and no fill color. Click the applicable swatch to specify a color. You can choose a color for the border and then choose a fill color, choose only a fill color, or choose none for both.

4. If you specify a border color, the Line Thickness option becomes available. Click the Line Thickness drop-down arrow and choose Thin, Medium, or Thick to specify the width of the border.

5. Click the Line Style drop-down arrow and choose Solid, Dashed, Beveled, Inset, or Underlined.

6. If the field type you choose has text, click the Font Size drop-down arrow in the Text area and choose a size from the drop-down menu. Alternatively, you can enter a value between 2 pts (points) and 300 pts. If you select Auto, Acrobat sizes the text to fit the field, with the exception of a text field set to display multiple lines, in which case the Auto option sizes the text to fit the field as the user enters it, with the text becoming smaller as Acrobat wraps the user's entry to another line.

7. Click the Text Color button and choose a color from the pop-up palette. Alternatively, you can click the Other Color button to create a custom color from the system color picker.

8. Click the Font drop-down arrow and choose a font. Note that if you select a font that isn't available on the user's system, the field font reverts to the user's default system font or, if possible, Acrobat renders a reasonable facsimile of the original font you specify. You can always embed the font, but be aware that font licensing issues may be involved and embedding fonts bloat the file size.

9. After you set appearance options for the field, click the other tabs, choose the parameters that apply, and then click OK to complete the field.

Tip After you create a field, align it, and set up all the parameters, you can prevent accidentally moving or otherwise editing the field by locking it. To lock a field, click the Locked check box in the form field's Properties dialog box.

Create a Button Field

You can use buttons for many things in Acrobat. You can use buttons for navigation devices, to submit forms, or to initiate an action. When you create a button, you can assign different actions to each state of the button. For example, you can have a sound play when the user rolls the mouse over the button. You can even change the appearance of the button based on the interaction of the user's mouse with the button. To create a button field, follow these steps:

1. Choose the Button command from the Add New Field section of the Tasks panel. Alternatively, choose the Button tool from the toolbar.

2. Drag diagonally on the document to define the dimensions of the button. After you release the mouse button, the Field Name dialog box appears.

3. In the Field Name field, enter a name for the field and then click Show All Properties to reveal the Button Properties dialog box.

4. Modify the parameters in the General section of the dialog box, as previously outlined in the section "Create Form Fields."

5. Click the Appearance tab and specify the applicable appearance options, as outlined previously in the section "Specify Field Appearance."

6. Click the Options tab, shown here.

7. Click the Layout drop-down arrow and, from the drop-down menu, choose one of the following options: Label Only; Icon Only; Icon Top, Label Bottom; Label Top, Icon Bottom; Icon Left, Label Right; Label Left, Icon Right; or Label Over Icon.

8. Click the Behavior drop-down arrow and choose one of the following options:

    - **None** The button appearance doesn't change when clicked.
    - **Push** You can change the button face in the Up, Down, and Rollover states.
    - **Outline** The button outline is highlighted when the button is clicked.
    - **Invert** The button colors invert when the button is clicked.

9. In the Icon And Label section, if you choose a layout with text, enter the button text in the Label field. If you choose a layout with an icon, click the Choose Icon button and follow the prompts to select an image for the button face.

10. If you chose Push for the Behavior option, click one of the three states (Up, Down, or Rollover) and, in the Icon And Label section, specify the text and icon decoration for the button when it's in this state, and then repeat for the other button states.

11. Click the Actions tab and specify the actions you want to occur when the user interacts with the button. Remember, you can apply multiple actions to the button for each state. For example, on Mouse Enter, you can have a sound play and a Tooltip appear; on Mouse Exit, you can hide the Tooltip and mute the sound. When you specify different actions and use the Push Behavior option, you create highly interactive buttons that pique user interest. When you add a sound file to a button, use a sound of short duration. Otherwise, the timing may be off, as Acrobat has to load the sound and the necessary libraries to play it. For more information on mouse events, refer to the section "Create Form Fields."

12. Click Close to complete the creation of the button.

After creating the button, you can forge ahead to the next field you need to create for the form. It's a good idea, though, to click Preview, select the Hand tool, and test the button to make sure it has the functionality you desire.

Rescale a Button Icon

When you create a button with an icon, Acrobat scales the icon to fit the area you designated when you created the button. After you test the button, you may find you need to fine-tune the size of the button icon. You can modify the size of the button icon by doing the following:

1. With the Button or Select Object tool, select the button you want to modify.
2. Right-click and choose Properties from the context menu.
3. Click the Options tab and then click the Advanced button to open the Icon Placement dialog box, shown here.
4. Click the When To Scale drop-down arrow and choose one of the following options:

   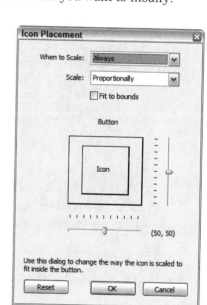

   - **Always** Acrobat always scales the icon to fit the area you specify, regardless of its size in relation to the form field.
   - **Never** Acrobat inserts the icon as originally sized. If the icon is too large for the field, it is clipped from top-left to bottom-right.
   - **Icon Is Too Big** Acrobat resizes the icon to the form field if it's larger than the form field dimensions.
   - **Icon Is Too Small** Acrobat resizes the icon to the form field if it's smaller than the form field dimensions. Note that if the icon is considerably smaller than the field size, the image will be pixelated.
5. Click the Scale drop-down arrow and choose one of the following options:
   - **Proportionally** Acrobat preserves the proportion of the original image when resizing it to fit the form field.
   - **Non-Proportionally** Acrobat resizes the icon to the proportions of the form field.
6. Drag the sliders in the Button area to determine icon placement in relation to the form field. By default, equal margins are preserved around the icon and the border of the button field. To modify the margin on the sides of the icon, drag the horizontal slider left or right. To modify the margin on the top and bottom of the icon, drag the vertical slider up or down.

7. Click the Fit To Bounds check box to constrain the icon image to the boundary of the button.

Click Reset to reset the icon placement to the default parameters.

8. Click OK to apply the parameters to the button icon.

You Can Use Button Fields for Navigation

When you create a multipage PDF document, readers can use Acrobat navigation tools to find their way around the document. If you distribute the document to casual Acrobat or Adobe Reader users who aren't familiar with all the navigation tools and menu commands, however, they may be unable to navigate the document. To solve this problem, create three buttons at the top of the page and label them Back, Next, and Home, respectively. Remember to assign a unique name to each button in the General tab of the Button Properties dialog box. Assign the Execute Menu Item action to each button. For the Back button, choose the View | Go To | Previous Page command. For the Next button, choose View | Go To | Next Page command. For the Home button, choose View | Go To | First Page command. Duplicate the buttons on all pages, as outlined in the "Duplicate a Form Field" section of this chapter. On the first page of the document, delete the Back and Home buttons and, on the last page of the document, delete the Next button. You now have a document that can be navigated by anyone.

Create a Check Box

You use check boxes to give the user the opportunity to choose more than one option. For example, if you create a questionnaire, you can use check boxes to collect information about which magazines the user reads. The user selects each applicable magazine and the results are sent to the location you specify when the form is submitted. To create a check box, follow these steps:

1. Select the Check Box tool from the Forms tools on the toolbar. Alternatively, you can click Tasks and choose Add New Field | Button.
2. Drag diagonally on the document to define the dimensions of the field. After you release the mouse button, the Field Name dialog box appears.

You can create a form field with the default size by selecting any form tool and clicking inside the document. You can manually resize a field by clicking the field with the Select tool and then dragging the handles until the field is the desired size.

3. In the Field Name field, enter a name for the field and then click Show All Properties to reveal the Check Box Properties dialog box.

4. Modify the parameters in the General section of the dialog box, as previously outlined in the section "Create Form Fields."

5. Click the Appearance tab and modify the parameters, as outlined previously in the section "Specify Field Appearance."

6. Click the Options tab, shown here.

7. Click the Check Box Style drop-down arrow and choose Check, Circle, Cross, Diamond, Square, or Star. This option determines what the check box looks like when selected. Note that some of these options may not render properly on different platforms. If possible, test the document on every platform your intended audience may use. When in doubt, Check is usually the best choice.

8. In the Export Value field, Yes is entered by default. This means the value of Yes will be exported when users select the check box. Enter different text to export a different value when users select the check box.

9. Select Check Box Is Checked By Default, and the check style you choose appears in the check box when the document loads. If you deselect this option, the check box is empty.

10. Click the Actions tab and specify the actions you want to occur when users interact with the check box.

11. Click Close to complete creation of the check box.

If you create a series of check boxes that are different options for a form element, such as a question, choose the same name for each check box, but specify a different export value. For example, if you're creating check boxes to gather a response for a simple question, you create two check boxes for each question and give one a Yes export value and the other a No export value.

Create a Drop-Down List

You can use a drop-down list to display a list of items when you want the user to select only one item from the list. A drop-down list functions like a drop-down menu, which can be accessed by clicking a down arrow. To create a drop-down list, follow these steps:

1. Select the Dropdown tool from the Forms tools on the toolbar. Alternatively, you can click Tasks and choose Add New Field | Dropdown.
2. Drag diagonally on the document to define the dimensions of the field. After you release the mouse button, the Field Name dialog box appears.
3. In the Field Name field, enter a name for the field and then click Show All Properties to reveal the Dropdown Properties dialog box.
4. Modify the parameters in the General section of the dialog box, as previously outlined in the section "Create Form Fields."
5. Click the Options tab, shown here.
6. In the Item field, enter the first item in your list.
7. In the Export Value field, enter the export value for the item. If no value is entered, the item is exported with the value listed in the Item field.
8. Click Add to add the item to the combo box.
9. Repeat steps 4 through 8 to add additional items to the list.
10. After adding all the items to the list, you can select the following options:
    - **Sort Items** Acrobat sorts the items numerically and then alphabetically.
    - **Allow User To Enter Custom Text** Users can enter their own value for the combo box.
    - **Check Spelling** Users can spell-check the custom text they enter. This option is selected by default.
    - **Commit Selected Value Immediately** Users' selections are saved immediately. Otherwise, the value is saved when the form is submitted. This option is handy when another field in the form will use the combo box export value.
11. If you didn't choose the Sort Items option, you can manually reorder the list. Select a list item and click the Up button to move the item one position higher in the list. Click the Down button to move the item one position lower in the list. If the item is at either extremity of the list, the applicable button is dimmed

out. Alternatively, you can click the Delete button to remove a selected item from the Combo Box list.

12. Click the Actions tab and specify the actions you want to occur when users interact with an item in the combo box. This step is optional.

13. Click the Format tab to specify the type of data that will be accepted in the field. For more information on formatting a field, refer to the upcoming section "Format Form Fields."

14. Click the Validate tab to restrict the range of data that can be entered in the combo box. For more information on this option, refer to the section "Validate Form Fields."

15. Click the Calculate tab if you want to use items from the combo box to perform a mathematical calculation. For more information on creating a calculating form field, refer to the section "Calculate Form Fields."

16. Click Close to complete the creation of the combo box.

Create a List Box

You create a list box when you want to enable users to select multiple items. When you create a list box, users can scroll through the list, as opposed to opening a drop-down menu with the combo box. Users cannot edit items in a list box, but they can select multiple items from the list, whereas they can select only one item from a combo box. You can use JavaScript to create a custom action when users change the list box selection. Here's how to create a list box:

1. Select the List Box tool from the Forms tools on the toolbar. Alternatively, you can click Tasks and choose Add New Field | List Box.

2. Drag diagonally on the document to define the dimensions of the field. After you release the mouse button, the Field Name dialog box appears.

3. In the Field Name field, enter a name for the field and then click Show All Properties to reveal the List Box Properties dialog box.

4. Modify the parameters in the General section of the dialog box, as previously outlined in the section "Create Form Fields."

5. Click the Appearance tab and define the appearance parameters for the list box, as discussed previously in the section "Specify Field Appearance."

6. Click the Options tab, shown here.

7. In the Item field, enter a name for the first item in the list.
8. In the Export Value field, enter the export value of the item. If you leave this field blank, the item name becomes the export value.
9. Click the Add button to add the item to the list box.
10. Repeat steps 5 through 9 to add additional items to the list box.
11. After you complete adding items to the list, you can choose the following options:
    - **Sort Items**   Acrobat sorts the list items in numerical and alphabetical order.
    - **Multiple Selection**   Enables users to make multiple selections from the list.

Note   If you select Multiple Selection, the Commit Selected Value Immediately option is no longer available.

    - **Commit Selected Value Immediately**   Users' selections are saved immediately; otherwise, the value is saved when the form is submitted.
12. If you didn't choose the Sort Items option, the Up and Down buttons are active. To move a selected item up one position in the list, click the Up button. To move a selected item down one position in the list, click the Down button. Alternatively, you can click the Delete button to remove a selected item from the list.
13. Click the Actions tab and specify the actions you want to occur when users interact with an item in the list box. This step is optional.
14. Click the Selection Change tab and, in the When The List Box Selection Changes section, choose one of the following options:
    - **Do Nothing**   This is the default option and, true to its name, nothing other than the selection change happens when you change a selection.
    - **Execute This Script**   Choose this option, and the Edit button becomes active. Click the Edit button to open the JavaScript Editor dialog box. Create the script that will execute when a list box item changes and then click OK to close the dialog box.
15. Click Close to complete the creation of your list box.

Create a Radio Button

When you create a group of radio buttons from which users can choose an option, only one button can be selected from the group, thus limiting users to one selection from the group. When you create a group of related radio buttons, each button has the same name, but a different export value. You'd use a group of radio buttons in conjunction with text labels. You'd create one label for the group and a separate label for each button. For example, if you needed to find the user's age, you'd create one label that reads "Age" and a label for each button that signifies the age choice for that button. If you're adept at JavaScript, your custom script can use the export value. To create a radio button, follow these steps:

1. Select the Radio Button tool from the Forms tools if displayed on the toolbar. Alternatively, you can click Tasks and choose Add New Field | Radio Button.
2. Drag diagonally on the document to define the dimensions of the field. After you release the mouse button, the Field Name dialog box appears.
3. In the Radio Button Choice field, enter text that describes the choice available for users. This is the value that will be exported for the button group when the form is submitted.
4. In the Group Name field, enter a name for the group. This is the value that will be exported with the choice when the form is submitted.
5. If desired, click the Required Field check box.
6. Click Add A Button.
7. Repeat steps 2 through 5 to configure the second button in the group.
8. Add additional buttons as needed.

After you create a group of buttons, they all have the same default properties. You modify the properties of the button group by doing the following:

1. Use the Select tool to select all buttons in the group.
2. Right-click to reveal the Radio Button Properties dialog box.
3. Click the Appearance tab and define the appearance parameters for the list box, as discussed previously in the section "Specify Field Appearance."

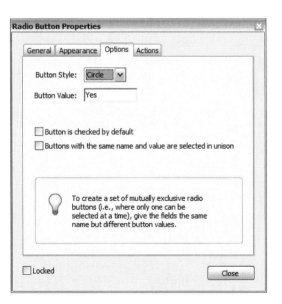

4. Click the Options tab, shown here.
5. Click the Button Style drop-down arrow and choose one of the following: Check, Circle, Cross, Diamond, Square, or Star. This option determines what the radio button looks like when selected.
6. Choose Button Is Checked By Default and, when the document loads, Acrobat will fill the field with the radio button style you selected in step 5. If you create a group of radio buttons with the same name, only one button can be set up with the Default Is Checked option. When you select a group of buttons, this option is applied to the first button selected.
7. Click the Buttons With The Same Name And Value Are Selected In Unison option if you have more than one radio button with the same name and export

value in the document. When you select this option, all buttons with the same name and export value are selected when the button you're creating is selected.

8. Click the Actions tab and specify the actions you want to occur when users interact with the button. This step is optional.

9. Click Close to complete modifying the properties of the radio button group.

Tip To create an exact copy of any field, select the field with the form tool with which it was created, and then, while pressing CTRL (Windows) or CMD (Macintosh), drag the form field. After you begin dragging the form field, press SHIFT to constrain motion vertically or horizontally. Release the mouse button to complete copying the field. If the copied field is part of a group of radio buttons, choose Properties from the context menu and change the export value of the field, but don't change the group name.

Create a Text Field

You can create text fields to accept user input or to display text strings, such as the current date. You can also use text fields to display multiple lines of text. You can limit the number of characters users can enter in the field and determine whether the field is visible. To create a text field, follow these steps:

1. Select the Text Field tool from the Forms tools if displayed on the toolbar. Alternatively, you can click Tasks and choose Add New Field | Text Field.

2. Drag diagonally on the document to define the dimensions of the field. After you release the mouse button, the Field Name dialog box appears.

3. In the Field Name field, enter a name for the field and then click Show All Properties to reveal the Text Field Properties dialog box.

4. Modify the parameters in the General section of the dialog box, as previously outlined in the section "Create Form Fields."

5. Click the Appearance tab and set the appearance options for the field, as outlined previously in the section "Specify Field Appearance."

6. Click the Options tab, shown here, to modify the following parameters:

- Click the Alignment drop-down arrow and choose to align the field contents to the left, center, or right.
- In the Default Value field, enter the default value for the field. This value is submitted unless the user enters different data. Alternatively, you can leave this field blank.

Tip   In the Default Value field, enter instructions on the type of information you want users to enter in the field.

- Enable the Multi-Line option to display the contents of the field on multiple lines. If this option is unchecked and the contents of the field exceed the width of the text box, the text is truncated.
- Enable the Scroll Long Text option, so users can scroll through the contents of a multiline text box. This option is selected by default. Users of the form can scroll through the field and edit the contents. Furthermore, if you use the text box to display read-only text and the Scroll Long Text option is deselected, users will be unable to scroll the contents of the field because no scroll bars will be present. If you create a read-only text box with multiple lines of text with this option deselected, be sure to properly size the box, so every line of text is visible.
- Enable the Allow Rich Text Formatting option to allow users to apply styles such as bold, italic, and underline to the text they enter in the field. Users with Acrobat Standard, Acrobat Pro, or Pro Extended can format text by choosing View | Toolbars | Properties Bar, selecting the text, and then selecting a style from the toolbar.
- To limit the number of characters a user can enter in the field, enable the Limit Of [ ] Characters option and enter a value in the field.
- Enable the Password option, and each character of text displays as an asterisk. This option is unavailable until you deselect the Check Spelling option.
- Enable the Field Is Used For File Selection option, and a path to a file can be entered as the value of the field, which enables a form to be submitted with the document. This option is dimmed out until you deselect the Scroll Long Text option. It is also unavailable if you enabled the Multi-Line, Limit Of Characters, or Password option. Likewise, this option is unavailable if you defined the field with formatting script.
- Enable the Check Spelling option (selected by default), and users can perform a spell check for the field.
- To spread a given number of characters evenly across the width in the field, enable the Comb Of [ ] Characters option and enter a value in the field. This option is available only if you deselect all other choices in the Options tab.

7. Click the Actions tab and specify which actions occur when a user's mouse interacts with the field. This step is optional.
8. Click the Format tab to specify the type of data that will be accepted in the field. For more information on formatting a field, refer to the upcoming section "Format Form Fields."

9. Click the Validate tab if you want to restrict the range of data that can be entered in the field. For more information on this option, refer to the upcoming section "Validate Form Fields."
10. Click the Calculate tab if the field will be used to perform a mathematical calculation. For more information on creating a calculating form field, refer to the section "Calculate Form Fields."
11. Click Close to finish creating the text box.
12. Select the Hand tool and click the text box to test it.

Create a Digital Signature Field

You can create a digital signature field when you want the user to sign the form. When you create a digital signature field, you can specify what occurs after the field is signed. To create a digital signature field, follow these steps:

1. Select the Digital Signature tool from the Forms tools on the toolbar. Alternatively, you can click Tasks and choose Add New Field | Digital Signature.
2. Drag diagonally on the document to define the dimensions of the field. After you release the mouse button, the Field Name dialog box appears.
3. In the Field Name field, enter a name for the field and then click Show All Properties to reveal the Digital Signature Properties dialog box.
4. Modify the parameters in the General section of the dialog box, as previously outlined in the section "Create Form Fields."
5. Click the Appearance tab and set the appearance options for the field, as outlined previously in the section "Specify Field Appearance."
6. Click the Actions tab and select the actions that occur when a user's mouse interacts with the field. This step is optional.
7. Click the Signed tab and choose one of the following options:
   - **Nothing Happens When Signed** Choose this default option, and the signature transmits with the submitted form, but nothing else happens.
   - **Mark As Read Only** Choose this option, and you can limit certain fields on the form to read-only status after the document is signed. When you select this option, choose one of the following from the drop-down menu: All Fields, All Fields Except These, or Just These. When you choose either of the latter options, click the Pick button to select the fields to include or exclude.
   - **This Script Executes When The Signature Is Signed** Choose this option to create a JavaScript that executes when the field is signed. After you choose the option, click the Edit button and create the JavaScript in the JavaScript Editor dialog box.
8. Click Close to complete the creation of the Signature field. For more information on digital signatures, refer to Chapter 10.

Did You Know?

Create a Barcode Field

If your organization distributes PDF forms that will be filled out in Acrobat or the Adobe Reader, printed, and then returned, you can greatly reduce processing time using a barcode field. As the form is filled out, the barcode appearance changes. To process a completed form, you simply scan the barcode. To integrate the Barcode tool into your workflow, purchase Adobe LiveCycle Barcoded Forms software. For more information, visit www.adobe.com/products/server/barcodedpaperforms.

Format Form Fields

When you create a form field that accepts data input, you can format the field for a specific type of data. For example, if the form field requests the user's fax number, format the field using the Phone Number option. If the user fills out the form and enters 5555551212, when the data is submitted, Acrobat reformats the entry to read (555) 555-1212. To format a form field, follow these steps:

1. Create a text or combo box field, as outlined previously in the section "Create Form Fields."
2. Click the Format tab in the form field's Properties dialog box.
3. The options in the Select Format Category drop-down list are None, Number, Percentage, Date, Time, Special, and Custom. Each category has different formatting options. The illustration here shows the available options for the Number category.
4. Choose the options that best suit the form you're creating.
5. If you chose the Custom category, click the Edit button beside Custom Format Script or click the Edit button beside Custom Keystroke Script to open the JavaScript Editor dialog box. Enter the script or paste an existing script into the dialog box, and then click OK.
6. Click Close to exit the form field's Properties dialog box.

Validate Form Fields

When you create a form field that accepts data, you can limit the amount of data the user enters by validating the form field. When you validate a form field, you specify a range of numerical data that can be entered, or you can create a custom JavaScript to limit the amount of data that can be entered. Validating a form field is useful when you put a form on the Internet. By limiting the amount of data you let the user enter, you eliminate a potential server bottleneck when a malicious user submits a form with copious amounts of data. You can only validate text and combo box form fields. To validate a form field, follow these steps:

1. Create either a text or combo box form field, as discussed in previous sections of this chapter.

2. Click the Validate tab in the form field's Properties dialog box, as shown in the illustration here. The options you have available vary, depending on the format you specify. The dialog box in this illustration is for a text field that accepts numeric input. By default, Acrobat doesn't validate the field.

3. If you choose either the number or percentage format (refer to the section "Format Form Fields"), you can limit the range of data the user can enter by clicking the Field Value Is In Range radio button and entering values in the From and To fields to define the acceptable range of data.

4. To create a validation script using JavaScript, click the Run Custom Validation Script radio button and then click the Edit button to open the JavaScript Editor dialog box. Enter the script you want to be used to validate the form field and then click OK.

5. Click Close to exit the form field's Properties dialog box.

Calculate Form Fields

When you create form fields with numeric data, Acrobat can calculate the value of two or more fields. You can choose from common arithmetic functions, or you can create a complex calculation using JavaScript. To calculate two or more form fields, follow these steps:

1. Create the form field that will display the result of the calculation, as outlined previously in this chapter.
2. Click the Format tab and choose Number from the Select Format Category drop-down menu.
3. Select the options that pertain to the calculation. For example, if you want to calculate a price, choose the appropriate style from the Currency Symbol drop-down menu.
4. Click the Calculate tab.
5. To use one of the present mathematical operations, choose the second option listed and, from the drop-down menu, choose the operation you want performed. You can choose from Sum (+), Product (×), Average, Minimum, and Maximum. Alternatively, you can choose Simplified Field Notation and then click Edit, which opens the JavaScript Editor dialog box, where you can enter a script to calculate the selected fields using simplified notation. Another option is to choose Custom Calculation Script, click the Edit button to open the JavaScript Editor dialog box, create the JavaScript to perform the calculation, and then click OK to close the dialog box and apply the custom calculation script.
6. Click the Pick button to display the Field Selection dialog box, which lists all the fields present in the document.
7. Click a field check box to use the field in the calculation.
8. Add the other fields necessary to perform the calculation and then click OK to exit the Select A Field dialog box.
9. Click Close to exit the form field's Properties dialog box.

Set Field Calculation Order

When you create a complex form with multiple fields of data that you call on for calculation, the order in which the calculation is performed may differ from the tab order of the fields. Follow these steps to change the order of the calculated fields:

1. Click Tasks and then choose Other Tasks | Edit Fields | Set Field Calculation Order to open the Calculated Fields dialog box, which shows all the calculable fields in your form and the order in which the calculations are performed on them.
2. To change a field's order in the list, select it and then click the Up button to move the field one position higher in the list. Click the Down button to move the field one position lower in the list.
3. Click OK when you finish reordering the fields.

Create a Reset Form Button

If you create a form with multiple fields, you may want to consider creating a reset button. Adding a reset button gives the user the option of starting over by clicking the button. When you create a reset button, you can specify which form fields are cleared when the button is used.

Here's how to create a reset button:

1. Create a button field, as outlined previously.
2. In Name field, enter a name for the field (Reset is a good choice) and then click Show All Properties.
3. Modify the button appearance and options to suit your form, as presented previously in the section "Create a Button Field."
4. Click the Actions tab and choose Mouse Up as the trigger.
5. Click the Select Action drop-down arrow and choose Reset A Form.
6. Click the Add button to open the Reset A Form dialog box, shown here.
7. Click Deselect All and then select the fields you want to reset. Alternatively, you can accept the default Select All option to select all form fields in the document.
8. Click OK to exit the Reset A Form dialog box, and then click Close to assign the action to the button.

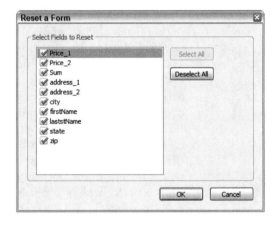

Create a Submit Form Button

When you create a form for use on the Internet or a local intranet, you can add a submit form button to transmit the results to a web server. You can specify the export format and specify which fields are submitted. To create a submit form button, follow these steps:

1. Create a button field, as outlined previously.
2. In Name field, enter a name for the field (Submit Form is a good choice) and then click Show All Properties.
3. Modify the button appearance and options to suit your form, as discussed previously in the section "Create a Button Field."
4. Click the Actions tab and choose Mouse Up for the trigger.
5. Click the Select Action drop-down arrow and choose Submit A Form.
6. Click the Add button to display the Submit Form Selections dialog box, shown on the next page.
7. In the Enter A URL For This Link field, enter the destination URL for the form results.
8. In the Export Format section, choose one of the following options:
   - **FDF Include** Acrobat exports the data as a Forms Data Format (FDF) file. With this format, you export field data and can choose to export comments, incremental changes to the PDF, or all the preceding. When you check the

Incremental Changes To The PDF box, data from digital signature fields can be exported in a manner recognized by a web server.

- **HTML**   Acrobat exports the form data in HTML format.
- **XFDF Include**   Acrobat exports the form data as an XFDF file. This file format is similar to FDF, with the exception that the file structure is XML. When choosing this option, you export Field Data and can choose to export Comments as well.

Note   When you choose the FDF or XFDF option, field data is exported by default. However, if you choose another option such as comments, you now have the option not to include field data.

- **PDF The Complete Document**   Acrobat exports the entire PDF file that contains the form data.

9. In the Field Selection section, accept the default All Fields option or click Only These. If you select the Only These option, click the Select Fields button to open the Field Selection dialog box. Click Select All to select all fields, or click the fields you want submitted when a user clicks the submit button. After selecting the fields, click the Include Selected radio button (the default) to include the selected fields when the form is submitted, or click the Exclude Selected radio button to exclude the selected fields when the form is submitted. If you choose the Empty Field option, fields with no data will be exported. Click OK to exit the Field Selection dialog box.

10. In the Date Options section, check Convert Dates To Standard Format to have Acrobat export date information in a standard format, regardless of what the user entered.
11. Click OK to apply the options.
12. Click Close to assign the action to the button.

How to... **Create a Form Table**

You can create a table of form fields by first creating a row or column of fields. Remember to give each field a unique name. Select the fields and then click Tasks | Other Tasks | Edit Fields | Place Multiple Fields to open the Create Multiple Copies Of Fields dialog box. From within the dialog box, you can specify the number of copies to make and the direction (above, below, left, or right) in which the new fields will be copied. By default, Acrobat provides a preview, so you can fine-tune the table before you exit the dialog box. When you click OK, Acrobat creates the multiple copies and appends the name of each copied field, so the field is unique.

Preview a Form

After you lay out and add form fields to a PDF document, your next step is to preview the form to test that everything works as expected. This is especially important if your form uses Actions. You can easily preview a form as follows:

1. Click Preview on the toolbar to display the form in Acrobat as your recipients will see it.
2. Fill out the form completely. As you fill out the form, pay attention to any problems that might occur, such as inconsistent type size, different font types, and so on.
3. If the form needs further editing, click Edit. Alternatively, if the form works as desired, click Edit and then choose Close Form Editing in the Tasks section of the Forms pane.

Spell Check Form Fields

You can spell check form fields and comments you create in a PDF document. You can add words to the Acrobat Spell Check dictionary and edit the dictionary as needed. To spell check form fields and comments in a document, follow these steps:

1. After creating your form, choose Close Form Editing from the Tasks panel of the Forms pane.
2. Choose Edit | Check Spelling | In Comments, Fields & Editable Text to open the Check Spelling dialog box.

3. Click Start to begin the spell check. When Acrobat finds a word that isn't in its dictionary, the word is highlighted in the Word Not Found field, as the following illustration shows. Acrobat supplies a list of suggested replacements in the Suggestions field. You can then take one of the following actions:

- Click Ignore to leave the highlighted word unchanged and continue with the spell check.
- Click Ignore All to leave the highlighted word and all future instances of the highlighted word unchanged.
- Edit the suspect word and then click Change.
- Edit the suspect word and then click Change All to change all instances of the suspect word to your edited text.
- Double-click a word from the Suggestions list to replace the highlighted word.
- Click Add, and Acrobat adds the word to your personal dictionary.
- Select one of the words from the Suggestions list and then click Change to replace the highlighted word.
- Select one of the words from the Suggestions list and then click Change All to change all occurrences of the highlighted word to the selected correction.

4. Click Done to end the spell check.

Specify Spell Check Preferences

Acrobat spell check is a powerful feature that you use to guard against typographical and spelling errors in your form fields and comments. You can configure the spell check feature to suit your preferences by following these steps:

1. Choose Edit | Preferences to open the Preferences dialog box.
2. Choose Spelling in the Categories list to open the dialog box, as shown on the next page.
3. Choose the Check Spelling While Typing check box (the default option) to have Acrobat underline any misspelled words with a squiggly red line immediately after you type them.
4. To change the underline color (red is the default), click the Underline Color button and choose a color from the pop-up palette.
5. To add a dictionary to the list, select one from the Dictionaries list and then click Check. The default dictionary is the language you selected when you installed

Acrobat. When you have multiple dictionaries, Acrobat searches the dictionary at the top of the list first.

6. To change the order in which Acrobat searches the dictionaries, select a dictionary from the Dictionaries list and then click the Up button to move the dictionary toward the top of the list. Click Down to move the dictionary toward the bottom of the list.
7. To remove a dictionary from the Dictionaries list, select it from the list (selected dictionaries are designated by an X between the < and > brackets) and then click UnCheck.
8. Click OK to apply the changes.

Edit the Dictionary

When you perform a spell check and Acrobat locates a word that isn't present in any dictionary in the Dictionaries list, you have the option to add the word to your personal dictionary. You can add or delete words from your personal dictionary when they're no longer needed by following these steps:

1. Choose Edit | Check Spelling | Edit Dictionary to open the Edit Custom Dictionary dialog box, shown next.

2. Click the Dictionary drop-down arrow and choose the dictionary you want to customize. Alternatively, you can accept the default All Languages option, and your changes will be applied to all Acrobat dictionaries you selected.

3. Choose an option from the second drop-down menu. Added Words is selected by default. Your alternative is to select Excluded Words.

4. To add a word to the dictionary, type it in the Entry field and then click Add.

5. To remove a word from the dictionary, select it from the list on the left and then click Delete.

6. To change a word in the dictionary, select it from the list on the left, make the desired change in the Entry field, and then click Change.

7. To exclude a word from the dictionary, choose Excluded Words from the second drop-down menu, type the word in the Entry field, and then click Add.

8. Click Done to finish editing the dictionary.

Note The Excluded Words option is only available when you select a specific dictionary. You can, however, add words to all dictionaries, such as the spelling of your name, your company, or any other word you want to appear in all dictionaries.

Use the Form Context Menu

You can find many of the commands needed to modify forms by choosing the desired command from the Forms menu or by using one of the Forms tools. You can also quickly access a command from the context menu. To modify a form field with a command from the context menu, select a form field with the Select Object tool and then right-click and choose a command from the context menu. Note that some of these commands are exclusive to the context menu. If you summon the context menu without selecting a form field, you have the option to add new form fields.

Tip When working in form-editing mode, double-click a form field with the Select Object tool to open the Properties dialog box for the field.

Use the Fields Panel

You can use the Fields panel to edit the form fields within your document. The Fields panel lists every field in your document. You can use the Fields panel to delete fields, navigate to fields, change field properties, and more. The Fields panel, shown here, is displayed on the right side of the interface beneath the Tasks panel.

To edit any field from the list in the Fields panel, select the field, right-click, and then choose a command from the context menu. Click a field in the Fields panel, and it is selected in the document.

Fields	
Sort By ▾	Tab Order ▾

- ⊟ ▢ Page 1
  - ▾ Dropdown2
  - Text1
  - Address 1
  - Address 2
  - State
  - City
  - Zip Code
  - Phone
  - eMail
  - Row1
  - Row1_2
  - Row1_3
  - Row1_4
  - Row2
  - Row2_2
  - Row2_3

Edit Form Field Properties

When a form works exactly as planned, it's time to move on to the next task—or take a quick break and bask in the glow of your accomplishment. More often than not, though, you'll need to tweak one or more properties of a form field. To edit form field properties, select the field with the form tool with which it was created, right-click, and then choose Properties from the context menu to open the form field's properties dialog box.

Delete a Form Field

When you revise a form and no longer need a particular form field, you can easily delete that form field. First, select it with the Select Object tool and then choose Edit | Delete. Alternatively, you can right-click the field and choose Delete from the context menu.

Align, Reposition, and Resize Form Fields

If you use the Layout Grid to align and size the fields in your form, you generally end up with a neatly laid-out form. However, you may still need to make some minor adjustments to the location or size of a field. You can resize individual fields or select multiple fields and then size and align them to each other.

To resize or reposition an individual form field, select the Select Object tool. After you select the field, eight handles appear around the field perimeter. You can then modify the field by doing any of the following:

- To reposition the form field, click the center of the field with the Select Object tool and drag the field to the desired location. As you drag the field, a bounding box gives you a preview of the current position of the field. When the field is in the desired position, release the mouse button.
- To resize the field, click any corner handle and drag. As you resize the field, a bounding box appears that gives you a preview of the current size of the field. Release the mouse button when the field is the desired size.

- To modify the field width, click the center handle on either side of the form field and then drag left or right to change the width of the field.
- To modify the field height, click the middle handle at the top or bottom of the field and drag up or down.

You can also modify the size and alignment of several fields. Use the Select Object tool to select any form field in the document. To add fields to the selection, press SHIFT and click the fields you want to add to the selection. The last form field you click is highlighted. All fields will be modified to the applicable parameter of the last field selected. After selecting two or more fields, you can do any of the following:

- To change the alignment of the selected fields, right-click and choose Align, Distribute, or Center. Then choose Align Left, Align Right, Align Bottom, Align Top, Align Vertically, or Align Horizontally.
- To center the selected fields to the current document, right-click and choose Align, Distribute, or Center. Then choose Center Vertically, Center Horizontally, or Both.
- To equally distribute the selected fields, right-click and choose Align, Distribute, or Center. Then choose Distribute Vertically or Distribute Horizontally. Note that the fields will be distributed relative to their center points.
- To change the size of the selected fields, right-click and choose Set Fields To Same Size. Then, choose Height, Width, or Both. Note that selected fields are sized to the last selected field.

Tip   You can set the tab order of form fields by opening the Fields section in the Forms pane. In the Tab Order section, choose Order Tabs By Row to set the tab order from left to right, Order Tabs By Column to tab order by columns from top to bottom, or Order Tabs By Structure to tab in the order in which the fields appear on the structure tree. Alternatively, you can select to set the tab order when working in form-editing mode by clicking Task and then choosing Other Tasks | Edit Fields | Show Tab Numbers. You can then move the fields to the desired positions in the document and change the tab order by selecting a field by name in the Fields panel and then dragging it to the desired position. The tab order is determined by the field's position in the panel.

Duplicate a Form Field

If the information or data entered in a form field needs to be in multiple locations of the document, you can duplicate the form field. You can duplicate a form field on the same page or across a range of pages. When you duplicate a form field, the field retains all the attributes you assigned to the original field. When you change a parameter in a field that was duplicated (in other words, a field with the same name that appears more than once in the document), the parameter changes in the duplicated fields as well. You can duplicate a single form field or a selection of form fields.

To duplicate form fields on a page, follow these steps:

1. If you're not already in form-editing mode, click Forms and then choose Edit.
2. Select the field using the Select Object tool.
3. Press CTRL (Windows) or OPTION (Macintosh) and drag the selected fields. To constrain the motion of the fields vertically or horizontally, press SHIFT (along with CTRL or OPTION) after you begin to drag the fields.
4. Release the mouse button. Acrobat then duplicates the selected fields where you released the mouse button.

Here's how to duplicate fields across a range of pages:

1. Select the field(s) you want to duplicate. When you work in form-editing mode, the Select Object tool is active. Click a field to select it. Alternatively, you can select the desired field by clicking its name in the Fields panel.
2. Click Tasks and then choose Other Tasks | Edit Fields | Duplicate to open the Duplicate Field dialog box, shown here.
3. Accept the All option (the default) to duplicate the field(s) on all document pages, or choose the From option and enter the range of pages on which to duplicate the field(s).
4. Click OK. Acrobat then creates the duplicates, per your specification.

Note When you're duplicating form fields, the names of the fields remain the same, but a hash/pound sign is appended to each name, along with a sequential index number.

Export Form Data

You can export data from a form for use in other PDF forms with the same field names. When you export data, you create a smaller file with data only. You can export the data as an FDF file, an XFDF file (an XML representation of the FDF data), an XML file, or a text file. To export form data, follow these steps:

1. Click Tools, click Forms, and then choose More Form Options | Manage Form Data | Export Data to open the Export Form Data As dialog box. This command is dimmed out when you work in form-editing mode.
2. Enter a name for the file and the folder where you want the data file stored. If you don't assign a name for the file, Acrobat uses the current name of the file by default.
3. Click the Save As Type drop-down arrow and select the desired file format.
4. Click Save.

Import Form Data

You can import form data to automatically fill in form fields using the following formats: Acrobat FDF files (.fdf), Acrobat XFDF files (.xfdf), XML files (.xml), FormFlow99 data files (.xfd), or text files (.txt). When you import form data, Acrobat automatically inserts the data in document form fields with the same names. To import data into a PDF document, follow these steps:

1. Click Tools, click Forms, and then choose More Form Options | Manage Form Data| Import Data to open the Select File Containing Form Data dialog box. This command is dimmed out when you work in form-editing mode.
2. Navigate to the file containing the data you want to import and select the file.
3. Click Select to open the file.

   You can also share form data with other users. For example, if you work in a corporate environment, you can post a form that contains fields pertaining to product information, such as current cost and list price. When the data needs to be updated, you can update the master version of the form and export the data. The version of the form posted on the corporate intranet can be programmed to automatically update using the Import Form Data action you program to execute when the page opens or when the user clicks a button. For more information on actions, refer to Chapter 7.

> **Tip** If you're working with multiple forms, you can merge them into a spreadsheet by clicking Tools, clicking Forms, and then choosing More Form Options| Manage Form Data | Merge Date Files Into Spreadsheet. The command opens the Export Data From Multiple Forms dialog box, which prompts you to add the PDF forms you want exported as CSV data. This can be viewed in a spreadsheet application such as Microsoft Excel.

Use JavaScript Actions

When you create a form field, you can use the Run A JavaScript Action command to create a custom script for the field. You can use the JavaScript Action to create JavaScript code and assign it to a button for use as navigation. You can also use JavaScript to augment Acrobat mathematical functions.

Use JavaScript to Subtract and Divide

In the section "Calculate Form Fields," you may have noticed Acrobat doesn't provide the capability to subtract or divide form fields. To perform either operation, you must use the JavaScript Action to create JavaScript code. To subtract a text field named Field B from a text field named Field A, follow these steps:

1. Select the Text Field tool.

2. Create a form field where you want the results of the calculation to appear. Enter a name for the field and then click Show All Properties.
3. Click the General tab and specify other parameters for the text field, such as the border color, fill color, font type, font size, and so on.
4. Click the Appearance tab and set the parameters for the field text, background color, and border color.
5. Click the Format tab and choose a format option for the field. Choose the same format as Field A and Field B. For example, if Fields A and B work with currency values, choose Number and then choose the currency symbol that applies.
6. Click the Calculate tab, choose Custom Calculation Script, click the Edit button, and then enter the following in the JavaScript Editor dialog box:

```
var a = this.getField("Field A");
var b = this.getField("Field B");
event.value = a.value - b.value
```

 If you create JavaScript in a word processing application, make sure you have smart quotes disabled. In JavaScript, smart quotes are illegal characters and will cause your script to fail.

7. Click OK to exit the JavaScript Editor dialog box.
8. You can modify the script to perform division by entering the following JavaScript in step 6:

```
var a = this.getField("Field A");
var b = this.getField("Field B");
event.value = a.value / b.value;
```

Note Division by a value of 0 isn't possible. If the user enters a value of 0 for the second field, an error message appears warning that the value doesn't match the format of the field. To guard against this, click the Validate tab and specify that the number must be greater than or equal to 1. Validating the field in this manner also results in an error message if the user enters a value less than 1. This includes dividing by negative numbers.

You can use JavaScript to perform complex calculations involving multiple form fields in a document. Simply create a variable for each form field and use the getField method to get the value of the field. To calculate the result, set the value method of the event object equal to a mathematical calculation using the value of each variable and the applicable operands. Here's an example:

```
var a = this.getField("Field A");
var b = this.getField("Field B");
```

```
var c = this.getField("Field C");
event.value = c.value * (a.value + b.value);
```

Distribute and Manage Forms

If you create a form for the purpose of gathering data, you can simplify the process of distributing a form and compiling data from returned forms. You manage forms with the new Forms Tracker, and you can export data from compiled forms as a spreadsheet.

Distribute Forms

When you have a form that needs to be distributed via e-mail to multiple recipients, you can easily do so within Acrobat. You can send the form immediately or save the form for future distribution. To distribute a form in Acrobat, follow these steps:

1. Create a form in Acrobat.
2. Add a submit button to the document. Instead of entering a URL in the URL field, enter **mailto:*myEmail@myserver*.com**.
3. Choose Forms | Distribute Form to display the Forms Distribution Options dialog box. Your choices for distribution are Automatically Download & Organize Responses With Acrobat.com, Manually Collect Responses In My Email Inbox, and Automatically Collect Responses On My Internal Server.

Note Acrobat.com is available on a trial basis with subscription fees that vary depending on the amount of features you need. For more information about Acrobat.com, visit https://acrobat.com/welcome.html.

4. Choose the method of distribution and then click Next to display the next page of the Distribute Form dialog box. The options you have available depend on the method of distribution you choose. If you choose Acrobat.com, you're prompted to log in to Acrobat.com using your Adobe ID. If you choose distribution via your internal server, you're prompted for the path to the folder in which you'll store the file. The steps that follow outline the process of collecting the information from e-mail. When you choose the option to collect data via e-mail, the Distribute Form dialog box reconfigures, as shown next.

5. Choose the manner in which you intend to distribute the form. Your choices are to send the form automatically using Adobe Acrobat, and to save a copy locally and manually send it later. If you choose to save a local copy and manually send it later, a Browse button appears that you use to specify the folder in which you save the file.

6. Click Next. The Distribute Form dialog box reconfigures, prompting you for your contact information, as shown next. This data is stored in the Acrobat Identity Preferences.

7. Enter your contact information and click Next. The following illustration shows the dialog box when the option to send the form via Acrobat is chosen.

8. Enter the e-mail addresses of the intended recipients. Separate each e-mail address with a semicolon, or press ENTER or RETURN after entering an e-mail address. Alternatively, click the To button and choose recipients from your e-mail address book.
9. Accept the default subject and message or enter your own information.
10. Accept the default option to collect the name and e-mail information to provide optimal tracking. This option stores the information in the Tracker.
11. Click Send to send the message. Acrobat displays a progress dialog box. After the form has been sent, the Tracker appears, provided you accepted the default option, to collect the name and e-mail information.

Note You may have to launch your default e-mail application and open the outbox to finish the distribution of the forms.

Compile the Data

After your form recipients fill out the forms and click Submit, the Send Form dialog box appears. After a recipient clicks Send, the completed form is returned to you via e-mail. The message in the body of the e-mail contains instructions to compile the data to a data set, as described next.

1. Download the e-mail with the returned form and double-click the attachment to display the Add Completed Form To Responses File dialog box, shown here.

2. Accept the default option, which adds the data to the data set created when you distributed the form.

Add Completed Form to Responses File

This file is a completed form and will be added to a responses file.

☉ Add to an Existing Responses File

`\C1RE2I08\Forms_distributed_distributed_responses.pdf` ▾   Browse...

○ Create a New Responses File

Browse...

Help   OK   Cancel

3. Click OK to display the Welcome To Your Form Response File dialog box and then click Get Started to display the home page of a PDF Portfolio that contains all responses to your distributed form.

4. Click Filter and then choose a field to filter the results by. After reviewing the results, click Done to return to the home page.

5. Click Export to export one or all results as CSV or XML data.

6. Click Archive to remove selected or all results as a new response file, or move the data to another file.

7. Click Add to add a PDF form file to the portfolio.

8. Click an icon to show the files in list view, preview a selected file, open the welcome page, save the Portfolio as a whole or save a file from the Portfolio, print some or all of the files in the Portfolio, share the Portfolio at Acrobat.com, or modify the Portfolio.

Did You Know?

Manage Forms

When you distribute forms, you can easily manage them using the Forms Tracker. From within the tracker, you can view responses, open the original form, e-mail all recipients, add recipients, or e-mail recipients who have not responded. The tracker also lists all recipients, whether or not they responded, and the date they responded.

Summary

In this chapter, you learned how to use Acrobat tools to add form elements to your PDF documents. You learned how to create and edit form fields that collect data, allow viewers to make a choice from a list or combo box, and choose items using radio buttons or check boxes. You also discovered how to create form fields that calculate numeric data and validate data. The final topics of discussion showed you how to distribute forms and compile returned forms into a data set. In the next chapter, you will learn how to optimize your PDF documents for print.

14

Batch Process and Optimize PDF Documents for Print

HOW TO...

- Use the Action Wizard
- Create PDF/X-compliant documents
- Perform a preflight check
- Preview print separations
- Preview transparency flattening
- Add information for the printer

Acrobat has a powerful timesaver known as batch processing that helps you automate tasks you need to perform on multiple documents. Batch processing is covered in detail in this chapter.

Acrobat X Pro provides robust tools for prepress print production. Document authors can create Portable Document Format Exchange (PDF/X)–compliant documents that are ideally suited for documents that will be printed commercially. The PDF/X format conforms to a set of rigid guidelines that ensures your printed document looks identical to the document you created in your authoring application. Before sending a document to a publisher or a printer, you can use the powerful set of prepress tools in Acrobat X Pro to perform sophisticated tests to ensure your document is ready for print. In this chapter, you will learn how to use these tools on your own documents before sending them to the printer.

Use the Action Wizard

When you prepare a large number of PDF documents for a specific audience or destination, you often end up performing the same task on every document—for example, optimizing several documents for Internet viewing. Instead of opening every document you need to modify and then repeat the same task, you can perform the same command on several documents at once by using the Action Wizard. You can choose from preset actions or create your action. When you create a custom action, you can specify the order in which the commands execute. You can also use batch processing to perform a specific sequence of commands on a single document or multiple documents.

Use Preset Actions

When you choose a preset action, you can run the action on an open file or choose a folder of files to process. If a command in the action requires user input, the applicable dialog box appears. Actions are particularly useful when you're doing final preparations on multiple documents stored in a folder. You can also perform an action on a single file. The following steps show you how to prepare a folder of documents. To perform a batch sequence, follow these steps:

1. Click Tools, click Action Wizard, and then choose the desired action. For the purpose of this demonstration, select the Prepare For Distribution action. After you select the action, the Action: Prepare For Distribution dialog box appears, as shown next. The dialog box differs depending on the action you choose.

Action: Prepare for Distribution   ✕

Description: This action allows you to add a header, footer,
                   watermark, bookmarks and remove hidden information.

Start with: A File Open in Acrobat

Steps:
                   1 Header & Footer (Add)

                   2 Watermark (Add)

                   3 Add Bookmarks

                   4 Remove Hidden Information

Save to: Ask When Action is Started

☐ Don't show again for this Action   Next   Cancel

---

2. Click Next to open the Select Files dialog box. This dialog box does not appear when you run the action on a document currently open in Acrobat.
3. Choose an option from the Add Files drop-down menu, as shown next.
4. After choosing the files upon which to run the action, click Next to open the Browse For Folder dialog box. This is where you choose the folder into which the processed files are saved.

5. Select or create a folder and then click OK.
6. At this stage, Acrobat opens the applicable dialog box for each step of the action. Follow the prompts to perform each step, and Acrobat performs the action on each file. Additional dialog boxes appear as needed for each step of the action. You're prompted when needed to move to another task in the action. After the action is complete, each file is saved to the specified folder.

Edit an Action

When you edit an action, you have several choices. You can edit the steps of the action, rename the action, copy the action to a different location, export the action as an SEQU file to share the action with colleagues, import an action that was exported as an SEQU file from a colleague's computer, or delete an action. To edit an existing batch sequence, follow these steps:

1. Click Tools, click Action Wizard, and then choose Edit Actions to open the Edit Actions dialog box, shown next.

2. Choose the action you want to edit. The steps to rename, copy, delete, export, or import are self-explanatory. The following steps focus on editing an action.

3. Click Edit to open the Edit Action dialog box. Shown next is the dialog box for editing the Create Accessible PDFs action.

4. Choose one of the following options from the Start With drop-down menu:

   - **Ask When Action Is Started** Prompts the user to select a file when the action is started.

- **File Open In Acrobat** The default choice for preset actions runs the action on a file that is currently open in Acrobat.
- **A File On My Computer** Prompts the user to open a PDF file on his computer.
- **A Folder On My Computer** Prompts the user to navigate to a file folder on her computer.
- **A Scanned Document** Prompts the user to scan a paper document. After the document is scanned, the action is executed on the resulting PDF.

- **Combine Files Into A Single PDF** Prompts the user to select files, which are converted into a PDF. The action is executed on the resulting PDF.

5. To change the options for a step, click the Options button. This opens a dialog box related to the action.
6. After changing options, click OK to exit the dialog box.
7. If the action you are modifying has instructions, you can modify the instructions by clicking the Information icon to open the Add/Edit Instructions dialog box.
8. Click Save to save the edited instructions.
9. To change the order in which the tasks execute, click and drag a task to a new location in the hierarchy.
10. To add additional instructions, click Add Instruction Step to open the Add/Edit Instructions dialog box.
11. Enter a name for the instruction step and then enter the instructions.
12. Click Save to save the additional instructions and close the dialog box.
13. Choose one of the following options from the Save To drop-down menu:
    - **A Folder On My Computer** The user is prompted to navigate to the desired folder on his computer.
    - **Ask When Action Is Started** The user is prompted for the location in which to save the file.
    - **The Same Folder As Selected At Start** This option saves the document in the folder from which it was opened.
    - **Don't Save Changes** If you choose this option, Acrobat won't save the changes or output the processed files. This option enables you to test the batch process. After you ascertain the batch sequence is working correctly, you can choose a different output location option and rerun the sequence.
14. Click the Output Options button to open the Output Options dialog box, shown here. In the Output Options dialog box, you can modify the filename and output options, as the following steps describe.
15. In the File Naming section, choose one of the following options:
    - **Keep Original File Names** Saves the batch-processed files with the same name as the original document.
    - **Add To Original File Names** Changes the original base filename. When you select this option, the Insert Before and Insert After fields become available, which enable you to add a prefix or suffix to the filename of the processed files.

16. In the Output Format section, accept the default Save Files(s) As Adobe PDF. Alternatively, deselect this option and proceed to step 19 to save the processed files in a different format.

17. Click Embed Index. Acrobat creates a searchable index for the files being processed and embeds the index with each file.

18. Choose the PDF Optimizer option, and all files processed with this batch sequence run through the PDF Optimizer. If you choose the PDF Optimizer option, the Settings button becomes available. Click the button to configure the PDF Optimizer for the batch sequence you're editing.

19. Click the Export File(s) To Alternate Format radio button and then choose one of the following options from the drop-down menu: Encapsulated PostScript, Excel Workbook, HTML, JPEG, JPEG 2000, Microsoft Word Document, PDF/A, PDF/E, PDF/X, PNG, PostScript, Rich Text Format, Text (Accessible), Text (Plain), TIFF, XML 1.0, or XML Spreadsheet 2003.

20. Click OK to close the Output Options dialog box and then click Save to open the Save Action dialog box. When you're editing an action, the name of the action is preserved and the text in the Action Description field is selected.

21. If desired, modify the action description.

22. Click Save to save your changes.

Create a New Action

You can create a new action and tailor it for operations you perform frequently on your PDF documents. When you create a new action, you specify the commands run when the action executes, the order they run in, the files upon which the action is executed, and how the processed files are saved. To create a new action, follow these steps:

1. Click Tools, click Action Wizard, and then choose New Action to open the Create New Action dialog box, shown next.

2. Choose one of the following options from the Start With drop-down menu:
   - **Ask When Action Is Started** Prompts the user to select a file when the action is started.
   - **File Open In Acrobat** This option runs the action on a file that is currently open in Acrobat.
   - **A File On My Computer** Prompts the user to open a PDF file on his computer.
   - **A Folder On My Computer** Prompts the user to navigate to a file folder on her computer.
   - **A Scanned Document** Prompts the user to scan a paper document. After the document is scanned, the action is executed on the resulting PDF.
   - **Combine Files Into A Single PDF** Prompts the user to select files, which are converted into a PDF. The action is executed on the resulting PDF.

3. Choose the steps that will run when the action is executed. To choose a step, click the left-pointing arrow next to one of the titles on the left side of the dialog box. You can add as many steps as needed to accomplish the task for which you're creating the action.

4. Click Options to open the Options dialog box as the first step in your action. This opens the dialog box for the first step in the action as seen when the action is executed.

5. Repeat step 4 for each step in the action you're creating.

6. If necessary, click the Prompt User check box. This check box is used when the step requires input from the user, such as choosing a range of pages when the Rotate Pages command is selected.

7. If desired, click Add Instruction Steps to open the Add/Edit Instructions dialog box. This option lets you leave instructions for one or more steps in the action.

8. Click Save to save the additional instructions and close the dialog box.

9. Choose one of the following options from the Save To drop-down menu:
   - **A Folder On My Computer** The user is prompted to navigate to the desired folder on his computer.
   - **Ask When Action Is Started** The user is prompted for the location in which to save the file.
   - **The Same Folder As Selected At Start** This option saves the document in the folder from which it was opened.
   - **Don't Save Changes** If you choose this option, Acrobat won't save the changes or output the processed files. This option enables you to test the batch process. After you ascertain the batch sequence is working correctly, you can choose a different output location option and rerun the sequence.

10. Click the Output Options button to open the Output Options dialog box, shown previously. In the Output Options dialog box, you can modify the filename and output options, as the following steps describe.

11. In the File Naming section, choose one of the following options:
    - **Keep Original File Names** Saves the batch processed files with the same name as the original document.

- **Add To Original File Names** Changes the original base filename. When you select this option, the Insert Before and Insert After fields become available, which enable you to add a prefix or suffix to the filename of the processed files.
12. In the Output Format section, accept the default Save Files(s) As Adobe PDF. Alternatively, deselect this option and proceed to step 13 to save the processed files in a different format.
13. Click Embed Index. Acrobat creates a searchable index for the files being processed and embeds the index with each file.
14. Choose the PDF Optimizer option, and all files processed with this batch sequence run through the PDF Optimizer. If you choose the PDF Optimizer option, the Settings button becomes available. Click the button to configure the PDF Optimizer for the batch sequence you're editing.
15. Click the Export File(s) To Alternate Format radio button and then choose one of the following options from the drop-down menu: Encapsulated PostScript, Excel Workbook, HTML, JPEG, JPEG 2000, Microsoft Word Document, PDF/A, PDF/E, PDF/X, PNG, PostScript, Rich Text Format, Text (Accessible), Text (Plain), TIFF, XML 1.0, or XML Spreadsheet 2003.
16. Click OK to close the Output Options dialog box and then click Save to open the Save Action dialog box. When you're editing an action, the name of the action is preserved and the text in the Action Description field is selected.
17. Accept the default option to overwrite existing files. This option will rewrite any file with the same name. It's advisable to deselect this option if you're saving files to the same folder.
18. Click Save to open the Save Action dialog box.
19. Enter a name and description for the action. You can also click the Run The Action after saving to test the action immediately.
20. Click Save. After you save the action, it appears in the Action Wizard for future use.

Optimize PDF Documents for Print

Commercial printing houses embrace the PDF format. When you create a document in an illustration program such as Adobe Illustrator, or a page design application such as InDesign, you can send the finished document to the printer in a PDF format that is tailored to the printer's needs. The following sections show you how to optimize PDF documents for a commercial printer.

Create PDF/X-Compliant Documents

PDF/X is now the standard for PDF documents destined for printers and publishers. The PDF/X format ensures the document will be printed correctly, while maintaining color and font integrity. The author creates the document using graphics and fonts in an illustration or publishing application and then exports a PDF document that's PDF/X compliant. You can export a PDF/X-compliant PDF document from the authoring application, or convert a PDF document to PDF/X standards within Acrobat 9 Pro and Acrobat Pro Extended.

Create a PDF/X-Compliant Document in an Authoring Application

You use an application's Print command to create a PDF/X-compliant document from within an authoring application using Adobe PDF as the printer. You can specify the version of PDF/X with which the document will be compliant in the Adobe PDF Document Properties dialog box. Here's how:

1. Choose your application's Print command and then choose Adobe PDF as the printer.
2. Click the Properties button to display the Adobe PDF Document Properties dialog box.
3. Click the Adobe PDF Settings tab.
4. Click the Default Settings drop-down arrow and choose one of the PDF/X conversion settings from the drop-down menu, shown here.

5. If necessary, click the Edit button to edit the conversion setting, as outlined in Chapter 11.
6. Exit the Adobe PDF Document Properties dialog box.
7. Print the document.

Print Production

When you prepare documents for print, you use the powerful tools in Acrobat X Pro to make sure your document is ready for the printer. The commands you use are found in the Print Production section of the Tools pane. To access the Print Production commands, click the Tools icon, click the Show or Hide Panels icon in the upper-right corner of the pane, and then choose Print Production to show the Print Production section, shown here.

Perform a Preflight Check

Within Acrobat, you can check an existing document to make sure it's compliant with the PDF/X format by performing a preflight check. When you perform a preflight check, you choose the version of Acrobat with which the document will be compliant. To perform a preflight check, follow these steps:

1. Open the PDF document you want to check.
2. Click Tools, click Print Production, and then choose Preflight. The Preflight dialog box appears and Acrobat begins loading profiles.

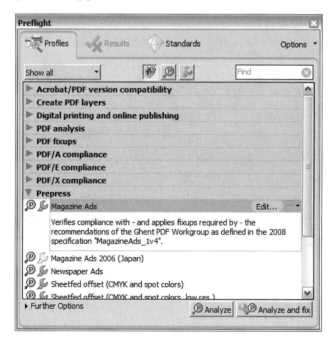

Note   After the profiles load, you might see a yellow exclamation point in the upper-right corner of the Preflight dialog box. Click the icon to open the Preflight: Display Settings Alert dialog box that warns you of any potential problems in the PDF, such as overprinting elements or present color management that doesn't have a corresponding embedded profile. Click Adjust to fix the conflict.

3. Click a drop-down arrow next to an option, select a Profile from the Acrobat/PDF Version Compatibility drop-down list (the version of Acrobat with which you want the document to be compatible), and then click Analyze or Analyze And Fix. The options vary depending on the profile you select.

4. If you choose Analyze, Acrobat analyzes the document for errors and displays the results, as shown next. You can embed the audit trail for the printer or create a report. If you choose Analyze And Fix, Acrobat analyzes and fixes the document for the selected profile. You are then prompted to save the document.

Preflight ☒

🔍 Profiles   ✖ Results   ◇ Standards   Options ▾

✖ Preflight profile "Verify compliance with PDF/X-1a" found the following errors:

📄 Pages 1 - 5 from "ProgramAssessment-PrinciplesofSuccess.pdf.pdf"
⊟ ✖ PDF document is not compliant with PDF/X-1a (2003)
    ⊞ ✖ OutputIntent for PDF/X missing
    ⊞ ✖ PDF/X version key (GTS_PDFXVersion) missing
    ⊞ ✖ Trapped key not true or false
    ⊞ ✖ Page does not have TrimBox or ArtBox (5 matches on 5 pages)
    ⊞ ✖ Uses device independent color (4 matches on 4 pages)
    ⊞ ✖ Font not embedded (88 matches on 5 pages)
⊞ 📊 Overview
⊞ Ⓟ Preflight information

🔍 Show in Snap   📝 Embed Audit Trail...   📋 Create Report...

Tip   In the Preflight dialog box, you also have the options to convert the document to PDF/X or PDF/A.

How to... Convert Colors

Sometimes the only thing preventing a document from being PDF/X compliant is the presence of RGB colors in the document. If this error appears on a Preflight report, or when you attempt to convert a PDF to PDF/X within Acrobat, you can convert the document colors to CMYK by clicking Tools, clicking Print Production, and then choosing Convert Colors. This opens the Convert Colors dialog box, as shown here. Choose the applicable options and then click OK. If you're unsure of which options to select, check with the service center or the publisher that will print the document.

Perform Prepress Production Tests

When you prepare a PDF document for a printer, you can perform several tests to make sure the document is as desired. You can preview the color separations and transparent areas of the document, add information for the printer, and so on. You can also specify the sizes of the crop, trim, art, and bleed boxes—information the printer uses when setting up the printing device and trimming the printed pages.

Preview Print Separations

You can preview print separations before sending your work to the printer to ensure the separation plates and ink coverage meet your requirements. You get your best results when previewing separations if you're working with a calibrated monitor. To preview print separations, follow these steps:

1. Click Tools, click Print Production, and then choose Output Preview. The Output Preview dialog box appears.
2. Choose a profile from the Simulation Profile drop-down list.
3. Check the Simulate Ink Black check box, and the document changes to show you how the black colors will appear when the document is printed.
4. Check the Simulate Paper Color check box, and the document changes to show how the white of the paper will appear when the document is printed.
5. To preview an individual process plate or spot plate in the document, deselect the other colors by clicking their check boxes in the Separations section.
6. To view the percentages of ink in a specific area, hover your cursor over the area you want to check, and the percentage of each ink appears to the right of its name in the Output Preview dialog box.
7. Click the Ink Manager button to open the Ink Manager, shown here, which enables you to convert spot colors to process and modify the

density of the inks used to print the document. The Ink Manager is primarily used by prepress service providers.

8. Click OK to exit the Ink Manager and then close the Output Preview dialog box.

Preview Transparency Flattening

Today's illustration and image-editing programs make it easy to include transparency in a document. For transparency to print properly on some PostScript printers, though, the transparency needs to be flattened or converted to raster images. Check with the service company handling your printing to see if transparency needs to be flattened. You can preview the way flattened transparency will appear and flatten transparency by doing the following:

1. Click Tools, click Print Production, and then choose Flattener Preview. The Flattener Preview dialog box is displayed.

2. Click the Highlight drop-down arrow and choose the desired option to highlight. The options vary, depending on the artwork in the document and the Flattener

setting specified in the Transparency Flattener section of the Acrobat Advanced Print Setup dialog box. The following is a list of all possible options:

- **None (Color Preview)** The default option doesn't highlight transparent objects in the document and shows a color preview of the entire document.
- **Rasterized/Complex Regions** Highlights the areas of the document that will be rasterized in accordance with the setting you specify with the Raster/ Vector Balance slider in step 6.
- **Transparent Objects** Highlights objects in the document with transparency, objects with blending modes, and objects with opacity masks. In addition, objects with styles and effects that contain transparency are highlighted.
- **All Affected Objects** Highlights all objects in the document that contain transparency, including objects that overlap transparent objects.
- **Expanded Patterns** Highlights all patterns that will be expanded if they contain transparency.
- **Outlined Strokes** Highlights all strokes that will be outlined if they contain transparency.

3. Click the Refresh button to refresh the preview and display the objects in accordance with the Highlight option you selected.

4. Click inside the preview window to zoom in. Each click zooms to the next highest level of magnification. While pressing the SPACEBAR, click and drag inside the preview window to pan within the document. CTRL-click (Windows) or CMD-click (Macintosh) to zoom out.

5. Choose an option from the Preset drop-down list. Your options are Low Resolution, Medium Resolution, and High Resolution. Use Low Resolution to create a quick proof for output on a desktop printer, or for PDF documents that will be published on the Web or converted to SVG format. Use Medium Resolution for creating proofs and for print-on-demand documents that will be output to PostScript color printers. Choose High Resolution for documents you're preparing for final press output.

6. Drag the Raster/Vector Balance slider to determine how much of the transparency will be converted to raster objects. Drag left to increase the number of raster objects or drag right to convert more transparent objects to vector objects. Click the Refresh button to preview the results.

7. Click the Line Art And Text Resolution drop-down arrow and choose an option. This setting determines the resolution in pixels per inch (PPI) for all line art and text in the document. Click the Refresh button to preview the results.

8. Click the Gradient And Mesh Resolution drop-down arrow and choose an option. This setting determines the resolution in PPI for complex objects in the document.

9. Specify flattening options:
   - **Convert All Text To Outlines** Converts any text in the document to graphic objects. This renders the text unsearchable.
   - **Convert All Strokes To Outlines** Keeps all stroke widths constant. Fine details such as thin lines and thin fonts may appear larger when this option is enabled.

- **Clip Complex Regions** Preserves the boundaries between vector objects and raster objects along object paths. Choose this option to reduce artifacts when part of an object is rasterized and other parts are vectors.
- **Preserve Overprint** Blends the color of transparent objects with the background color to produce an overprint effect.

10. Click Refresh to refresh the preview based on your current settings.

You can save your current settings as a preset by clicking Save and then following the prompts to name and then save the preset.

11. In the Apply To PDF section, choose an option to determine whether flattening is applied to the entire document, the currently selected page, or a page range.
12. Click Apply to apply transparency flattening to the document.
13. Click OK to exit the dialog box.

Add Information for the Printer

When you have a document that contains artwork, such as the graphics for a business card, and you use an application's Print command to convert the document to PDF, it appears on an 8.5 × 11–inch page, unless you specify a different size. The additional white space around the graphic isn't wasted because you can add valuable information for the printer. But before you can add the printer's information, you must specify the size for the trim box, the art box, and the bleed box.

Modify the Trim Box, the Art Box, and the Bleed Box

Before you can add printer marks to a document with art smaller than the page size, you must specify the size of the trim box (the size to which the printer will trim the printed document). At the same time, you can also specify the size of the art box (the actual size of the artwork) and bleed box (the extended area beyond the trim box to which content is clipped if a bleed area is present). You set the sizes for the trim box, art box, and bleed box as follows:

1. Click Tools, click Print Production, and then choose Set Page Boxes to open the Set Page Boxes dialog box, shown in Figure 14-1.
2. Click the Units drop-down arrow and choose the document's unit of measure.
3. Choose ArtBox from the Boxes drop-down list.
4. In the Margin Controls area, enter the Top, Bottom, Left, and Right values. These values crop the art box from the document size to the actual artwork. To arrive at these values, subtract the size of the artwork from the size of the document, divide the difference in the width by 2 to determine the Left and

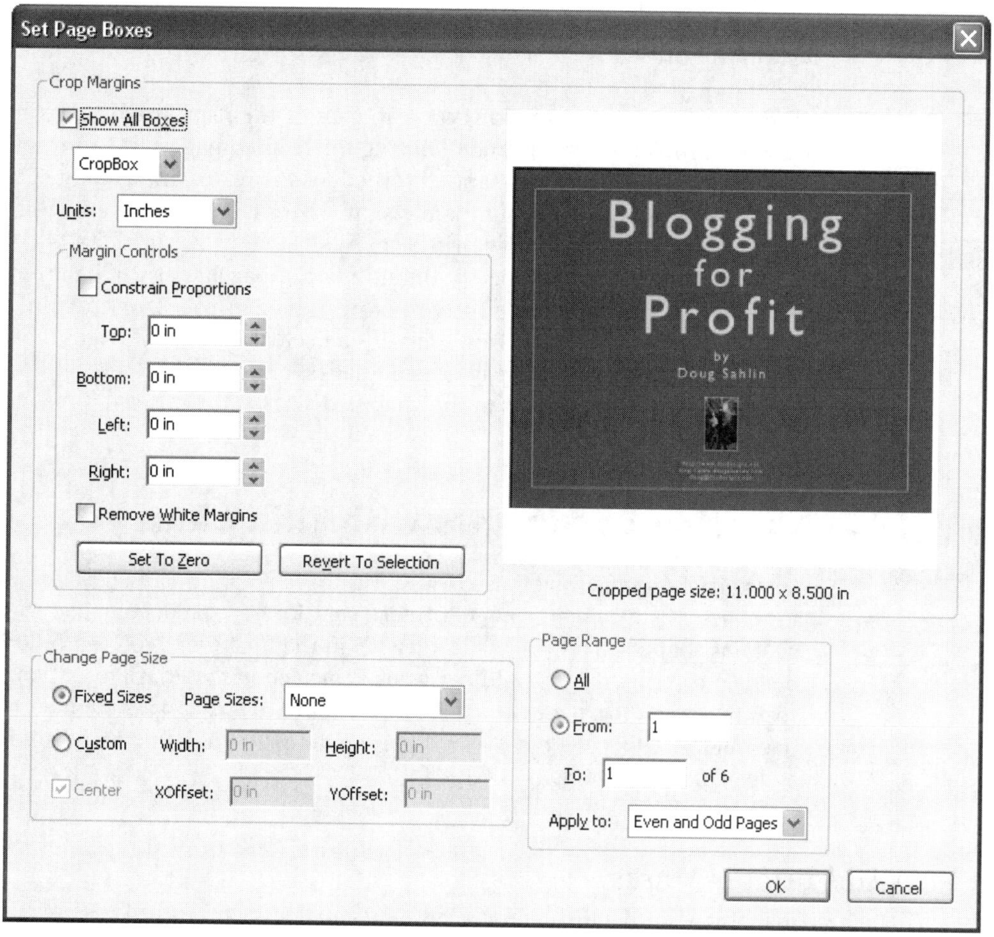

FIGURE 14-1   Specifying the size of the trim box, art box, and bleed box.

Right values, and then divide the difference in the height by 2 to determine the Top and Bottom values. For example, if you're specifying trim values for a 2 × 3.5–inch business card on an 8.5 × 11–inch page, the values for Left and Right are 3.25 inches, and the values for Top and Bottom are 3.75 inches.

5. Choose TrimBox from the Boxes drop-down list and enter the Top, Bottom, Left, and Right values to specify the trim box size.

6. Choose BleedBox from the Boxes drop-down list and enter the Top, Bottom, Left, and Right values to specify the bleed box size.

Note   When you specify the values for cropping margins and deselect the Show All Boxes option, the color of the border surrounding the artwork changes when you select an option from the Boxes drop-down list. In the preview window, a blue rectangle shows the current bleed box size, a green rectangle shows the current trim box size, and a red rectangle shows the current art box size. The dimensions are noted beneath the artwork.

7. In the Change Page Size section, you can change the page size by clicking the Page Sizes drop-down arrow and choosing the desired page size. Alternatively, click the Custom radio button and enter values for Width and Height. This option is handy if the document is the same size as the artwork and you need additional white space to show printer marks.

8. In the Page Range section, specify the number of pages that will be cropped in the document. You can crop all pages, crop a range of pages, or crop only the pages you selected from the Pages tab. If you select a range of pages, you can specify whether to crop odd pages, even pages, or both.

9. Click OK to crop the margins to the specified sizes.

Printing Documents with Thin Lines

Commercial printers sometimes have difficulty when printing a document with thin lines. If you're preparing a PDF document for print production and it contains thin lines, they may not show up in the final print. You can fix this problem by using the Fix Hairlines menu command in the Print Production section of the Tools pane, which identifies hairlines and assigns them a thicker line weight, which you can specify. The tool also fixes hairlines in Type 3 fonts and PostScript patterns.

Add Printer Marks

Before finalizing your document for print, you can add printer marks such as trim, bleed, and registration marks as described in this section. This information ensures the document is printed to your specifications. Here are the steps to follow:

1. Click Tools, click Print Production, and then choose Add Printer Marks. The Add Printer Marks dialog box opens, as shown on the next page.

2. Choose from the following options:
   - **All Marks** Adds all printer marks to the document.
   - **Trim Marks** Adds a mark at each corner of the trim box.
   - **Bleed Marks** Adds a mark at each corner of the bleed box.
   - **Registration Marks** Adds marks outside of the trim box area, which are used by the printer when aligning separations for a color document.
   - **Color Bars** Adds a small bar for each spot or process color. Your printer uses these marks to adjust ink density when setting up the printer for your document.
   - **Page Information** Places information such as the filename, current date, and page number outside of the trim box.

3. Click the Style drop-down arrow and choose the desired mark style. Your choices are printer mark styles used by Adobe InDesign, Adobe Illustrator, and Adobe QuarkXPress. If you choose the Default style, Acrobat uses generic printer marks that are universally recognized by printers.

4. Click the Line Weight drop-down arrow and choose the desired weight for the lines used to create the printer marks.

5. The Embed Printer Marks With Layers option is selected by default. This option embeds printer marks on a layer, which you can show or hide using the Layers pane.

6. In the Page Range section, specify the number of pages in the document that will have printer marks. You can choose from the following: All, Selected, and From, which enables you to specify a range of pages. Selected is dimmed out if you haven't selected page thumbnails from the Pages panel.

7. Choose an option from the Apply To drop-down menu to determine whether printer marks are added to odd pages, even pages, or odd and even pages.

8. Click OK to add printer marks to the document.

How to... Create a JDF File

Job Definition Format (JDF) files are electronic job tickets. JDF files can be embedded in the file when the artwork is created in an illustration application, or you can create a JDF file in Acrobat. This file enables you to specify information such as the product name, job ID, job ID part number, and so on. You can also embed a preflight profile and a PDF conversion setting with a JDF. You create a JDF file within the Edit JDF Definitions dialog box. To create or edit a JDF file, click tools, click Print Production, and then choose JDF Job Definitions to open the JDF Job Definitions dialog box. Click New, and then follow the prompts. Check with your service center to see if it supports JDF files.

Summary

In this chapter, you learned how to prepare a document for a commercial printer. You saw how to perform a preflight check, convert a PDF file to a PDF/X file, and convert colors. You also learned how to flatten transparency, how to specify the size of the trim box, art box, and bleed box, as well as how to add printer marks to a document. In the next chapter, you will learn how to add multimedia to your PDF documents.

15

Add Multimedia Elements
to PDF Documents

HOW TO...

- Work with images
- Extract images from documents
- Add sound to documents
- Add movies to documents

When most people think of creating multimedia presentations, they think of an application such as Microsoft PowerPoint. Indeed, PowerPoint is one of the most frequently used programs to create full-fledged multimedia presentations. However, with a bit of imagination and Acrobat X Pro, you can create impressive multimedia presentations.

When you create a multimedia presentation for CD-ROM, file size generally isn't an issue. A CD-ROM can hold 700 MB of data, which means you can fill your PDF documents with stunning full-color images, audio files, and full-motion video. In this chapter, you learn how to integrate multimedia files into your PDF documents to create multimedia presentations that will impact your viewing audience.

Work with Images

When you create a multimedia PDF presentation, images are a must. Whether you're creating a corporate portfolio presentation, educational media, or a product catalog, images add visual spice that piques user interest and makes the presentation a success. When you prepare images for multimedia PDF presentations, you can use high-resolution images and save them in file formats that aren't compressed. Alternatively, if you use an image file format that compresses images, you can apply less compression to create a sharper image.

If you create documents with images and intend to use these as the basis for a multimedia PDF, and you're not using one of the newer word processing applications with improved layout tools, consider investing in a page-layout program such as Adobe InDesign. When you use a page-layout program, you have better control over image placement, especially when you want text to wrap around the image. In lieu of a page-layout program, many popular word processing applications support embedding images in documents. If the authoring program supports PDF export, you should export the document with little or no image compression. If PDF export isn't supported, choose Adobe PDF as the printing device to convert the document to PDF format, and use the High Quality conversion setting.

Tip When you're working with a PDF document with images you want to use in another document, you can export the images by clicking Tools, clicking Document Processing, and then choosing Export All Images. This opens a dialog box you use to specify the export format for the images and the folder in which you want to store the images.

How to... ## Optimize Images for Multimedia PDF Presentations

If you have image-editing software, such as Adobe Photoshop CS5 or Adobe Fireworks CS5, scan your images into the program with a resolution of 300 dpi (dots per inch). This is more than you need for monitor viewing, but it allows the image to be magnified in the resulting PDF with negligible loss of quality. If you're capturing images with a digital camera, shoot them at the highest resolution possible. Resample the image to the desired size for your presentation. Ultimately, your presentation will be viewed on a 72- or 96-dpi monitor, but you can leave the resolution at a higher value and the images will look better when your viewers magnify the document. Export the finished image as a BMP file (Windows) or an uncompressed TIFF file (Macintosh and Windows) for the best results.

Add Sound to Documents

No multimedia experience is complete without sound. When you add sound to a presentation, you involve another one of the viewer's senses, which makes the experience more complete. You can use sounds in a variety of ways, including with buttons, when a page opens, or when a page closes. Acrobat now supports sounds for all popular formats, including MP3.

When you add a sound file to an Acrobat document, you can choose whether or not to embed the file. When you embed a sound file in a document, it's saved with the document. When a sound file isn't embedded with a document, Acrobat records the path to the sound file and the file plays when the trigger you specify occurs. If you move a sound file that isn't embedded in a document to a different folder on your computer, or to a different URL, it won't play. Adding a sound file to a document you plan to display on the Internet would result in an extremely long download for users with a slow Internet connection, unless the sound file is extremely small. Alternatively, you can include the path to a streaming audio file on a website. When you create a PDF document and add sound files for a multimedia file you're creating for distribution on CD or DVD disc, file size is no longer a concern.

Add Sound to a PDF Document

You can use the Sound command to add sound to a PDF document. When you use the Sound tool, you create an activation area that, when clicked, plays a sound. This is useful when you want to augment an image with a prerecorded narration or perhaps a song. When you use the Sound command, you enable viewers to play a sound on demand.

You can also play a sound when a page opens or closes by using the Play Media (Acrobat 6 And Later Compatible) action. This action gives you complete control over the sound file you want the user to hear when the page opens. Depending on the type of presentation you create, you can have a short musical piece play when a page opens or have a vocal introduction. You can also use a sound when the page closes. (For more information on actions, refer to Chapter 6.) When you use the Play Media (Acrobat 6 And Later Compatible) action and choose Page Close as the trigger, you can choose to play a sound that has been added to the page by using the Sound command, as outlined in the next section.

Tip Sound can enhance your presentation, but the blatant use of sound will have your viewer turning down the speaker volume or, worse yet, exiting your presentation before it's finished.

Adding a button is another method you can use to add sound to your PDF presentation. Create a button and then use an action to play the sound when the button is clicked or when a user pauses his or her cursor over the button. You can use an action to play a sound during the Mouse Enter event to alert viewers that the button warrants their attention. Alternatively, you can play the sound during the Mouse Down event, which alerts the viewers that the button has successfully been clicked. For more information on buttons and events, refer to Chapter 13.

Caution If you use sounds for both events, and the sound assigned to the Mouse Enter event is longer than the sound you use for the Mouse Down event, the first sound plays until conclusion. This means the button action may execute before the second sound ever plays.

If you're creating a product catalog or an educational tool for distribution on CD or DVD disc, you can have a product description or tutorial play when an image is clicked. To have a sound play when an image is clicked, select the Link tool and create a hotspot around the image, as outlined in Chapter 6. In the Create Link dialog box, choose Invisible Rectangle from the Link Type drop-down list and then choose the Custom Link option. In the Actions tab, choose Play A Sound from the Action Type drop-down menu and then select the sound you want to play when the image is clicked.

Use the Sound Command

When you use the Sound command, you define an active area of the document that viewers can click to play a sound file. You can choose to embed the file with the document or not. When you don't embed the sound file with the document, Acrobat plays the sound from the folder where it resides on your computer or from the website where the sound file is stored. If you intend to send a PDF document with a nonembedded sound to someone, you have to send the sound file as well. Alternatively, you can upload the sound to a website and enter the URL to the sound file when you specify sound properties. As long as your recipient has a reasonably fast Internet connection and is online when viewing the document, he or she will be able to hear the sound file. The only times you should consider not embedding a sound file is when the document is for playback on your own computer or for a CD-ROM compilation where the sound file will be used by several documents, or if you've uploaded a streaming sound file to a website. When you compile the assets for burning the presentation to a CD or DVD disc and you have PDF documents with sounds that aren't embedded, be sure to include the folder with the audio clips. You also have to maintain the same relative path to the sound files. In other words, if the sound files are in a subfolder to the parent directory named Sounds, you must create a subfolder named Sounds at the website or on the CD or DVD disc from which the PDF presentation will be viewed.

To add a sound to a document by using the Sound tool, follow these steps:

1. Navigate to the page to which you want to add the sound file.
2. Click Tools, click Content, and then choose | Multimedia | Sound.

If you use multimedia in many PDF documents you author, right-click the Multimedia section in the Content section of the Tools pane and choose Add To Quick Tools from the context menu.

3. Drag diagonally inside the document to define the active area that will play the sound when clicked. This opens the Insert Sound dialog box.
4. Click the Browse button to open the Select A File dialog box. Next, select the desired sound file and then click Open to exit the dialog box.
5. Click Show Advanced Options. This gives you options to add a poster frame for the sound, determine what activates the sound, and so on. You can still add sound to the document without enabling this option. However, you do have more control over the final output if you use the advanced options, as shown next.

6. In the Enable When drop-down menu of the Activation Settings section, choose one of the following options:
   - **The Content Is Clicked**   Plays the audio file when a user clicks the activation area in the document.
   - **The Page Containing The Content Is Opened**   The sound plays when the page is opened.
   - **The Page Containing The Content Is Visible**   The sound plays when the page containing the media is visible.
7. From the Disable When drop-down menu of the Activation Settings section, choose one of the following options:
   - **'Disable Content' Is Selected From The Context Menu**   The file stops playing when a user chooses Disable Content from the file's context menu.
   - **The Page Containing The Content Closes**   The file stops playing when the page closes.
   - **The Page Containing The Content Is No Longer Visible**   The content stops playing when the page is no longer visible.
8. Choose one of the following options from the Playback Style drop-down menu in the Activation Settings area:
   - **Play Content On Page**   Choose this option, and Acrobat embeds the player at the position on the page where you dragged your mouse after invoking the Sound command.

- **Play Content In Floating Window**   The file plays in a floating window when the content is activated. If you choose this option, the Width and Height text boxes become available. These determine the size of the player.

9. Choose one of the following options from the Border Width drop-down menu:
   - **No Border**   Displays no border around the player.
   - **Thin**   Displays a thin border around the player.
   - **Medium**   Displays a medium border around the player.
   - **Thick**   Displays a thick border around the player.

10. In the Poster Image section, you can specify what viewers see when a multimedia file is embedded in a document. By default, the first frame of a video file is displayed. This is also know as the "Poster." To specify a poster, choose one of the following options:
   - **Keep Current Poster**   This option is grayed out for a sound file because there is no poster frame in a sound file.
   - **Retrieve Poster From Media**   If you choose this option with a sound file, you end up with a white rectangle and the border option you specify in step 9.
   - **Create Poster From File**   If you select this option, the Browse button becomes available. Click the button and select an image that will designate the active area for the sound file. Note that when you select an image, its dimensions are reconfigured to fit the area you defined with the Sound tool.

11. Click OK to finish adding the sound to the document and close the Insert Sound dialog box.

Note   If you use an image as a poster for a sound object, you may have to resize the area to conform to the dimensions of the image by clicking the poster after invoking the Sound command or by clicking the poster with the Select Object tool and then dragging the handles around the perimeter of the object until the image is no longer distorted.

Viewers can play the sound by clicking the active area with the Hand tool.

Create Audio Tracks for Your PDF Documents

Acrobat doesn't have the capability to edit soundtracks. If you intend to use sound extensively when creating multimedia PDF presentations, you may want to consider investing in sound-editing software. You can use sound-editing software to record your own sound clips and then edit them to fit your presentation. Most popular sound-editing software can be used to enhance a recording, remove noise from a recording, add special effects (such as echo or reverb) to a sound recording, and much more. Some sound-editing programs enable you to mix soundtracks with other recordings. Software is also available to create musical soundtracks. Adobe sells an application called Soundbooth CS5, which enables you to create music soundtracks for your applications and record soundtracks. For more information on Adobe Soundbooth CS5 visit www.adobe.com/products/soundbooth/.

Sony also makes an application that enables you to create music soundtracks from royalty-free music samples. Sony's ACID Music comes in several different versions to fit any budget. To find out more about Sony's ACID Music family of products, visit http://www.sonycreativesoftware.com/products/acidfamily.asp.

Did You Know?

Insert Flash Content into a PDF Document

With Acrobat X Pro, you can embed Flash content in a PDF document. If you use Flash to create animations or applications, you can embed the resulting SWF file in a PDF. You can also embed Flash Video (FLV files) into a PDF document. In addition, you can embed Flash Widgets in a PDF document. A Flash Widget is a Flash application in the SWF format. If you're a savvy Flash programmer, you can create your own Flash Widgets. You can also find Flash Widgets that perform many functions by performing a search in your favorite search engine. To add a Flash SWF file to a document, click Tools, click Content, and then choose Multimedia | SWF.

Add Video Clips to PDF Presentations

You can add full-motion video to your PDF documents by using the Video tool. When you add a movie to a PDF document and choose Acrobat 6 (And Later) Compatible Media, you can choose whether or not to embed the movie with the document. You can also specify multiple versions of the movie that are tailored for playing from a CD disc, DVD disc, or from an Internet website.

Add Movies to Documents

You use the Video command to add movies to your document. You can add videos in the following file formats: FLV, F4V, MOV, MP4, M4V, 3GP, and 3G2. After embedding a video in the document, you can use the Multimedia Operation page action to play, pause, rewind, advance to the next chapter point, advance to the previous chapter point, advance to a specific time, mute the audio, display a volume control, or create a custom action when the page opens or closes. By default, Acrobat X Pro snaps the movie window to the size of the movie and uses the first frame of the movie as a poster in the document. To add a movie to a PDF file, do the following:

1. Click Tools, click Content, and then choose Multimedia | Video.
2. Click and drag inside the document to specify the position in which the poster frame of the movie appears. You don't have to worry about sizing the area. By default, Acrobat snaps the activation area to the dimensions of the movie. After you release the mouse button, the Insert Video dialog box appears. The default version of the Insert Video dialog box makes it possible for you to insert a video

that will be playable in the published document. However, you have more control over the process if you use the advanced options for video. The following steps show you how to use the advanced controls.

3. Click Advanced Controls.
4. Select the desired file, or enter the URL where the video can be found, and then click OK to display the Insert Video dialog box shown next.

5. In the Enable When drop-down menu of the Activation Settings section, choose one of the following options:
   - **The Content Is Clicked**   Plays the video file when a user clicks the activation area in the document.
   - **The Page Containing The Content Is Opened**   The video plays when the page is opened.
   - **The Page Containing The Content Is Visible**   The video plays when the page containing the media is visible.
6. From the Disable When drop-down menu of the Activation Settings section, choose one of the following options:

- **'Disable Content' Is Selected From The Context Menu**   The file stops playing when a user chooses Disable Content from the file's context menu.
- **The Page Containing The Content Closes**   The file stops playing when the page closes.
- **The Page Containing The Content Is No Longer Visible**   The content stops playing when the page is no longer visible.

7. Choose one of the following options from the Playback Style drop-down menu in the Activation Settings area:
   - **Play Content On Page**   Choose this option, and Acrobat embeds the player at the position on the page where you dragged your mouse after invoking the Video command.
   - **Play Content In Floating Window**   The file plays in a floating window when the content is activated. If you choose this option, the Width and Height text boxes become available. These determine the size of the player.

8. Choose one of the following options from the Border Width drop-down menu:
   - **No Border**   Displays no border around the player.
   - **Thin**   Displays a thin border around the player.
   - **Medium**   Displays a medium border around the player.
   - **Thick**   Displays a thick border around the player.

9. In the Poster Image section, choose one of the following options:
   - **Keep Current Poster**   This option is grayed out when you first insert the file, but is available as an option when you edit the video annotation.
   - **Retrieve Poster from Media**   This displays the first frame of the video. If the first frame of your video is blank, you may want to consider choosing the Create Poster From File option.
   - **Create Poster From File**   If you select this option, the Browse button becomes available. Click the button and select an image that will designate the active area for the sound file. Note that when you select an image, its dimensions are reconfigured to fit the area you defined with the Video tool.

10. Click the Controls tab. This section of the dialog box lets you configure the playback controls, as shown on the next page. By default, the controls are displayed when a user pauses his cursor over the video.

11. Choose an option from the Skin drop-down menu. This gives you the option to display all controls, or you can choose which controls are visible. There is also an option to display no controls, which is useful if you use a Page action to play the movie when the page opens.

12. Click the color swatch to specify the color of the controls. The default color for the playback control background is black. Choose a color that's harmonious with the content that's in your video.

13. Enter a value for Opacity. The default value of 75 percent displays 25 percent of the underlying video. Specify a higher value to make the controls more visible, or a lower value to make the underlying video more visible. You can also use the spinner controls to specify a value.

14. Uncheck Auto-Hide Controls to display the video controls at all times.

Insert Video

File: F:\MysticalMyakka.mp4 [Browse...]

☑ Snap to content proportions

Launch Settings | Controls | Video

Playback Controls

Skin: [All Controls ▾] Color: [ ] Opacity: [75 ⬍]

☑ Auto-hide controls

[Help]   ☑ Show Advanced Options   [OK] [Cancel]

15. Click the Video tab. If the video you're adding to the document has chapter points, they are listed in this tab. If you prepare your videos, you may be able to add chapter points in your video-editing software. Check your user manual for more information. If the video has chapter points, you can use the chapter point as a trigger for an action, as shown in step 16. If your video has no chapter points, proceed to step 17.

16. Select a chapter point, click Actions, and then select the action you want to occur when the video reaches the chapter point.

17. Click OK. Acrobat adds the movie to the document and displays a poster according to the options you selected.

Did You Know?

Adding 3D to PDF Documents

For those of you who work with 3D applications, you'll be happy to know you can add 3D content to your PDF documents. With Acrobat X Pro, click Tools, click Content, and then choose Multimedia | 3D to add *U3D and *PRC files to a PDF document.

Edit Multimedia Annotations

After you add a multimedia element to a document, you may find it necessary to edit the annotation. You can change player options, change the manner in which the multimedia file is played, and more. To edit a multimedia annotation, right-click it and choose Properties from the context menu. This opens the applicable dialog box, where you can modify the parameters to suit the document and your vision.

Summary

In this chapter, you learned how to add multimedia elements such as sound, video, and SWF and 3D files to your PDF documents. You learned how to configure the parameters for each element to suit your document.

Index

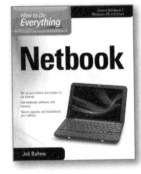